# MEDIEVAL ASPECTS OF RENAISSANCE LEARNING

# MEDIEVAL ASPECTS OF RENAISSANCE LEARNING

Three Essays by PAUL OSKAR KRISTELLER

Edited and translated by Edward P. Mahoney

COLUMBIA UNIVERSITY PRESS  NEW YORK

Columbia University Press Morningside Edition
Columbia University Press
New York   Oxford

Morningside Edition with new preface
Copyright © 1992 Columbia University Press
Copyright © 1974 Duke University Press

Library of Congress Cataloging-in-Publication Data

Kristeller, Paul Oskar, 1905–
    Medieval aspects of renaissance learning : three essays /
  by Paul Oskar Kristeller;
  edited and translated by Edward P. Mahoney.
        p.   cm.
    Originally published: Durham, N.C. : Duke University Press, 1974.
    Includes bibliographical references and index.
    ISBN 0-231-07950-8 : —ISBN 0-231-07951-6 (pbk.):
    1. Philosophy, Renaissance.
    2. Thomas, Aquinas, Saint, 1225–1274.
    3. Latin language, Medieval and modern—History.
    4. Monasticism and religious orders—History.
    I. Mahoney, Edward P., 1932–   .  II. Title.
B775.K69   1992
001.2′09′02—dc20
92-1764   CIP   AC

Printed in the United States of America
c 10 9 8 7 6 5 4 3 2 1
p 10 9 8 7 6 5 4 3 2 1

# TABLE OF CONTENTS

# EDITOR'S PREFACE

This book brings together three essays which emphasize certain medieval aspects of the Renaissance. It should therefore be equally of value to those scholars and students who are interested in the Middle Ages and to those who are interested in the Renaissance itself. The book evolved out of my judgment that Professor Paul O. Kristeller's essay on Thomism in the Italian Renaissance, which was originally written and published in French in 1967, was of such importance and general interest to historians and philosophers, as well as to their students, that it should be made available in English. It was appropriate that the English version was originally published in 1974 during the seven-hundreth anniversary of Saint Thomas's death. In like fashion, since the first essay seemed at that time to be unique in its treatment of a topic that is significant both for medievalists and Renaissance scholars, namely, the interrelationship of literary structure and audience in the Late Middle Ages and the Renaissance, it too seemed to merit translation so that it could be drawn to the fuller attention of English-speaking scholars and students. The third essay provides both a clear and concise survey for the general reader of the contribution of religious orders to learning during the Renaissance and also an excellent reference tool for scholars who are especially interested either in Renaissance humanism or the history of religious orders. The appendix listing humanists who were members of religious orders was thoroughly reworked and greatly expanded by Professor Kristeller for the original publication of this book in 1974. Both he and I have now co-authored supplements to the first and third essays for this reprint edition by the Columbia University Press that appear as "Addenda et Corrigenda". Particularly noteworthy are the entries added for those members of religious orders who engaged in humanistic and other scholarly pursuits and who were not listed in the 1974 printing.

In order to bring the essay on Saint Thomas and the Renaissance up-to-date, I have prepared a bibliographical survey of the scholarly literature on Saint Thomas and his influence during the Italian Renaissance that has appeared since 1974. Mr. James B. South, my student at Duke University, has collaborated with me in preparing this survey which we have entitled "Studies on Saint Thomas and the Italian Renaissance (1974–1991): An Overview." It should be carefully noted that we have deliberately restricted ourselves to Italy, thus excluding the rich scholarly literature on Spanish Thomism during this period as well as the many fine studies on Thomism in France and Germany during the Late Middle Ages. If we have included some figures such as Francisco Suarez, we did so on the grounds that part of his teaching career was at the Jesuit Roman College. Some articles and books relevant to Saint Thomas's influence in Italy during the Late Middle Ages and the Renaissance bearing the date of 1991 may not appear in our overview simply because they were not yet available to us when we ended our search for appropriate material in June 1992. We hope that those scholars who may not find their articles or books mentioned will understand the difficulty of producing a truly exhaustive account. It is also necessary to warn the reader that the index contained in this volume is identical to that printed in the original edition of 1974. Consequently none of the references either to late Medieval and Renaissance figures or to modern scholars that are found in the supplements to the first and third essays or in the overview on recent scholarship on Saint Thomas and the Renaissance will appear in the index. Unfortunately rather serious practical considerations excluded the possibility of reworking the index for this edition.

This book originally appeared as the first volume in a series published by the Duke University Press entitled Duke Monographs in Medieval and Renaissance Studies. I wish to restate my gratitude to John O. Blackburn and Frederic N. Cleaveland, who at that time served respectively as Chancellor and Provost at Duke, for their warm support and encouragement. My translation of the second essay from the original French was carefully studied by my friend and colleague, Professor Ronald Witt, who made valuable suggestions for its improvement. Professor Kristeller kindly studied that translation and also the translation of the first essay from German and suggested valuable refinements in both translations. Mr. Ashbel G. Brice and Mr. William N. Hicks, who were then on the staff of the Duke University Press, provided me with sound editorial advice.

The reprinting of this book by the Columbia University Press seems particularly appropriate since Professor Kristeller's first book in English, *The Philosophy of Marsilio Ficino*, was published by the Press almost fifty years ago. I am grateful to Mr. John Michel, the editor of the Morningside Books series, and also to Mr. John Moore, Director of the Press, for their patience, support and practical help in bringing this project to a successful conclusion. Mr. Michel generously accepted my condition for involvement, namely, that the reprint edition contain a supplementary study surveying the many scholarly contributions to the history of Thomism in Italy during the late Middle Ages and the Renaissance that have been published since 1974. I am grateful to him for allowing extra time to complete that survey.

Professor Paul O. Kristeller was himself the determined prime mover in securing the Columbia University Press as publisher for this reprint edition of *Medieval Aspects of Renaissance Learning*. I wish to thank him for garciously accepting my judgment that such a reprint had to contain a supplementary overview of recent scholarship on Thomas and the Renaissance if the needs of students and scholars were to be served. It is clear that his own study on Saint Thomas and the Italian Renaissance has been one of the reasons for the growth of interest in the topic. It is my hope that his study and the accompanying overview will interest and encourage younger scholars to engage in serious examination of the influence of Saint Thomas and other medieval thinkers on the Renaissance. Much remains to be done.

Duke University                                    EDWARD P. MAHONEY
*June 10, 1992*

# PREFACE TO THE MORNINGSIDE
# EDITION

This volume, edited and partly translated by Edward P. Mahoney, was first published by the Duke University Press in 1974. It was then very well received, and it has been widely used and quoted, and its conclusions and implications have been accepted by some scholars and ignored by others. After it went out of print in 1988, the Columbia University Press agreed to republish it in both a cloth and paperback edition.

The volume consists of three essays which are quite different in origin, length and content, but are all related to a common theme: the continued presence of some typically medieval traits in the civilisation of the Renaissance. I do not deny, on the other hand, that these medieval traits underwent some transformation during the Renaissance, or that they coexisted at the same time with some other features that are unmedieval or even antimedieval.

The first essay, "The Scholar and His Public during the Late Middle Ages and the Renaissance," tries to show that the use of the vernacular and of Latin, either scholastic or humanistic, especially in Italy, was not due to a political or ideological contrast between vernacular and Latin authors, as is often believed, but that both languages were used simultaneously by the same authors, depending on the reading public or audience which they wanted to reach in each particular case.

The second essay, "Thomism and the Italian Thought of the Renaissance," deals with the history of late scholasticism and tries to show, with the help of original documents and of bibliographical, textual and lexicographical evidence, that Thomism came to be the generally accepted philosophical doctrine of the Catholic Church only in the late nineteenth century and was for many centuries merely one of several options available to Catholic philosophers and theologians. On the other hand, Thomism became the official doctrine of the Dominican Order as early as 1286, and became increasingly influential also outside the Order after Thomas's canonization in 1323. During the fourteenth, fifteenth and sixteenth centuries, Thomas was highly respected and followed, not only among many theologians outside his order, but also among many philosophers and humanist scholars. On the other hand, a strong attack was directed against the Thomists by Baptista Mantuanus, a beatified Carmelite who was renowned as a Latin poet rather than as a theologian or philosopher.

Of special significance for Renaissance Thomism is a treatise on the superiority of the intellect over the will, written against Marsilio Ficino and dedicated to Lorenzo de'Medici, by Vincenzo Bandello da Castelnuovo, a theologian who later became General of the Dominican Order. It survives in two manuscripts, both of them once preserved in the library of S. Marco, Florence and edited by me in 1967. Bandello directed his attack against a letter of Ficino to Lorenzo, entitled *Epistola de felicitate* and probably written in 1473, which served as the basis for part of Lorenzo's poem *L'Altercazione*, composed during that year. It seems significant that a typically scholastic problem, the relative superiority of the intellect or of the will, which was debated by Thomas and Duns Scotus and by their followers, remained an important issue for the Platonic Academy of Florence in the late fifteenth century. The arguments used on both sides are of great interest for the thought of the late fifteenth century. On the other hand, we know from other passages in Ficino's works that he oscillated on this very topic and even argued in some of his other works for the superiority of the intellect, a fact evidently unknown to Bandello. I discussed Bandello's treatise in "A Thomist critique of Marsilio Ficino's Theory of Will and Intellect: Fra Vincenzo Bandello da Castelnuovo O.P. and His Unpublished Treatise Addressed to Lorenzo de'Medici," in *Harry Austryn Wolfson Jubilee Volume on the Occasion of His Seventy-Fifth Birthday*, English Section, vol. II (Jerusalem, 1965), 463–494, which will reappear shortly without any bibliographical additions or other modifications in my *Studies in Renaissance Thought and Letters*, III (Rome: Storia e Letteratura), 147–172. Although there is some overlap with the second essay in this volume, "A Thomist Critique" is far narrower in scope. Moreover, the second essay in this volume was revised and the footnotes were brought up to date in 1974 by supplementary data provided by Professor Mahoney, who had translated it from the original French. These bibliographical additions are not to be found in the original French version (1967). The English translation is the definitive version of my study on Thomas and the Renaissance.

The third and longest essay, "The Contribution of Religious Orders to Renaissance Thought and Learning," does not deny the fact that many theologians and clerics of the Renaissance were opposed to the lay culture, and especially to the classical studies of their time, or that there were, among thinkers and writers of the period, many whom we might call anticlerical. Yet we try to show that there were many monks and friars (and the same may be said of many secular clerics) who took an active part in the secular literature, learning and thought of their period, whether humanistic or scholastic. I should like to single out Antonius Bargensis OSB Congr. Olivet. whose writings, some of which I edited (*Studies in Renaissance Thought and Letters*, II, [Rome, 1985], pp. 531–560), included what is perhaps the earliest humanist treatise on the dignity of man which seems to have influenced both Bartolomeo Fazio and Giannozzo Manetti.

What the three essays have in common, and what I hope they show, is the continued presence of medieval themes, doctrines and literary genres in the midst of Renaissance thought and learning, and the frequent interchange of ideas between the laymen and the clerics of the period.

I should like to thank all those who have made the publication of this book possible: the publishers and editors who originally gave their permission to include the three essays in this volume; Mrs. Joanne Ferguson of the Duke University Press, who gave permission to have the volume reprinted; Mr. John Moore, Miss Luna Carne-Ross and Mr. John L. Michel of the Columbia University Press for having agreed to include the volume in their paperback series, called Morningside Books. I am especially grateful to my friend and colleague, Prof. Edward P. Mahoney, who took time from his own research to act as an editor of this new edition. Professor Mahoney organized and verified the data and then wrote the "Addenda and Corrigenda" to the first and third essays. He also provided a good deal of valuable additional information. Moreover, both he and his student at Duke University, Mr. James B. South, have done a valuable service by preparing a supplement to the second essay in which they give an overview of articles and books published during the years 1974 to 1991 that relate to Saint Thomas's influence during the Renaissance.

*Columbia University*                                    PAUL OSKAR KRISTELLER
*June 10, 1992*

# THE SCHOLAR AND HIS PUBLIC
# IN THE LATE MIDDLE AGES
# AND THE RENAISSANCE

If we want to understand the learned literature of the declining Middle Ages and the Renaissance in its content and significance, we must especially keep in mind a fundamental fact: from the twelfth century, and above all from the rise of the universities, scholarly teaching was no longer encyclopedic as in the preceding centuries, but was divided into a number of clearly distinct subjects. There were still of course encyclopedic reference books, just as there are today. There were also individual scholars, especially during the Renaissance, who aimed at a universal knowledge, and a great many who had a mastery of several scholarly disciplines at the same time or who combined all sorts of scholarly interests in unexpected ways. Finally, there were more or less original thinkers and authors, whose works cannot be reduced to established disciplines but in the truest sense of the word do not fit into a framework. But there is a frame here and it must serve at least as a kind of system of coordinates in which most of the learned writers of the time take their clearly determined places. The most important subjects that are in question are theology, jurisprudence,

The basis of this essay is a lecture which the author gave to the Medieval Seminar of Columbia University on April 14, 1959. To the best of my knowledge, the topic has not yet been treated in a comprehensive way, although there exists for many of the particular questions that have been raised a more or less extensive specialized literature from which I shall cite the most important contributions. This essay, however, is essentially an attempt to synthesize from a new point of view the impressions and recollections that I have accumulated over decades of study; some of these could be demonstrated only with difficulty and at great length. For many details, may I be permitted to refer to my earlier works, especially *The Classics and Renaissance Thought* (Cambridge, Mass., 1955), *Studies in Renaissance Thought and Letters* (Rome, 1956), and *Renaissance Thought: The Classic, Scholastic and Humanistic Strains* (New York, 1961). The most important study on our topic is a recent book of Erich Auerbach with which I became acquainted only after having completed this essay (*Literatursprache und Publikum in der lateinischen Spätantike und im Mittelalter*, Bern, 1958, especially ch. IV, 177–279; "Das abendländische Publikum und seine Sprache"; see now the English version, *Literary Language and its Public in Late Latin Antiquity and in the Middle Ages*, trans. Ralph Manheim, New York, 1965, ch. IV, 235–338: "The Western Public and its Language"). Auerbach enters into the period after 1300 only at the conclusion of his exposition (233 ff.; English version: 306 ff.) and at the same time he completely restricts himself to the vernacular languages and their literature. In his treatment of the preceding centuries, purely linguistic, stylistic and literary points of view are in the foreground for him, and he touches only slightly on literary genres and scholarly literature in particular. He seems to view the relation of humanism to scholasticism and to Italian literature in a manner not unlike the one presented in this essay (207 ff. and 243 ff.; English version: 273–275 and 318–320). Cf. also Fritz Schalk, *Das Publikum im italienischen Humanismus* (Krefeld, 1955). I am indebted for valuable suggestions to Jean Monfrin.

medicine, mathematics (along with astronomy and astrology), philosophy (above all logic, natural philosophy and metaphysics), and finally the so-called humanistic subjects (*Studia humanitatis*), to which belong above all grammar, rhetoric, poetry, history and ethics. This scheme, with slight variations, underlies the scholarly teaching of the universities and secondary schools and we also find it again in the library catalogues of the period as well as in the occasional attempts to establish a systematic classification of all the sciences. I have attempted on several occasions to trace the opposition of humanism and scholasticism, especially for Italy, back to the rivalry between the philosophical and rhetorical professional traditions, and I believe that a similar demonstration could be produced also for Germany and the other European countries. Nevertheless, there are some characteristic differences between Italy and the other European countries which are based on the different organization of the universities and go back to the High Middle Ages: in the Italian universities, in contrast with Paris and the other northern universities, theology was scarcely represented. The accent lay from the very first on jurisprudence, medicine and rhetoric, and for that reason philosophical studies did not develop in connection with theology but in conjunction with medicine and to a lesser degree with rhetoric.[1] I should like to presuppose these facts as well-known, especially since, in regard to the treatment of scholarly literature, I have in view primarily the philosophical and rhetorical literature of Italy, which I know best from direct acquaintance.

If we inquire about the scholar and his public, then we obviously think of the communication and transmission of scholarly material to others, namely, first of oral communication, especially through teaching and public addresses, and further of written communication through the diffusion of scholarly works. Both forms of communication are intimately connected with one another, as we shall soon see. At least a considerable part of the scholarly literature arose from teaching and oral lecturing, and at least a part of this oral instruction was set down in works of scholarly literature. For that reason it seems right, in the case of the question regarding the public, to start from the different forms of oral and written communication. I do not believe that there was a uniform public for all oral and literary discussions of philosophical and rhetorical themes. Rather it seems to me that differ-

1. Hastings Rashdall, *The Universities of Europe in the Middle Ages*, ed. F. M. Powicke and A. B. Emden, 3 vols. (Oxford, 1936), especially I, 233 ff.

ent literary genres were intended for different groups of readers. We can even go a step further and conjecture that some literary genres owe their origin and development to a concern for a definite public. In any case, an author certainly often chose a definite literary genre to address a definite reading public that was accustomed to this genre. I am convinced, however, that this problem can be investigated still more thoroughly by the techniques of comparative literature and esthetic theory. Problems of this sort have been somewhat neglected in recent decades, primarily through the influence of Benedetto Croce, who proscribed the concept of literary genre. Croce's attitude was to an extent justified since his concern was with describing the artistic contents of some masterpieces of poetry, and he justly remarked that the conventional rules that had been drawn up for certain literary genres did not suffice for this task. Our task is much more modest. We have to deal with a large mass of little known and in part quite mediocre literary works and we want first of all to gain a preliminary overview of this still unsorted mass. In doing so it seems to me that the concept of literary genres is altogether indispensable.

The most important literary genres (*Literaturgattungen*) for the scholarly literature of the late Middle Ages, and in particular for the written works of scholastic philosophy, are the textbook, the commentary, the *Quaestio* and the treatise. Humanistic literature likewise includes textbooks, commentaries and treatises, which are nevertheless distinct in content and style from the scholastic ones, and to these we must add the oration, the letter, the dialogue and the translation, especially from Greek. Other forms of humanistic literature, in particular the history and the poem, I pass over to concentrate on our theme, although many works of historical writing and didactic poetry must also be designated as scholarly. Since we have considered among all these genres the Latin works above all, we must then add as still a third group the scholarly literature in the vernacular languages. This literature essentially takes over the humanistic forms, at least in Italy. Besides all these genres, there arise in the sixteenth century two new genres, the lecture and the essay.

Let us begin with the scholastic literary genres. It is obvious that the textbook was written for the use of schoolboys and university students. Such manuals of logic, rhetoric and other school subjects served primarily for private study; they were no doubt also intended to prepare for examinations and were distributed by the university bookstore. As one can see from the prefaces, the author recommends himself to his readers above all by the claim that he treats in a brief and concise manner a subject matter that is otherwise only found scattered in much longer works. The success and the diffusion of these textbooks differ in each case. An author naturally provided for the circulation of his textbooks by taking them as a basis for his own courses. It sometimes happens (usually after the death of the author) that a textbook was officially prescribed in the statutes of the university as the basis for specific courses. When a textbook held its ground in many schools and for a long period of time, as for example the works of Gratian, Peter Lombard or Peter of Spain, it then acquired the same recognition as the didactic writings of the Greek and Arab "authorities" and became itself the basis of an extensive literature of commentaries.[2]

The commentary should probably be considered as the most important form of scholarly literature of the Middle Ages. It has a long historical development which in many respects is still in need of more detailed investigation.[3] The grammatical as well as the philosophical commentary had already been fully developed in Greek antiquity, and this inheritance was mediated to the Latin Middle Ages, above all through the Roman grammarians and through Boethius. From the time of the specialization of learning in the twelfth century, the commentary form was in like manner used in all branches of knowledge and it was cultivated without interruption until the sixteenth century and beyond. The methods of explanation and the doctrinal content as offered were naturally subject to constant change. Nevertheless, the continuity of literary form itself remains visible right into the Renaissance, above all in the thematic division of the introductory section, which was called *Accessus* in the Middle Ages. Notwithstanding this tradition of literary form, the commentary develops down to recent times from the oral exposition, namely, in the class lecture as it was delivered day in and day out in the schools and universities throughout the

2. On the use of the textbooks of Paul of Venice and other authors at Padua, see Rashdall, I, 247.

3. Gustavus Przychocki, *Accessus Ovidiani* (Cracow, 1911); Edwin A. Quain, "The Medieval Accessus ad Auctores," *Traditio* 3 (1945), 215–264; Richard W. Hunt, "The Introduction to the Artes in the Twelfth Century," in *Studia Mediaevalia in honorem . . . Raymundi Josephi Martin* (Bruges, 1948), 85–112; R. B. C. Huygens, *Accessus ad Auctores* (Berchem and Brussels, 1954; rev. ed. Leiden, 1970). For further examples, see *Catalogus Translationum et Commentariorum*, ed. P. O. Kristeller (I, Washington, 1960; II, 1971).

years.[4] This class lecture was organized in such a fashion that the teacher first read aloud (hence the name *Lectura*) a section from the prescribed or selected text for his course and then explained it in detail.[5] If one considers how many courses of that kind were given everywhere over the centuries, it becomes clear that the extant or even merely attested commentaries have preserved for us only a small part of this teaching activity. The extant commentaries are frequently nothing but classroom notes, that is, notes which one student wrote down during the class lecture and in most cases later revised, occasionally with the help of other students or the professor himself.[6] Obviously such *Reportata* or *Recollecta* are to be used with caution, since the comprehension and memory even of the best university student has its limits, but in many cases they are still important documents, not only for the thought and learning of the professor in question, but also in general for the history of learning and of the teaching system at that time. In other cases, we have before us the detailed lecture notes of the professor himself, and this second form of commentary is of course still more valuable, since this is an original work of a scholar which has not passed through other hands. In any case, commentaries on the works of Aristotle and on the logic of Peter of Spain constitute right into the seventeenth century a broad and important branch of philosophical literature that has not yet been sufficiently explored, particularly for the later centuries.[7] The manu-

4. *Editor's footnote*: On Professor Kristeller's suggestion, I have translated *die Vorlesung* here as "class lecture" and will also translate it on occasion as "course." On the other hand, I will translate *der Vortrag* almost always as "lecture." This will enable us to keep distinct the "class lecture" in the university and the "lecture" in the academy. (E. P. M.)

5. Gérard M. Paré and others, *La Renaissance du XIIᵉ siècle, les écoles et l'enseignement* (Paris and Ottawa, 1933); A. M. Landgraf, *Einführung in die Geschichte der theologischen Literatur der Frühscholastik* (Regensburg, 1948).

6. Numerous examples can be found in Martin Grabmann, *Mittelalterliches Geistesleben*, 3 vols. (Munich, 1926–56). For the sixteenth century, the lectures of Pietro Pomponazzi are a good example. Cf. P. O. Kristeller, "A New Manuscript Source for Pomponazzi's Theory of the Soul from his Paduan Period," *Revue internationale de philosophie* 5 (1951), 144–157; "Two Unpublished Questions on the Soul by Pietro Pomponazzi," *Medievalia et Humanistica* 9 (1955), 76–101; 10 (1956), 151; Bruno Nardi, *Studi su Pietro Pomponazzi* (Florence, 1965); Pietro Pomponazzi, *Corsi inediti dell' insegnamento padovano*, ed. Antonino Poppi, 2 vols. (Padua, 1966 and 1970); Antonino Poppi, *Saggi sul pensiero inedito di Pietro Pomponazzi* (Padua, 1970).

7. Joseph P. Mullally, *The Summulae Logicales of Peter of Spain* (Notre Dame, 1954), 138–158. This list needs to be further supplemented, as Professor Wilhelm Risse has informed me. See now Risse's *Bibliographia Logica*, I (Hildesheim, 1965). See also the work of Charles Lohr, cited below, p. 52.

scripts in which these commentaries have come down to us are by no means always or even chiefly the original manuscripts of the teacher or student. In most cases, they are copies. The diffusion of the commentaries in question can be determined by the number of preserved copies, as also later by the number of the printed copies. They obviously served not as textbooks, but rather as study aids for students and as teaching aids for other professors, who could obtain from the commentaries of their predecessors or colleagues different explanations of contested passages of the text and the arguments and proofs adduced for them.

The most important literary genre in scholasticism after the commentary was the *Quaestio*.[8] It appears above all as a separate piece of inquiry, but frequently also in collections, which either are of miscellaneous content (*Quaestiones quodlibetales*), or attach themselves to one text in commentary form, or finally comprise a whole branch of knowledge in a systematic arrangement (as for example the *Summa theologiae* of Thomas Aquinas). The question also has its ancient and medieval antecedents—one may think of the *Problemata* and *Aporiai* of Aristotle, of the *Questions* of Augustine or of the so-called school dialogues which are composed of questions and answers in a schematic form. On the other hand, however, the true scholastic question exhibits a new and peculiar structure which was probably first developed in the twelfth century. That is to say, a proposition (thesis) is first laid down, then arguments which support it are presented, then some counterarguments, and finally the counterarguments are refuted and the proposition thereby declared as proven. Just as the commentary

8. See note 5 above. Martin Grabmann, *Die Geschichte der scholastischen Methode*, 2 vols. (Freiburg im Breisgau, 1909–1911; repr.: Graz, 1957), II, 151 ff. Also fundamental are the studies of Palemon Glorieux. See his *La littérature quodlibétique de 1260 à 1320* (Kain, 1925), ch. I: "Le Quodlibet: Sa structure" (11–58), and ch. II: "Le Quodlibet: Sa valeur" (59–95), and also his article, "Le Quodlibet et ses procédés rédactionnels," *Divus Thomas* (Piacenza) 42 (1939), 61–93. See also Glorieux's more recent article, "L'enseignement au moyen âge. Technique et méthodes en usage à la Faculté de Théologie de Paris, au XIIIᵉ siècle," *Archives d'histoire doctrinale et littéraire du Moyen Age* 35 (1968, pub. 1969), 65–186, especially 123–136. On the *Quaestio* form in legal literature, see Hermann Kantorowicz, "The Quaestiones Disputatae of the Glossators," *Revue d'histoire du droit* 16 (1938), 1–67, as well as the book Kantorowicz wrote in collaboration with William W. Buckland, *Studies in the Glossators of the Roman Law: Newly Discovered Writings of the Twelfth Century* (Cambridge, 1938; repr.: Aalen, 1969), 81–82, 130–131, 181–205. For the history of the *Quaestio*, see also Harry Sebastian, "William of Wheteley's (f. 1309–1316) Commentary on the Pseudo-Boethius' Tractate 'De Disciplina scolarium' and Medieval Grammar School Education" (Ph.D. diss., Columbia University, 1970).

grew out of the lecture course, so another form of medieval school and university activity is the basis of the question, namely, the disputation. The disputation on individual or miscellaneous theses is part of the prescribed exercises of candidates for examinations and also of university teachers, as it followed precisely determined rules whereby the counterarguments were generally expounded by an opponent. Later the disputations relating to a text formed an indispensable supplement to the respective lecture course. The preserved questions are never "stenographic" transcripts of the actual disputation, since the name of the opponent is to my knowledge never indicated, and the counter-arguments are always worked into the text. It also happens here that the transcript of a student underlies the written, preserved question,[9] though in contradistinction to the commentary the professor himself is generally responsible for the editing and collecting of his questions, and for that reason they are in general more reliable than the commentaries as a testimony of his teachings. As a literary genre, the question also was addressed primarily to students, who of course were also in many cases the professors of the next generation. From the questions they got to know the arguments which were employed for the discussion of specific problems that were debated again and again, and they were also able with their help to practise the technique and method of disputing, which of course constituted an indispensable part of their professional education and career.

The monographic treatise, as we have it before us in the *Opuscula* of Thomas or in the main writings of Pomponazzi, often developed out of the discussion of individual passages of a text or out of the debate on a favorite thesis, but in contrast with the commentary and the question it shows no close connection with oral teaching. Most treatises were written primarily to be read, frequently at the request of a specific patron or student. Nevertheless, by reason of the content and the method of presentation, it is clear that also these works were written primarily for specialists, that is, for scholars and students, and were essentially read only by them.

Summing up, we must consider all literary genres examined up to now as forms of professional literature which were written by specialists for their students and professional colleagues. The stylistic character of these works also bears this out. They place no worth whatever on literary elegance, but make use, on the contrary, of an

9. See note 6 above.

extremely refined terminology and method of proof which must often have been unintelligible to the layman. On the other hand, this public of scholars was not restricted to a city or a country but was completely international. Students of all countries flocked together, especially at Paris and the Italian universities, and professors frequently taught outside their native land. It was thus no wonder that this scholarly literature also spread from the universities where it originated over all Europe. The geographical distribution of the manuscripts and printed books in which these writings have been preserved enables us to recognize this to some extent even today, especially if it is supplemented in the appropriate way by the history of individual collections and even of individual volumes.

If we turn from the scholarly literature of scholasticism to the literature of the humanists, we encounter to some extent the same literary genres that we already know. Here too there are textbooks and treatises, especially on themes of rhetoric and moral philosophy, just as there is a great mass of commentaries on ancient authors. These humanistic commentaries also resulted from the teaching activity of their authors in the schools and universities. They differ to some extent from the scholastic commentaries in the choice of authors commented upon, but above all, even when it is a question of the same author, in the method of interpretation. Grammatical and historical interpretation for the most part takes the place of dialectical analysis and argumentation, more value is placed on style, and the terminology of scholastic learning is rather avoided.

The form of the question is almost completely disregarded by the humanists, and this reflects their antipathy to the disputation, which is well-known to us from many works on method and pedagogy. In its place the oration becomes an important literary form, one that often serves as well for the formulation of philosophical and scientific ideas. The orations of the humanists were almost always delivered orally and were composed for a specific occasion that occurred only once. In the Renaissance there was a series of typical events at which an oration was regularly presented, and to which the most numerous forms of oration correspond. Above all there were the funeral oration and the marriage oration, the oration of an ambassador and the welcoming oration to a newly appointed official or to a princely visitor. There was, moreover, a great mass of school and university orations: solemn orations at the opening of the school year or of a special course of lectures, orations of professors and of candidates following the successful conclusion of a doctoral examination, and a few others.[10] The number of these orations over the course of the centuries was enormous, and only a small part of them has come down to us. In contrast with the commentaries, the preserved orations were only rarely written down by members of the audience, as frequently happened with sermons. On the contrary, in most cases we have the text as the author wrote it down, and in fact before he actually made the speech. In this way, then, the orations, unlike the letters, were afterwards but only rarely revised or collected by their authors. Their diffusion was dependent on the public success of the oration, which was indeed regarded by the audience as a public entertainment like a theater performance or a concert, as well as on the fame of the speaker.[11] Many orations were preserved only in the autograph sketch of the author or in the copy of a friend or student; others, on the contrary, are preserved in numerous copies. If one asks why such orations found so great a diffusion, one must come to the conclusion that they were evidently read with pleasure, a pleasure which the modern reader no longer always shares. On the other hand, the interest of the school also plays a role here, just as in the scholarly literature of scholasticism. The young schoolboy as well as the university student needed a model from which he could learn how one wrote a speech, and even the full-grown humanist needed patterns on which he could rely when he had the opportunity to deliver an oration on a similar theme himself. Humanist orations only rarely had the political interest for their contemporaries that we connect with the speeches of our own time, and even the great historical interest that they often possess for the modern reader played hardly any role for contemporaries.

Still more important than the oratory of the humanists is their extremely rich and often interesting epistolary literature. Here we must make a clear distinction between letters of state and private letters.

10. Georg Buchwald and Theo Herrle, *Redeakte bei Erwerbung akademischer Grade an der Universität Leipzig im 15. Jahrhundert, Abhandlungen der Philologisch-Historischen Klasse der Sächsischen Akademie der Wissenschaften*, XXXVI, no. 5 (Leipzig, 1921).

11. For humanistic orations and letters, see Jakob Burckhardt, *Die Kultur der Renaissance in Italien*, 13th ed. (Stuttgart, 1922), 167 ff.; *The Civilization of the Renaissance in Italy*, trans. S. G. C. Middlemore (London, 1955), 137 ff.; Georg Voigt, *Die Wiederbelebung des klassischen Alterthums*, 3rd edition, ed. M. Lehnerdt (Berlin, 1893), II, 414 ff.; Vittorio Rossi, *Il Quattrocento* (Milan, 1933); Karl Müllner, *Reden und Briefe italienischer Humanisten: Ein Beitrag zur Geschichte der Pädagogik des Humanismus* (Vienna, 1899).

Letters of state were composed by the chancellor, who regularly had, during the Renaissance, a humanist education and who therefore placed a certain value on style and expression. At the same time, however, legal and political points of view played a commanding role. State letters were often publicly circulated by the government in whose name they were sent in order to make known or to justify its policy, and in this way they served as political propaganda, as one can see in the instance of Salutati. Nevertheless, they generally were not subsequently revised or collected. As soon as the political moment for which they were written was past, only a formal, literary interest remained. They served, as did the orations, primarily as models or examples for other humanists, and they were often copied without the original names and dates, like the medieval state documents in the *Artes dictaminis*, with which the humanistic literature also exhibits some formal similarities in other respects.

The private letters of the humanists, like the letters of all periods, were above all personal communications of the sender, but from the first they had at the same time a literary appearance. The humanist wrote his letters with his reading public in mind, and in this he followed a tradition of the art of letter-writing which can be followed from antiquity down through the entire Middle Ages. The writer as well as the addressee gladly showed around an interesting or beautifully written letter, and with Petrarch there begins the long line of humanists who collected their own letters and at the same time carefully polished and revised them.[12] Some collections of letters, and even many individual letters, found an extremely wide diffusion, as can be seen from the manuscript tradition of the letters of Bruni, Poggio and Guarino.[13] One factor in this was the interest in the actual content of the letter. The letter often played at that time the role of the newspaper: it was quickly read and copied on account of the news it contained. In many cases, the letter had a scholarly or philosophical content and was really nothing but a treatise to which the form of the letter gave as it were a personal tone, as the humanists liked to do. In fact it is not always easy to draw the line between letters of this kind

12. Francesco Petrarca, *Le familiari*, 4 vols., ed. Vittorio Rossi and Umberto Bosco (Florence, 1933–42).
13. Guarino Veronese, *Epistolario*, ed. Remigio Sabbadini, 3 vols., *Miscellanea di Storia Veneta*, VIII, XI and XIV (Venice, 1915–19); Leonardo Bruni Aretino, *Humanistisch-Philosophische Schriften*, ed. Hans Baron (Leipzig and Berlin, 1928).

and treatises, which are likewise addressed for the most part to a specific person. The sole, half-way safe criterion is generally the size. In other respects, the private letter served more than the state letter, and like the oration, as a literary model for students and other humanists. This is also the chief reason why they were copied and later printed.

In all these cases, a specific, concrete occasion is at the root of the finished literary work, even though it was generally more or less thoroughly revised for the purpose of publication. On the other hand, the humanistic dialogue or treatise, like the scholastic treatise, is essentially "purely literary," that is, written from the start to be read. In the case of the dialogues, the author always pretends to reproduce the substance of a conversation that actually took place. But one has good reason to assume that the dialogue deviates much further from a conversation that actually took place than was the case with orations or letters, and also that in many cases it is a question of pure fiction. The popularity of the dialogue is explained, just as in the case of the letter, by the predilection for personal, subjective expression, as well as by the admiration for famous ancient examples. Since a specific occasion for writing a commentary, an oration, or even a letter, was lacking in the case of the dialogue, it must thus be assumed in most cases that an author wrote a treatise or dialogue on his own, in order to state openly his views on specific themes. As is to be expected, the success of such writings with the public was quite diverse. Many of them are transmitted only in one manuscript apiece, and yet this in no way signifies that they are lacking in interest for us; on the other hand, others are found in numerous copies and printed editions. Their success depended to some extent on the importance of the contents, as well as on the quality of the style and on the fame of the author. A further factor was the popularity of the theme. Even a mediocre author could achieve great success with one work on a fashionable theme, as for example Bonaccursius with his work *De nobilitate*.[14]

If one wishes to understand which public the author of a treatise has in mind, one must examine the prefaces and dedications with which almost all humanist treatises, and in general all published writings of the Renaissance, were introduced. The custom of dedicating one's works to a patron or friend and of putting a preface in the form of a dedica-

14. Rossi, *Il Quattrocento*, 132–133; P. O. Kristeller, *Renaissance Thought II* (New York, 1965), 85–86.

tory letter at the head of these works had its prototypes in late antiquity and is also frequently met in the Middle Ages,[15] but it apparently finds general diffusion for the first time with humanism.[16] At the same time both the character of the addressee of the dedication and also the wording of the dedication play a role. The dedicatory prefaces of the Renaissance are generally addressed to princes or other influential personages, and according to a widespread view of the time the author thereby rendered a great honor to the person being addressed. It was therefore also customary that the prince or patron who had been honored with a dedication rewarded the author either by a gift of money or in some other way, and an author even counted on this and made his choice with this in view and sometimes even inquired in advance whether the proposed patron was disposed to accept the dedication. If on the other hand an author was already permanently in the service of a patron, he expected no new reward, but rather treated the dedication as payment of a debt already existing beforehand. Accordingly, the author also had to obtain the permission of his patron if he wanted to dedicate a work to someone else, and he provoked the dissatisfaction and the displeasure of his patron if he did this without his permission. From the contents of the prefaces we also see that the author tries to create the impression that he had composed his work at the special wish of the addressee, which was occasionally, but not always, the case, or that he had reluctantly decided, upon the urgent request of the addressee, to make his work accessible to the reading public. Occasionally the author asks the addressee in the preface to read his work, supposing that his pressing duties allow him the time for it, and then to decide himself whether it merits to be read by others as well. In other cases, the author explains that he is too timid to expose himself alone to public criticism, and he expresses the hope that the name of the addressee, supposing that he does accept the

15. Ernst R. Curtius, *Europäische Literatur und lateinisches Mittelalter* (Bern, 1948), 94–95; *European Literature and the Latin Middle Ages*, trans. Willard R. Trask (New York, 1963), 86–88; R. Graefenhain, *De more libros dedicandi apud scriptores graecos et romanos obvio* (Marburg, 1892); J. Ruppert, *Quaestiones ad historiam dedicationis librorum pertinentes* (Leipzig, 1911).

16. A rich collection of humanistic dedicatory prefaces is to be found in *Bibliotheca Smithiana*, ed. Giovanni B. Pasquali (Venice, 1755), pars. sec. lxvii–cccxlviii. See also Karl Schottenloher, *Die Widmungsvorrede im Buch des 16. Jahrhunderts* (Münster, 1953); Eugene F. Rice, Jr., *The Prefatory Epistles of Jacques Lefèvre d'Etaples and Related Texts* (New York and London, 1972). For the dedications of Marsilio Ficino, see my *Supplementum Ficinianum*, 2 vols. (Florence, 1937; repr. 1973).

dedication, will persuade the public of the worth of his work so that even possibly envious people and unfriendly critics will thereby be reduced to silence. Such turns of expression are in part suggested by ancient prototypes, in part occasioned by given relationships, and they contain at the same time a good dose of conceit and false modesty. But behind it all there still remains, nevertheless, the idea that the patron who accepted a dedication thereby assumed at the same time a certain responsibility for the publication of the work. This can occasionally be demonstrated even for the age of manuscripts, in that the patron had the richly decorated dedicatory manuscript, which was solemnly presented to him as the first copy of the work and which often served as the model for all the other copies of the same work, produced at his own expense. When printing later stepped into the place of the manuscript, it then became customary for the patron to whom a work was dedicated also to bear the printing costs, as we can clearly demonstrate in many cases. If an author had more self-confidence, or dared show it more openly, he also alluded in the preface to the fact that the addressee would gain glory and honor as a result of such an excellent work being published bearing his name and under his auspices, and posterity has actually endorsed this judgment in many cases. The number and quality of the works which are dedicated to individual Renaissance popes or members of the Medici family are also for us a measure of the range of their intellectual and literary interests. This is a theme that has not yet been completely dealt with and that can be further advanced, like so many problems of the history of ideas during the Renaissance, only by a thorough examination of manuscripts and rare books.[17]

Finally, we must still mention briefly a group of humanistic works which forms an important part of humanist literary production and concerns as much the history of the literature as the history of the philosophy of the time, namely, the Latin translations from the Greek. The fifteenth and sixteenth centuries generated a veritable flood of such translations and in this way many writings were made accessible

17. For the dedications to Lorenzo de'Medici and to Leo X, see the old biographies of Angelo Fabroni (*Laurentii Medicis Magnifici vita*, 2 vols., Pisa, 1784; *Leonis X Pontificis Maximi vita*, Pisa, 1797) and William Roscoe (*The Life of Lorenzo de'Medici*, 2 vols., Liverpool, 1795, and other editions; *Vita di Lorenzo de'Medici*, trans. Gaetano Mecherini, 4 vols., Pisa, 1816; *The Life and Pontificate of Leo the Tenth*, 4 vols., Liverpool, 1805 and other editions; *Vita e pontificato di Leone X*, trans. Luigi Bossi, 12 vols., Milan, 1816–17).

to the Western world for the first time, just as many already previously known works were circulated in supposedly better translations. These translations were directed to the large number of readers who had a humanistic education and could read Latin well, but who had only a small command of Greek or none at all. They served school and university instruction only in individual cases, as for example the writings of Aristotle or of the Greek medical writers. It can be shown that many of these translations were prepared at the wish of princely patrons, as perhaps the translations of various philosophers and historians prepared for Pope Nicolaus V, and all are introduced by dedicatory prefaces which tell us something about the history of the origin of the translations in question. At the same time, these prefaces are a proof that the translations were viewed by contemporaries as a valuable literary accomplishment of the translator, which one judged no less by their literary style than by the faithful rendering of the Greek original. According to the testimony of manuscripts, printed editions and old library catalogues, the translations of the humanists in general had a greater circle of readers than their own original treatises. This is of course connected with the classicism of the Renaissance and forms part of a broader problem that has not yet been adequately examined, namely, in what ratio was the interest of the reading public of the time distributed among ancient, medieval and contemporary authors and texts.[18] The humanistic translations of ancient Greek authors occupy a special position, since they were so to speak not only ancient but also contemporary.

Summing up, we can say of humanistic literature that it was certainly also read by schoolboys and university students, but unlike scholastic literature it directed itself primarily to a highly cultured lay public, namely, to princes and statesmen, ecclesiastics and merchants, as well as to doctors and lawyers, and also to scholars and academicians of the various disciplines, all of whom had in common with one another a classical-humanistic education. The form and the content of this literature are also very closely connected with this fact. Every effort is made to avoid the "barbaric" technical language and the overly rigorous methods of proof of scholastic learning, and to write, with more or less success, a classical or even a Ciceronian Latin. Moral problems

18. Pearl Kibre, *The Library of Pico della Mirandola* (New York, 1936); Victor Scholderer, "General Introduction," in *Catalogue of Books Printed in the XV[th] Century now in the British Museum*, VII (London, 1935), ix–xxxvii.

and practical wisdom, not logical subtleties or metaphysical speculations, are the focus of interest. This reading public also was not tied to specific regions or countries, but was, on the contrary, international. It comprised all the educated persons who participated in the classical-humanist culture of the time. On the other hand, one can perceive as it were in the geographic and professional diffusion and distribution of humanistic literature how the intellectual movement which took its beginning with the Italian humanists of the fourteenth and early fifteenth century gradually gained ground in the remaining European countries and at the same time found acceptance in Italy as well as in the other countries in the various professional and social classes.[19]

After the scholastic and humanistic literature, both of which were essentially Latin, we must still enter briefly into the scholarly literature in the vernacular, above all in Italy.[20] It is striking, to begin with, that we encounter for the most part the same literary genres that were also cultivated by the humanists, namely, letters, orations, dialogues, treatises and, finally, translations from Greek (and Latin). The state of affairs is further complicated by the fact that the Tuscan dialect was employed much earlier than the remaining dialects for literary and especially scholarly prose and also by the fact that this dialect was accepted as the foundation of a common Italian literary language only in the sixteenth century. At all events, scholarly literature in Italian was intended not for an international reading public, like Neolatin literature, but essentially for an Italian, or even only a Tuscan reading public. For the first time in the sixteenth century Italian as a literary language also found many readers outside Italy, in a manner analogous to French, which already occupied a similar position from the High Middle Ages, whereas the remaining European languages were understood and read almost solely in their own countries. The scholarly literature in Italian was not intended for uncultured readers, as has occasionally been thought, but rather for cultured and inquisitive read-

19. Besides the translation and the commentary, the Florentine Platonists cultivated not only the humanistic literary forms of the letter and the oration but also the scholastic treatise (Ficino's *Theologia Platonica*) and the disputation (Pico's "Theses" and *Apologia*). They created the love treatise, prepared for the development of the Academy lecture and also took part in the development of vernacular literature. This peculiar combination of heterogeneous elements is in complete accordance with the position of these thinkers in the history of ideas. See my *Studies*, 35 ff. and 99 ff.

20. Leonardo Olschki, *Geschichte der neusprachlichen wissenschaftlichen Literatur*, 3 vols. (Heidelberg, 1919—Halle, 1927; repr. Vaduz, 1965).

ers who nevertheless lacked both a humanistic school training and a professional university education. From the dedicatory prefaces we can recognize the groups involved: princes and noblemen, women, business men, artists, and artisans appear most frequently. In the sixteenth century, there arises in addition the conscious ambition to make the vernacular equal to Latin in the treatment of scholarly subjects, and at that time Italian actually made great advances at the expense of Latin, but in no way did it fully drive Latin out of literature, as is frequently asserted by modern historians. Inasmuch as this Italian literature was connected with well identified groups, we must therefore above all take into consideration, up to the fifteenth century, the lay religious guilds. There was in fact a vast quantity of spiritual letters and sermons and other devotional writings in Tuscan which in many cases originated in the circle of these religious confraternities. In the fifteenth century, the Tuscan writings and translations of the humanists and Florentine Platonists still exhibit certain reminiscences of the popular religious literature of the preceding decades which one will seek in vain in their Latin writings. The same connection is also confirmed by the manuscript tradition, in that the Tuscan writings of the humanists are often found together in the same manuscripts with the spiritual letters and sermons of the older theologians. These writings are usually intended for devotional reading, and they obviously have nothing to do with the school or the university. Nevertheless, already in the fifteenth century the use of Tuscan for certain kinds of letters and speeches became more and more frequent, and certainly many Tuscan letters and speeches, which appear with a characteristic frequency in the manuscripts, served as models for the beginning orator and letter writer, as did their Latin counterparts.[21]

Another Tuscan literary genre, which can be traced back to Dante and the early fourteenth century, is the commentary on poetry. Commentaries on the *Divine Comedy*, from the fourteenth century onwards, form a compact genre which was plainly influenced by the Latin commentaries of the grammarians and in many ways itself grew out of school and university instruction—already in the fourteenth century there were regular lecture series on Dante at Florence and elsewhere.[22] Another genre is that of the commentaries on lyrical poems

21. Emilio Santini, *Firenze e i suoi "Oratori" nel Quattrocento* (Milan, 1922).
22. Bruno Sandkühler, *Die frühen Dantekommentare und ihr Verhältnis zur mittelalterlichen Kommentartradition* (Munich, 1967).

and groups of sonnets, some of which were composed by the poet himself, such as Dante's *Convito* and *Vita Nuova*, whereas others were composed by other expositors such as, perhaps the first examples, the commentaries on Guido Cavalcanti's *Canzone*.[23] In the case of these commentaries, a connection with the school is excluded; they were probably written solely for reading. In many cases, they may be based on a recitation, followed by a discussion, in a private group. All these forms of commentaries on poetry were also fostered in the fifteenth century and they received a new impetus, especially in the sixteenth century, through the academies. In their name, the academies reflected, of course, an ancient prototype, but in their essence they were a new creation of the fifteenth and sixteenth centuries.[24] They call to mind in part the social clubs of later periods, in part the learned societies or academies as we know them. The innumerable academies which sprang up everywhere in Italy, especially in the sixteenth century, differed widely from one another in their programme, but there was, nevertheless, a large and important group among them which above all made the cultivation of the Italian language and literature their duty. In the academies, the commentary on poetry continued to be cultivated. Moreover, a new literary form also arose there, namely, the lecture and the series of lectures. The lecture exhibits a certain kinship with the oration, and the series of lectures is to be compared in several respects with the university course. However, they are to be distinguished from these Latin counterparts not merely by the use of the Italian language. In contrast to the university course, the academy lecture was not necessarily bound to a text. It was in principle detached from the strict pattern of scholastic argumentation, and it was in most cases dedicated to the candid discussion of a freely chosen literary or philosophical theme. The wider range of chosen themes is also, after the use of the vernacular, the main difference between the academy lecture and the humanist oration, with which it otherwise has many features in common, since the humanist oration was strictly limited in its range of themes by the conventional forms and occasions of public orations.

The remaining forms of scholarly Italian prose literature of the sixteenth century also stand, at least in their choice of themes, in a loose relationship with the academies, namely, the moral treatises, the

23. John C. Nelson, *Renaissance Theory of Love* (New York, 1958), 15 ff.
24. Michele Maylender, *Storia delle Accademie d'Italia*, 5 vols. (Bologna, 1926–30).

innumerable literary treatises, and finally, the philosophical love treatises, a favorite fashionable genre that was modelled on Plato's *Symposium* and on Ficino's commentary on this work.[25] In any case, this literature was directed toward the same public of literati and dilettantes who also, as members or listeners, gave to the entertainments of the academies, to their discussions and lectures their peculiar character. We must at the same time bear in mind that the diverse literary genres, which we have tried to separate sharply, were sometimes cultivated by the same authors, and that one and the same person frequently belonged to several groups of readers, each of which was characterized by different interests. One could quite easily be an academic dilettante and at the same time a humanist or school philosopher, and sometimes one was all of these together.

The last literary genre which we shall consider is the essay: nothing definite can be stated about its reading public at least until the end of the sixteenth century. The genre first begins just then with Montaigne, who was at the same time its first important representative. Later on, this type was destined to have an important development, and the question, for which reading public the literature of the essay was intended, must best be decided by seventeenth and eighteenth century specialists. I would only like to add that the essay of Montaigne had its ancient prototypes and its humanistic precedents. In his range of themes, Montaigne is in accord with the moral treatises of the humanists, just as he is in his mania for quotations. The choice of French instead of the Latin language is of comparatively little consequence. The Montaignian essay, in its loose composition and its subjective-personal form of expression, appears to be fastened to the humanistic letter. The difference between them consists not in the length, since there are also very long letters of humanists, but simply in the omission of the addressee. The personal communication to a living friend becomes a lonely soliloquy or, if you wish, a communication to an anonymous and unknown reader.[26]

Now that we have become acquainted with the scholarly literature of the late Middle Ages and the Renaissance in its most important genres, I would like, in conclusion, to say something further about

25. John C. Nelson, 67 ff.
26. Peter M. Schon, *Vorformen des Essays in Antike und Humanismus: Ein Beitrag zur Enstehungsgeschichte der "Essais" von Montaigne* (Wiesbaden, 1954).

the history and diffusion of individual texts, at least so far as something that is of general validity can be observed about it. In many cases, there is first an oral communication to a circle of listeners, for example a class lecture, disputation, oration or public lecture. The written text that we have before us was either taken down in accordance with the spoken word, as in the case of the class notes of students, or it was formulated beforehand in writing by the author as the first draft for his oral presentation, as were most of the questions, speeches, and lectures, as well as the professors' lecture notes. The first draft was then later frequently revised by the author, and for that reason there are in numerous texts of our period often quite interesting author's variants, a phenomenon in the face of which, at least until quite recently, classical p..i.ologists were very sceptical. When the revision of the text was finished, the author generally added a dedicatory preface to it and presented at the same time his work to his reading public. The publication of a work in the age of the manuscript book signified that the author released for copying his original manuscript, which did not always need to be in his own hand.[27] With this there began the diffusion in manuscript of a work. This diffusion resulted either spontaneously from the interest of readers and bibliophiles or was organized, on the other hand, by booksellers. There were, above all at the universities, officially recognized booksellers, the so-called *stationarii*, who kept in stock for the students not only the prescribed textbooks but also the most important commentaries.[28] Nevertheless, we learn from information found in many manuscripts about the person who copied or first owned them that poor students copied their textbooks themselves, while rich students had their books copied by professional scribes. Outside the universities there was, in the Italian cities of the fifteenth century, a group of famous calligraphers who primarily produced luxurious manuscripts for wealthy book collectors. Many of them were permanently employed by princeiy bibliophiles, as we know for example in regard to the Aragonese kings in Naples.[29] On the other hand, there was, especially in Florence, a

27. *Studies*, 123 ff.

28. Jean A. Destrez, *La Pecia dans les manuscrits universitaires du XIIIᵉ et du XIVᵉ siècle* (Paris, 1935); Miroslav Bohaček, "Zur Geschichte der Stationarii von Bologna," *Eos* 48, fasc. 2 (1956; published Warsaw, 1957), 241–295; *Handbuch der Bibliothekswissenschaft*, 2nd ed., I (Wiesbaden, 1952), 849 ff.

29. Tammaro De Marinis, *La biblioteca dei Re d'Aragona*, 4 vols. (Milan, 1947–52).

regular trade in manuscripts, or at least we know one famous example of this in the person of Vespasiano da Bisticci, who supplied primarily the libraries of Federico of Urbino and Matthias Corvinus of Hungary and who personally knew most scholars of his day and was also prominent himself as an author.[30] Moreover, it happened that students or young scholars earned their money through copying, while most scholars and even many businessmen assembled their libraries by copying books themselves. Of more particular interest is the type of miscellaneous manuscript in which many often wholly heterogeneous short texts are copied in the same hand, since here the range of interests of the scribe or of the original owner is reflected in the combination of the contents of the manuscript. The extent of the manuscript diffusion of a text naturally depends on its success and it can therefore serve as a measure of this success. However, this success does not always correspond to the importance which modern historians ascribe to the author or text in question, and in this respect our literary histories are frequently very misleading. Many interesting and even famous texts appear surprisingly rarely in manuscripts of the time, while other works, which today are completely or almost forgotten, are to be found time and again in hundreds or even thousands of copies.

The manuscript book immediately found its way into a library. Besides the church libraries, the princely collections also gained in importance in the late Middle Ages. In that period they filled the function of public libraries, since they stood open for the use of scholars and frequently even lent important manuscripts to them.[31] For that reason it is quite erroneous to believe, as has often happened, that a text which was found at that time in one or two princely libraries remained unknown like an unpublished manuscript in the desk of its author.[32] In addition to the princes and the ecclesiastical institutions, there were many private libraries, above all those of nobles and wealthy citizens, but also those of scholars and businessmen. We are quite

30. *Handbuch*, loc. cit.; Enrico Frizzi, *Di Vespasiano da Bisticci e delle sue biografie* (Pisa, 1878); Rossi, *Il Quattrocento*, 36 ff. and 191 ff.

31. Maria Bertòla, *I due primi registri di prestito della Biblioteca Apostolica Vaticana, Codices e Vaticanis selecti*, XXVII (Vatican City, 1942).

32. Giannozzo Manetti's translations of the Bible are an important example. Cf. P. O. Kristeller, "Renaissance Research in Vatican Manuscripts," *Manuscripta* 1 (1957), 77; Salvatore Garofalo, "Gli umanisti italiani del secolo XV e la Bibbia," in *La Bibbia e il Concilio di Trento*, Scripta Pontificii Instituti Biblici, 96 (Rome, 1947), 38–75, which appeared earlier as an article in *Biblica* 27 (1946), 338–375.

well informed regarding these libraries,[33] since some of them have maintained themselves as unbroken units even to the present day,[34] while there are old inventories for others,[35] and in still other cases the former content of an old collection has been painstakingly reconstructed from the subscriptions and the owner's notes of manuscripts now widely dispersed.[36] Nevertheless, there is still much to be done in this area, since the available material is still far from completely known or systematically utilized.

This whole concept of books, as we have described it up to now, was completely transformed from the middle of the fifteenth century through the introduction of printing, even though the manuscript book did not make way for the printed book as quickly and completely as is frequently assumed. For our purpose, however, it is important to understand that recognized scholars began to publish their own writings very soon, around 1470; they had the printing financed by their patrons and read the galley-proofs themselves.[37] In this manner the scholarly literature of the time found its way into the different libraries, just as it had done before through manuscripts. New centers of the book trade, which were simultaneously centers of printing, developed in the process, above all Venice, Lyons and Basel.[38]

The success or influence of a scholarly work after its publication can be estimated in several ways. Occasionally, we learn something about the size of an edition. A good measure is the bibliography of editions, translations included, as well as the number and distribution of copies in libraries of different countries, much like the distribution of manuscript copies. Since many copies are lost or inaccessible, it is thus advisable to draw once again on old library catalogues as a supplement. Naturally there are still other pieces of circumstantial evidence. Specific works created a following and were therefore regularly

33. Cf. *Handbuch*, III, pt. 1 (1955), 243 ff. and 499 ff.

34. As above all the Biblioteca Laurenziana in Florence, the Biblioteca Malatestiana in Cesena and the Fondo Urbinate of the Vatican Library.

35. For bibliographical evidence, see Carlo Frati, *Dizionario bio-bibliografico dei bibliotecari e bibliofili italiani dal secolo XV al XIX*, ed. Albano Sorbelli (Florence, 1934).

36. De Marinis (see above note 29); André de Hevesy, *La bibliothèque du roi Matthias Corvin* (Paris, 1923); V. Fraknói and others, *Bibliotheca Corvina* (Budapest, 1927).

37. For Marsilio Ficino, see my *Studies*, 123 ff.

38. See now Curt F. Bühler, *The Fifteenth-Century Book* (Philadelphia, 1960); Rudolf Hirsch, *Printing, Selling and Reading 1450–1550* (Wiesbaden, 1967).

read or used in certain circles. Others were imitated or copied without always being cited by name, or they were repeatedly cited without on that account always being read. Another form of success was when a work formed the starting-point of a controversy. In the sixteenth century it sometimes happened, just as later in the eighteenth, that a controversial work remained unprinted out of caution, but was circulated so much the more widely in manuscript copies.[39] The diffusion and the influence of a work is likewise not a purely quantitative matter, but is further subject in other respects to interesting variations. It is important to establish, as far as our material permits, whether the distribution of a work exhibits temporal or geographical limits, or whether it seems to conform to definite ideological, professional or social divisions. From all these factors something can be inferred about the reading public of a given work. In the cases in which a work enjoyed a long-lasting popularity, its reading public was naturally much wider than the public for which the author had originally intended his work.

The topic which I have treated here only in brief outline would certainly deserve at some time a more extensive presentation, and it would be necessary to examine many sources and problems still more thoroughly than has been done, as far as I know, up to now. For all that, it can perhaps be said in summation that in the late Middle Ages and the Renaissance there were primarily three types of scholarly and especially of philosophical and rhetorical literature which were intended for three different groups of readers. The scholastic literature directed itself to the specialists of the different disciplines and to their students; the humanistic literature was of course also written for professional humanists and their students, but at the same time for a wider circle of humanistically educated readers as well; the vernacular literature, on the other hand, was read by readers who possessed neither a professional university training nor a humanistic secondary school education but who had, nevertheless, sufficient intellectual curiosity and interest to be willing as laymen to inform themselves about scholarly and philosophical questions. In other words, if we want to employ modern terms, there was a special literature for professionals, further a literature for readers with a classical secondary education,

39. As for example Pomponazzi's De fato. See now the critical edition of Richard Lemay, Petri Pomponantii Mantuani libri quinque de fato, de libero arbitrio et de praedestinatione (Lugano, 1957).

and finally a specifically popular literature for laymen. It is in the nature of things that each of these literary types exhibits its peculiar characteristics, advantages and disadvantages. The scholastic literature was distinguished by a precise terminology and by ingenious argumentation, but it was criticized by its enemies because it supposedly got lost in hairsplitting and debated useless problems which were not of common interest. The humanistic literature possessed an elegant style, historical and philological erudition, and sometimes even practical wisdom, but it was frequently bitingly ridiculed on account of its empty rhetoric, its artificial classicism and its conceptual vagueness. The vernacular literature recommended itself through the charm of a fresh and spontaneous language, and it merits our respect since it set about a difficult problem which would be of great future importance, namely, to express for the first time in a modern language abstract concepts and complicated thoughts. On the other hand, owing to its undeveloped vocabulary and its still somewhat fluid syntax, this new language was in the meanwhile at a great disadvantage vis-à-vis Latin. Indeed, only rarely does the scholarly literature in the vernacular contain ideas which had not already been previously articulated in Latin and in a much more exact formulation. Each of these three literary forms performed a legitimate function in the compass of its time. If it sometimes happened that they were more or less ardent rivals, we cannot forget, on the other hand, that for the most part they peacefully continued side by side, and that it even happened quite frequently that one and the same author, depending on the theme that he was treating and the circle of readers to whom he wished to address himself, wrote some of his works in scholastic or humanistic Latin and some in the vernacular. As historians, therefore, we should not for our part attempt, as so often happens, to take sides in a quarrel that faded away long ago. We should rather calmly watch the spectacle from afar.

# THOMISM AND THE ITALIAN
# THOUGHT OF THE RENAISSANCE

The Institut d'Etudes Médiévales has accorded me a great honor, of which I am acutely aware, in inviting me to address in French its distinguished audience for the Albert-le-Grand Lectures. I am to discuss a field of inquiry which is of interest to us all, since it brings together, it seems to me, the vast sphere of your long and difficult researches with the equally vast, although less well-known, field of my own modest studies. I feel somewhat embarrassed, however, to touch upon problems which have great importance from the historical, philosophical, and theological perspectives before colleagues better in-

I want to express my deep gratitude to all those from whom I have received help during the preparation of the present study. In the first place, to the directors of the Institut d'Etudes Médiévales of the University of Montreal who, by inviting me to speak within the framework of the annual lectures dedicated to the memory of Saint Albert the Great, thereby afforded me the opportunity to develop a topic which is rather neglected and yet of great interest for the history both of Thomism and of the thought of the Italian Renaissance. And then to my friend, Rev. Albert-M. Landry, O.P., whose generous cooperation made possible the preparation and publication of the original French version. It is likewise a pleasure for me to thank many other friends who have aided me by their advice and furnished valuable bibliographical references: the late Mrs. Zofia Ameisenowa (Cracow), Giuseppe Billanovich (Università Cattolica, Milan), Mrs. J. M. Dureau, Myron P. Gilmore (Harvard University), Rev. Thomas Kaeppeli, O.P. (Santa Sabina, Rome), Stephen Kuttner (University of California at Berkeley), Edward P. Mahoney (Duke University), Sesto Prete (University of Kansas), Serafino Prete (Bologna) and Paul Lawrence Rose (New York University). I owe a special debt of gratitude to the following libraries which, by furnishing me with references, microfilms, or photocopies, enabled me to clarify a good number of details and to cite and also edit some rare or unknown texts: Archivio di San Domenico, Bologna (Rev. Abele Redigonda, O.P.); Biblioteca Comunale dell'Archiginnasio, Bologna (Dott. Gino Nenzioni); Harvard University Library, Cambridge, Mass.; Newberry Library, Chicago (Mr. James M. Wells); Biblioteca Comunale Ariostea, Ferrarra (Dott. Luciano Capra); Biblioteca Medicea Laurenziana, Florence (Dottoressa Irma Merolle Tondi); Hessische Landesbibliothek, Fulda (Dr. Eickermann); Biblioteca Comunale, Mantua (Prof. Ubaldo Meroni); Biblioteca Ambrosiana, Milan (Msgr. Angelo Paredi); Biblioteca Estense, Modena (Dott. Pietro Puliatti); Bodleian Library, Oxford (Dr. Richard W. Hunt); Bibliothèque Nationale, Paris (Mme. Denise Bloch); Biblioteca Angelica, Rome; Württembergische Landesbibliothek, Stuttgart (Dr. Wolfgang Irtenkauf); Biblioteca Apostolica Vaticana (Rev. Alfonso Raes, S.J.); Catholic University of America Library, Washington; and the Carmelitana Collection, Washington (Rev. Scott Robinson, O. Carm.). For photographs I would like to thank Mme. Sylvie Béguin of the Musée du Louvre, Dott. G. B. Pineider and Fratelli Alinari of Florence and Sig. Giovetti of Mantua. I have made full use of the libraries of New York City, which are rather well supplied with materials relating to the present study, especially the Columbia University Libraries and the Library of Union Theological Seminary. Thanks to the generosity of the Columbia University Council for Research in the Social Sciences, I was able to procure the necessary photocopies and microfilms.

formed about them than I am. Not only in preparation for this lecture but for many years before that, I have devoted serious efforts to learning as much as possible about the history of Thomism, but this history has never been the principal object of my concern and investigation. Consequently, in speaking to you today about some marginal aspects of the history of Thomism which are related to my own area of research—Italian thought of the fifteenth and early sixteenth centuries—I can simply hope to add some clarifications and explanations to the more comprehensive and central theme that Thomism and its history represent. If it happens then that one or the other of my observations seems false, or at least strange to you, I beg you to excuse the deficient state of my knowledge of a tradition that, I repeat, has not been the principal object either of my early training or of my later studies. I hope you will also keep in mind the fact that the study of the Italian Renaissance cannot help but lend a somewhat different perspective even to such a precise and well-known phenomenon as Thomism. You of course understand that, although it represents only one limited, marginal aspect of the history of Thomism, the subject I propose to discuss, which involves a large number of features and details still unknown or insufficiently explored, remains too vast and complex to be developed fully within the framework of only one lecture. I shall therefore limit myself only to some particular aspects which I have been able to observe and study. In so doing, I hope, nonetheless, by the utilization of several yet unedited or little known sources, to be able to complete or even correct the conventional image of the history of Thomism to which we have, until now, been accustomed.

It is generally recognized that the thought and work of Saint Thomas were among the consummate achievements of medieval thought and of all Western thought. In fact, Thomism and Neo-Thomism have constituted the central current of Catholic thought in modern times, influencing even some Protestant, Jewish, and agnostic thinkers. The renaissance of Thomism, which must be dated from the famous encyclical, *Aeterni Patris*, published by Leo XIII in 1879, imparted also a new and powerful impetus to historical studies devoted not only to the thought of Saint Thomas but to all aspects and currents of medieval thought. Among the historical disciplines, the history of medieval thought in particular has enjoyed remarkable progress and success in the discovery of new sources, in the refinement of research methods, in textual criticism and interpretation, and in the revision of judgments and general theories. But unless I am mistaken, the history of Thomism and the influence of Saint Thomas—a history that would trace in a continuous fashion the developments connecting the work of Saint Thomas with that of his modern disciples—has not been fully studied. We do have some very valuable and complete studies on certain phases of this history, as we shall see later; but there are other phases, including that with which we shall occupy ourselves, that have remained relatively obscure. The most recent work on the whole history of Thomism was published in 1859,[1] thus long before the renaissance of Thomism and of medieval studies, and although it is not without value, the point of view it presents and the information to be found in it are no longer sufficient.

The lack of a complete modern treatise on the history of Thomism is a surprising fact that should serve as an excuse for the vagueness and uncertainty of my remarks on several points. I will accordingly indicate here and there, without elaboration, certain problems which should be made the object of further research.

Most certainly the lack of studies on the history of Thomism, or at least on some phases of this history, may appear strange when we consider the substantial number of works and articles published during the last eighty years on Saint Thomas, Thomism, and many other aspects of medieval thought. But we may better comprehend this phenomenon by remembering that an analogous situation exists for certain other schools of philosophy, for example that of Kant. Thomism, like Platonism and Aristotelianism, represents one of the great traditions of Western thought, and although it has recently received the name *philosophia perennis* after seven centuries of existence, and after even

1. Karl Werner, *Der heilige Thomas von Aquin, vol. III: Geschichte des Thomismus* (Regensburg, 1859; reprint: New York, 1963). For the general bibliography relating to our subject, one should consult: P. Mandonnet and J. Destrez, *Bibliographie Thomiste* (Kain, 1921); V. J. Bourke, *Thomistic Bibliography, 1920–1940* (St. Louis, 1945); P. Wyser, *Thomas von Aquin* (Bern, 1950); idem, *Der Thomismus* (Bern, 1951). For general treatments of the subject, other than the histories of medieval philosophy by M. de Wulf, Ueberweg-Geyer, E. Gilson and A. Maurer, see P. Mandonnet, "Frères Prêcheurs (*La théologie dans l'Ordre des*)," in *Dictionnaire de théologie catholique*, 6 (1920), 864–924; R. Garrigou-Lagrange, "Thomisme," ibid., 15 (1950), 823–1023; C. Fabro, "Santo Tommaso d'Aquino," in *Enciclopedia Cattolica*, 12 (1954), 252–298; M. Grabmann, *Geschichte der katholischen Theologie seit Ausgang der Vaeterzeit* (Freiburg, 1933; reprint: Darmstadt, 1961); W. A. Wallace and J. A. Weisheipl, "St. Thomas Aquinas," in *New Catholic Encyclopaedia*, 14 (1966), 102–115; J. A. Weisheipl, "Thomism," ibid., 126–135; C. Giacon, "Tomismo," in *Enciclopedia filosofica*, 2nd ed., 6 (1967), 505–510.

older antecedents, it has suffered the fate of all other philosophical and intellectual traditions, that is to say, it has experienced more or less profound developments and transformations through the centuries. The philosopher who follows the authority of a master (and it is of little importance whether this master be Plato or Aristotle, Saint Thomas or Kant, Dewey or Wittgenstein or Heidegger) is strongly inclined to understand and interpret the master with the help of his own powers of vision and according to his own conception of truth. He must clarify the ambiguities, obscurities, and inconsistencies he discovers in the text and thought of the master, must fill his gaps, and apply his principles to the solution of new problems as well as to the refutation of new rival positions not known or not studied by the master. There is also the temptation to attribute to the master all the other truths deduced more or less consciously from arguments and sources which are not the master's, but which appear to be compatible with the central idea and fundamental principles of his work. This was the procedure already proposed by Origen for the interpretation of the Bible.[2] For the philosopher who attempts to discover the truth and for whom historical expressions of this truth are simply an aid for discovering it, the attitude that we have been attempting to describe is almost unavoidable, and the historian who would interfere with it will find himself obstructing the very process of philosophical thought. But the historian, and even the philosopher as historian, is obliged to make the effort (which cannot of course always attain its goal) to distinguish the authentic thought of a past thinker from the transformations brought to it by his school and by the tradition that makes use of his name as well as of his authority.

The problem that we have attempted to define exists for all great thinkers in regard to the schools that have grown up around them. In the case of Saint Thomas and Thomism, however, there are certain additional interrelated difficulties of a semi-historical, semi-philosophical kind. Saint Thomas' thought represents a synthesis of a very special sort which contains a great diversity of historical and philosophical elements. Moreover, commentators on Saint Thomas, as well as Thom-

---

2. *Periarchon*, I, Praef. 10: "Oportet igitur velut elementis ac fundamentis huiusmodi uti . . . ut manifestis et necessariis assertionibus de singulis quibusque quid sit in vero rimetur et unum . . . corpus efficiat exemplis et affirmationibus, vel his quas in sanctis scripturis invenerit vel quas ex consequentiae ipsius indagine ac recti tenore reppererit." Origenes, *Werke*, V, ed. P. Koetschau (Leipzig, 1913), 16 (cf. p. 9).

ist thinkers, have committed themselves to very different courses, according as they have given more or less weight to these various elements.[3] The decisive influence of Aristotle's writings on the thought of Saint Thomas has been justly pointed out, but once this fundamental fact was accepted, intense discussion centered on the differences that distinguish Aristotle from Saint Thomas and Saint Thomas from Aristotle. Saint Augustine's influence on the theological thought of Saint Thomas has been noticed, but it has often been denied in relation to the more properly philosophical points of Thomas' thought. Now we know this problem is related to the much discussed question of the influence exercised by Neoplatonism on Saint Thomas' thought, an influence that has been alternately denied and affirmed by scholars of great authority.[4] Furthermore, setting aside the influence that Aristotle and Neoplatonism had on him, and with a view to determining his role in the history of humanism, scholars have wondered what knowledge he could have had of Cicero and the classical world.[5] It has also

3. E. Gilson, *Le Thomisme*, 5th ed. (Paris, 1944); idem, *The Christian Philosophy of St. Thomas Aquinas*, trans. L. K. Shook (New York, 1956); C. Fabro, "Santo Tommaso d'Aquino," in *Enciclopedia Cattolica*, 12 (1954), 252–298.

4. A. C. Pegis, *Saint Thomas and the Greeks* (Milwaukee, 1939): D. A. Callus, "Les sources de saint Thomas," in the volume *Aristote et Saint Thomas d'Aquin* (Louvain, 1957), 93–174; F. van Steenberghen, *Aristote en Occident* (Louvain, 1946), 170–172; idem, *Aristotle in the West*, trans. L. Johnston (Louvain, 1955; 2nd ed., 1970); L. de Raeymaker, *Introduction to Philosophy* (New York, 1948), 177; J. Santeler, *Der Platonismus in der Erkenntnislehre des heiligen Thomas von Aquin* (Innsbruck, 1939). When, after Saint Thomas' death, the masters of the faculty of arts of Paris requested a few of his still unknown philosophical writings from the Dominican chapter in Lyons, this list included an "Expositionem Tymei Platonis." See H. Denifle and E. Chatelain, *Chartularium Universitatis Parisiensis*, I (Paris, 1889), 504–505, n. 447 (May 2, 1274). According to A. Birkenmajer, this refers to a Latin translation of Proclus by William of Moerbeke. Cf. "Der Brief der Pariser Artistenfakultät über den Tod des hl. Thomas von Aquino," in his *Vermischte Untersuchungen zur Geschichte der mittelalterlichen Philosophie* (Münster, 1922), 1–35; "Neues zu dem Briefe der Pariser Antistenfakultaet über den Tod des hl. Thomas von Aquino," in *Xenia Thomistica*, III (Rome, 1925), 57–72. At Naples, Saint Thomas was a student of Peter of Ireland, whose orientation toward medicine rather than theology has been pointed out by C. Baeumker, "Petrus de Hibernia der Jugendlehrer des Thomas von Aquino und seine Disputation vor Koenig Manfred," in *Sitzungsberichte der Bayerischen Akademie der Wissenschaften, Philosophisch-philologische und historische Klasse* (Munich, 1920), n. 8. Cf. M. Grabmann, *Mittelalterliches Geistesleben*, I (Munich, 1926), 249–265.

5. E. K. Rand, *Cicero in the Courtroom of St. Thomas* (Milwaukee, 1946). Cf. W. Jaeger, *Humanism and Theology* (Milwaukee, 1943). *Contra gentiles*, I, 5, presents a curious problem where the Leonine edition (XIII, 1918, p. 14) gives as the text: "Cum enim Simonides quidam homini praetermittendam divinam cognitionem persuaderet." The variation offered by some manuscripts: "Simonides cuidam homini," would make Saint Thomas appear more humanist. The name "Simonides" is not found in the text of Aristotle quoted by Saint Thomas (*Eth.*

been necessary to determine, independently of the philosophical or Neoplatonic speculations of Saint Augustine, what role properly Christian ideas played in the development of Saint Thomas' thought as a result of his study of scripture, the Fathers of the Church and the *Sentences* of Peter Lombard.[6] Considering all these problems, it is evident that a sound method requires that judgment on the relative importance of sources be made only by relying on texts and terminology, and that a privileged place may not be granted certain of them to the prejudice of others, which seems to have been done in some cases.

The influence exercised by Christian ideas upon the thought of Saint Thomas is closely linked to another problem much discussed by his recent followers, namely that of the relationship between philosophy and theology in his work. It would be very difficult, I believe, to deny that in his works the distinction between faith and reason, between theology and philosophy, is very clear. This distinction may be seen as much in the sort of studies he pursued, in his teaching, and in the division of his works, as in his explicit statements themselves. It must be admitted that the introduction of philosophical arguments to confirm or defend theological truths does not allow treating this distinction of his as if it were a question of a complete separation. It must also be admitted that, for him, properly metaphysical problems sometimes involve theological as well as philosophical elements. But in his thought Christian theology is supported by an Aristotelian and universal philosophy. It is not by chance that the expressions "Christian philosophy" and "Catholic philosophy" are not found in his writings, anymore than in those of other medieval scholastic thinkers.[7] The attempt to present Thomism as a Christian philosophy may appear

---

*Nic.*, X, 7, 1177b31–33), nor in the commentary of Michael of Ephesus (ed. G. Heylbut, Berlin, 1892, 591–592). But see Aristotle, *Metaph.*, I, 2, 982b30–32.

6. The idea of being is considered properly Christian by E. Gilson (cf. *L'esprit de la philosophie médiévale*, 2nd ed., Paris, 1948, 39–62; *The Spirit of Medieval Philosophy*, trans. A. H. C. Downes, London, 1936, repr.: New York, 1940, 42–63), and as derived from Greek thought by Cornelia de Vogel, " 'Ego sum qui sum' et sa signification pour une philosophie chrétienne," *Revue des sciences religieuses* 35 (1961), 337–355.

7. "Notes bibliographiques pour servir à l'histoire de la notion de philosophie chrétienne," in E. Gilson, *L'Esprit. . .* , 413–440. Gilson cites no text between Saint Augustine and Erasmus. Some texts of Justin, Petrarch and Calvin could be added to his list. The term *christiana philosophia* is also used in the famous decree in which Pietro Barozzi, bishop of Padua, condemned Averroism in 1489 (G. Di Napoli, *L'immortalità dell'anima nel Rinascimento*, Turin, 1963, p. 186). I am indebted to Professor Edward P. Mahoney for this last reference.

legitimate from a certain modern point of view, but it represents a transformation of the original position of Saint Thomas and encounters both historical and philosophical difficulties. Besides, it has not been accepted by all Catholic or Thomist thinkers.[8] We cannot deny that Saint Thomas was Christian at the very moment he was dealing with philosophy, nor that his religious beliefs exerted an influence on certain of his philosophical positions. But it has been rightly observed that the insistence on the Christian content and basis of philosophy severs all communication between Christian philosophers and those who are either non-Christian or who are unwilling to accept religious authority in the domain of philosophy.[9] A similar, perhaps even greater, difficulty arises from the attempt to define Thomism as a "Christian humanism" or "integral humanism." Not only do the term and the idea of "Christian humanism," or even of "humanism" itself, not occur in the writings of Saint Thomas and his contemporaries, but there is also the additional difficulty that the word "humanism" has acquired such vague and varied meanings in our time that its use leads to considerable confusion if we do not attempt to limit it by means of rigorous definition. The humanism of the Renaissance, of which we shall have to speak, was perhaps neither "true" nor "integral"; it is possible to debate in what sense and to what degree it was Christian. But it has had a very precise significance in the history of scholarship and of literature and if we are to accord Saint Thomas a place in the history of humanism thus understood, this place can be neither as central nor as important as that which he justly occupies in the history of philosophical and theological thought.[10]

It is neither possible nor necessary to present a great deal of evidence to support the fact that the interpreters of Saint Thomas have given more or less weight to certain of his philosophical ideas and that the differences of interpretation are linked to the diversity of emphasis given to certain sources of his thought. It suffices to mention the long discussions that have been dedicated to the doctrine of the analogy of being, a doctrine that has often been considered as a sufficient answer for all problems of modern thought. While deriving

8. A. Renard, *La querelle sur la possibilité de la philosophie chrétienne* (Paris, 1941); M. Nédoncelle, *Existe-t-il une philosophie chrétienne?* new ed. (Paris, 1959) (*Is there a Christian Philosophy?* trans. I. Trethowan, New York, 1960).

9. F. van Steenberghen, "La philosophie en chrétienté," *Revue philosophique de Louvain* 61 (1963), 561–582.

10. P. O. Kristeller, *Renaissance Thought* (New York, 1961).

from Aristotle, it finds more support in the texts of Cajetan than in those of Saint Thomas himself.[11] On the other hand, the doctrine of participation, clearly derived from Neoplatonism, has rarely been mentioned by those of his interpreters who have insisted on his Aristotelianism. Nevertheless this doctrine is considered as central and it is analyzed with great finesse by several recent commentators who are not afraid of emphasizing some elements of strong Neoplatonic origin in his thought alongside the Aristotelian and Christian doctrines. But after all this is not surprising, since he had access to several texts of Proclus and the *Liber de Causis*, in addition to the writings of Saint Augustine, Boethius, the Areopagite, and several Arabian sources with the same tendencies.[12]

Great caution should be exercised in examining the history of Saint Thomas' tradition and influence. The first thing to avoid—and this

11. E. Gilson, *Le Thomisme*, 5th ed. (Paris, 1944), 153; idem, *The Christian Philosophy of St. Thomas Aquinas*, 105–106. See also the comprehensive study of George P. Klubertanz, *St. Thomas Aquinas on Analogy: A Textual Analysis and Systematic Synthesis* (Chicago, 1960).

12. C. Fabro, *La nozione metafisica di partecipazione secondo S. Tommaso d'Aquino* (Milan, 1939); expanded ed. (Turin, 1950; 3rd ed., Turin, 1963); idem, *Participation et causalité selon S. Thomas d'Aquin* (Louvain, 1961); idem, "Participation," in *New Catholic Encyclopedia*, 10 (1966), 1042–46; idem, "Platonismo, neoplatonismo e tomismo: Convergenze e divergenze," in his *Tomismo e pensiero moderno* (Rome, 1969), 435–460; idem, "Platonism, Neo-Platonism and Thomism: Convergences and Divergences," *The New Scholasticism* 44 (1970), 69–100; L.-B. Geiger, *La participation dans la philosophie de S. Thomas d'Aquin* (Paris, 1942; 2nd ed., 1953). Cf. Arthur Little, *The Platonic Heritage of Thomism* (Dublin, 1949); W. Norris Clarke, "The Meaning of Participation in St. Thomas," in *Proceedings of the American Catholic Philosophical Association* 26 (1952), 147–157; idem, "The Limitation of Act by Potency: Aristotelianism or Neoplatonism," *New Scholasticism* 26 (1952), 167–194; idem, "The Platonic Heritage of Thomism," *Review of Metaphysics* 8 (1954–55), 105–124; idem, "St. Thomas and Platonism," *Thought* 32 (1957), 437–443; John S. Dunne, "St. Thomas' Theology of Participation," *Theological Studies* 18 (1957), 481–512; H. H. Berger, "Partizipationsgedanke im Metaphysik-Kommentar des Thomas von Aquin," *Vivarium* 1 (1963), 115–140; J. Durantel, *Saint Thomas et le Pseudo-Denis* (thesis, Paris, 1919; reprint: Dubuque, Iowa, 1964); K. Kremer, *Die Neuplatonische Seinsphilosophie und ihre Wirkung auf Thomas von Aquin* (Leiden, 1966), a much discussed book in which the concept of participation is also treated; Joseph chiu yuen Ho, "La doctrine de la participation dans le commentaire de saint Thomas d'Aquin sur le Liber de causis," *Revue philosophique de Louvain* 70 (1972), 360–383. R. J. Henle's very useful book (*Saint Thomas and Platonism*, The Hague, 1956) is limited to a study of the texts of Saint Thomas in which he speaks explicitly of Plato or the Platonists. Gilson discusses participation in Saint Thomas only in a short note (*Le Thomisme*, p. 182, n. 3) and asserts "que participer, en langage thomiste, ne signifie pas être une chose, mais ne pas l'être." (*The Christian Philosophy of St. Thomas Aquinas*, p. 461. n. 115: "that to participate, in Thomistic language, does not mean to be a thing, but rather means not to be it.") Now in Platonic language, to participate signifies to be a thing and not to be it at the same time, and the resemblance of a copy to its archetype does not imply a reciprocal likeness.

has not always been done—is to attribute to his influence the presence in the thought of the following centuries of a large number of ideas which are indeed found in his work, but which are not in fact peculiar to him. Rather, they are common to many other medieval thinkers or they are derived from ancient sources just as accessible to his successors as to himself. It is also advisable to point out that a great number and a great variety of problems and doctrines in his very vast work are not closely linked one with another. The attempt has been often made to establish a clear distinction between orthodox Thomists and eclectic Thomists. If by orthodox is meant the thinker who is content to reaffirm the doctrines contained in the master's work without adding anything, it is indeed difficult to find any Thomist other than Saint Thomas himself. It is important to distinguish clearly those authors who rely principally on his authority and who tend to support most of his major and characteristic doctrines from those who combine his ideas with other ideas that are either original or from another source, or who are content simply to borrow certain of his ideas or assertions without giving them a central position in their own writings or thought. When dealing with the history of Thomism, it is obviously necessary to consider all of these various factors.

In tracing Saint Thomas' influence on the centuries following him, it is necessary to distinguish the authority attributed to the Saint and to his doctrine by the Dominican Order, of which he had been a member, from that accorded him by theologians of the Catholic Church in general who were not Dominicans and, finally, from that ascribed to him by those philosophers and other scholars not especially concerned with theology. In his Order, the authority of Saint Thomas was established rather quickly after his death, as is easily shown by the decrees on the subject made by a good number of general and provincial chapters of the Order.[13] At first it was merely a question of defending the person and doctrine of the master against the attacks of a few Dominican theologians (1278–79).[14] But even as early as 1286 all Dominican theologians were invited to promote and defend his

13. Mandonnet, in *Dict. de théol. cath.*, 6 (1920), 888–890; C. Douais, *Essai sur l'organisation des études dans l'ordre des Frères Prêcheurs au treizième et au quatorzième siècle* (Paris-Toulouse, 1884); A. Walz, "Ordinationes capitulorum generalium de Sancto Thoma eiusque cultu et doctrina," *Analecta Sacri Ordinis Fratrum Praedicatorum* 31 (1923), 168–173.

14. *Acta Capitulorum Generalium Ordinis Praedicatorum*, I, ed. B. M. Reichert (Rome, 1898), 199 and 204.

doctrine.[15] Then, in 1309, they were asked to teach and resolve every theological question according to his doctrine and works,[16] a prescription that was often repeated in succeeding decrees.[17] Instructions were also given all libraries of the Order to obtain his writings,[18] and, as early as the fourteenth century, Dominican theologians began to be designated by the name of Thomists.[19] The Order of Friars Preachers very early organized a system of instruction that it utilized in its local and provincial schools as well as in its *studia generalia* and in the chairs entrusted to its theologians at the University of Paris and the other universities endowed with faculties of theology.[20] As a result of this system, from at least the fourteenth century on, every Dominican student and every other student of a Dominican school or professor was required to study Thomist doctrine. This applied to philosophy as well as to theology. We should note, however, that in the schools of the Order philosophy was taught only as a subject preliminary to theology, and that in the universities themselves, the teaching done by Dominicans and members of other religious orders was generally limited to theology, and did not extend to philosophy. Moreover, the courses in theology given in the universities and Dominican schools were based exclusively on the Bible and the *Sentences* of Peter Lombard. The teaching of Thomist doctrine thus consisted in using Saint Thomas' commentaries and other writings for interpreting the Bible and the *Sentences*, to which was added, in the schools of the Order alone, the independent study of his other writings.[21] All this explains why a vast theological and philosophical literature was produced by the Dominicans in the fourteenth century, a literature that has been the subject of much research. There was, first of all, a group of polemical treatises

15. Ibid., 235: ". . . doctrinam . . . Thome de Aquino . . . promovendam et saltem ut est opinio defendendam."

16 Ibid., II (Rome, 1899), 38: ". . . quod legant et determinent secundum doctrinam et opera . . . Thome de Aquino, et in eadem scolares suos informent . . ."

17. Ibid., 72 (1314), 81, (1315), 191 (1329), 196 (1330), 262 (1340), 280 (1342), 297 (1344), 303, 308 (1346), 313 (1347), 350 (1353), 367 (1355), 391 (1361).

18. Ibid., II, 83–84 (1315). Cf. Walz, 172. For an excellent recent study of the Dominican Library at Padua, see L. Gargan, *Lo Studio teologico e la Biblioteca dei Domenicani a Padova nel Tre e Quattrocento* (Padua, 1971).

19. F. Ehrle, "Arnaldo de Villanova ed i 'Thomatiste,'" *Gregorianum* 1 (1920), 475–501; idem, *Der Sentenzenkommentar Peters von Candia* (Münster, 1925), 263.

20. Douais, 113–138.

21. Douais, 97–102. The 1308 decree of the provincial chapter of Perugia should be noted: ". . . quod lectores et baccellarii legant de Sententiis et non de Summa Thome." Cf. *Acta Capitulorum Provincialium Provinciae Romanae*, ed. T. Kaeppeli and A. Dondaine (Rome, 1941), 169.

written to defend Saint Thomas' doctrines.[22] Later there were commentaries, questions, and treatises that followed the Thomist position in its key doctrines. A certain number of concordances, summaries, and tables, which reflect the use of his works in the schools, have also been found. These evidently served as tools for study and reference.[23] There also exists at least one commentary on the *De ente et essentia* which dates from the first half of the fourteenth century.[24] This first period of the history of Thomism may be considered to extend to the first half of the fifteenth century, that is, until John Capreolus, the *Princeps Thomistarum*, finished his monumental defense of Saint Thomas' theology at Toulouse around 1432.[25]

Outside the Dominican Order, the influence of Saint Thomas during this first period manifests itself in the discussion of particular doctrines upheld or criticized by masters of the other orders or by secular masters.[26] The diffusion of his works was evidently not limited to the libraries of the various monasteries of his order. To determine the extent of this diffusion precisely, it would be necessary to publish a list of all extant manuscripts of his works, not only of the oldest, which must be used in any critical edition of his works,[27] but also of those which came after them, and even of those which preserve the text in a defective state. These manuscripts would indicate the presence of the texts at a certain moment and in a certain milieu, and the possibility of their use by certain scholars. It would be necessary, moreover,

22. F. Ehrle, "Der Kampf um die Lehre des hl. Thomas von Aquino in den ersten fuenfzig Jahren nach seinem Tod," *Zeitschrift für katholische Theologie* 37 (1913), 266–318. P. Mandonnet, "Premiers travaux de polémique thomiste," *Revue des sciences philosophiques et théologiques* 7 (1913), 46–70, 245–262.

23. Grabmann, *Mittelalterliches Geistesleben*, II (1936), 424–489.

24. M.-H. Laurent, "Armand de Belvézer et son Commentaire sur le 'De ente et essentia,'" *Revue Thomiste* 25 (N.S. 13, 1930), 426–436. The commentary, written between 1323 and 1328, was printed at Padua in 1482 (edited by Andrea da Urbino, O.P., *Gesamtkatalog der Wiegendrucke* 2505) and reprinted, after that of Cardinal Cajetan, at Venice in 1496 (Hain 1504). Still to be studied is the problem of knowing when the term *esse*, which was utilized by Saint Thomas and his first successors, was replaced by *existentia*, the term utilized by William of Moerbeke in his translation of Proclus' *Tria Opuscula* (1280) to render the Greek term ὕπαρξις, which the Neoplatonists borrowed from the Stoics and which is not found in Plato or Aristotle. Cf. Procli Diadochi *Tria Opuscula*, ed. H. Boese (Berlin, 1960), and my review in the *Journal of Philosophy* 59 (1962), 74–78.

25. Grabmann, *Mittelalterliches Geistesleben*, III (1956), 370–410.

26. Cf. the letter of the Paris masters, note 4 above.

27. For a model study of some early manuscripts of Saint Thomas, see A. Dondaine, *Secrétaires de saint Thomas* (Rome, 1956). See now H. F. Dondaine and H. V. Shooner, *Codices Manuscripti Operum Thomae de Aquino*, Tomus I (*Autographa et Bibliothecae A-F*) (Rome, 1967).

to complete the information provided by such a list with an inventory of destroyed and dispersed manuscripts.

But the event which did most to determine Saint Thomas' role in the Church outside his order was his canonization, declared in 1323 by John XXII after a long process.[28] A consequence of the canonization was the revocation by the bishop of Paris of the condemnation of those of Saint Thomas' positions which had been included in the condemnation of 1277.[29] There is no doubt that the canonization contributed in an indirect, but effective, manner to the increase of the Saint's doctrinal authority among theologians and scholars outside the Dominican Order. The Dominicans immediately instituted an office for the new saint, whose feast-day was fixed as March 7,[30] and already in the fourteenth century there were sermons containing eulogies to him.[31]

What may be called the second period of the history of Thomism is marked by the tendency to adopt the *Summa Theologiae* instead of the *Sentences* as the basic text in theology.[32] This movement, whose existence must be established from school and university documents, as well as from manuscript and printed commentaries, began according to the results of the most recent research with which I am acquainted, in the Dominican convents of Germany during the second

28. *Acta Sanctorum*, Martii Tomus I, 653–733; *Fontes vitae S. Thomae Aquinatis*, ed. D. Prummer and M.-H. Laurent (Toulouse, 1912–37), 265–531. For the bull of canonization of John XXII (July 18, 1323), cf. *Bullarium*, IV (Turin, 1859), 302–308; *Bullarium Ordinis FF. Praedicatorum*, II (Rome, 1730), 159–162; A. Walz, "Historia canonizationis S. Thomae Aquinatis," in *Xenia Thomistica*, III (Rome, 1925), 105–188; cf M. Grabmann, "Die Kanonisation des hl. Thomas von Aquin in ihrer Bedeutung fuer die Ausbreitung und Verteidigung seiner Lehre im 14. Jahrhundert," *Divus Thomas*, 3rd ser., 1 (1923), 233–249.

29. Denifle-Chatelain, II (1891), 280–281, n. 838 (February 14, 1325).

30. Walz, *Ordinationes*, 173.

31. Jean de Cardailhac delivered seven sermons on Saint Thomas at Toulouse (cf. Douais, 101–102, who cites Bibliothèque Nationale, Fonds Latin, ms. 3294, and Toulouse ms. 342). On three sermons delivered by Pierre Roger (Clement VI) between 1324 and 1340, cf. M.-H. Laurent, "Pierre Roger et Thomas d'Aquin," *Revue Thomiste* 36 (N.S. 14, 1931), 157–173; B. Guillemain, *La cour pontificale d'Avignon* (Paris, 1962), 117. Before the canonization of Saint Thomas in July 1323, two eulogies were delivered by the pope himself (cf. Guillemain, p. 128) and another by Raymond Bequin (ibid., 384). I am indebted to my friend Giuseppe Billanovich for having brought Guillemain's book and other important sources to my attention.

32. Mandonnet, in *Dictionnaire de théologie catholique*, 6 (1920), 906–907; Ricardo G. Villoslada, *La Universidad de Paris durante los estudios de Francisco de Vitoria* (Rome, 1938), 279–307; Grabmann, *Mittelalterliches Geistesleben*, III (1956), 411–448.

half of the fifteenth century and a little later in Italy. It spread, thanks to Dominican professors, from the convents to the universities, especially in Germany.[33] Then, it was introduced at the University of Paris by Peter Crockaert around 1510 and at Salamanca by his student, Francis de Vitoria, around 1530. During the sixteenth century, the *Summa* was also adopted as a text by the theologians of the new Order of the Jesuits in their college and university teaching, and their example was followed by other Catholic theologians. The study of university documents and the compilation of a bibliography of the commentaries are not yet completed, but we have the impression both that the use of the *Summa*, especially in Spain, Portugal, and their colonies, was very widespread after the second half of the sixteenth century, although study of the *Sentences* had not been completely abandoned, and also that the Franciscans in particular never forsook their Scotist orientation.[34] The notable importance accorded Saint Thomas at the Council of Trent is an indication that his authority had become more general, if not exclusive, in the area of Catholic theology. To the same period, namely to the sixteenth century and the first half of the seventeenth century, also belong numerous commentaries on the *Summa* and on some other works, in particular on the *Summa contra Gentiles* and the *De ente et essentia*.[35] A complete inventory of these published and unedited commentaries has yet to be made, but their importance may be appreciated if we consider the influence exercized by the commen-

33. Grabmann, ibid. For Italy, I am chiefly acquainted with the example of Pavia where we find several times, beginning with 1480 and until at least 1498, some Dominican professors of theology mentioned in the *rotulus* with the note: ". . . qui legat opera Beati Thomae de Aquino" or ". . . sub ea lege quod opera Beati Thomae Aquinatis legat." Cf. *Memoire e documenti per la Storia dell'Università di Pavia*, I (Pavia, 1878), 189–191. The name of the professor teaching in 1498 was Thomas de Vio Caietanus. On the special case of Padua, see below.

34. F. Stegmueller, *Filosofia e teologia nas Universidades de Coimbra e Evora no século XVI* (Coimbra, 1959); idem, *Repertorium Commentariorum in Sententias Petri Lombardi*, 2 vols., (Würzburg, 1947). I am indebted to my friend F. Stegmueller for the additional information that he was kind enough to communicate to me by letter.

35. M. Grabmann, *Mittelalterliches Geistesleben*, I (1926), 314–331; II (1936), 602–613; III (1956), 411–448; idem, "De commentariis in opusculum S. Thomae Aquinatis de ente et essentia," in *Acta Pont. Academiae Romanae S. Thomae Aq. et Religionis Catholicae*, N.S., 5 (1938), 7–20; K. Feckes, "Das Opusculum des hl. Thomas von Aquin 'De ente et essentia' im Lichte seiner Kommentare," in *Aus der Geisteswelt des Mittelalters* (Münster, 1935), I, 667–681; A. Michelitsch, "De commentariis in summam Theologiae S. Thomae Aquinatis," in *Xenia Thomistica*, III (Rome, 1925), 449–458. The work of Henry of Gorrichem (Gorkum) (d. 1439) is not a commentary but a summary of the *Summa*. Cf. Grabmann, II, 440–443.

taries of Cardinal Cajetan, Sylvester of Ferrara, Francis of Vitoria and the other theologians of Salamanca and Coimbra, as well as by those of John of St. Thomas.

Although it is a subject not lacking in interest, the influence that Saint Thomas exerted, outside theological and even Catholic circles, on medieval philosophy and on early modern philosophy has not yet been sufficiently studied.[36] I am referring here, of course, to an influence exercised by means of texts and particular doctrines rather than to a solid current of thought. Saint Thomas' prestige, however, was always great, and beginning with the sixteenth century it often happened—as it never did during the Middle Ages—that the ordinary reader who was not a theologian, and even the reader who was neither a Catholic nor a philosopher, considered Saint Thomas to be the sole representative of medieval philosophy and theology who deserved to be excluded from the general contempt for that tradition.

The third period in the history of Thomism is that in which we are still living today. It began in 1879 with the encyclical *Aeterni Patris*.[37] Saint Thomas thereby became the principal master in Catholic schools, not only in theology but also in philosophy. This event must have had a profound influence on the teaching of these subjects in all Catholic institutions, and it did have very salutary effects on Catholic scholarship, particularly in the area of the history of medieval philosophy and theology. I am sure I will be allowed to note, however, that the position of Thomism, even within the Catholic Church, has since 1879 become very different from what it had been previously. In order to form a correct idea of the history of Thomism and of Saint Thomas' influence during the periods prior to 1879, it is necessary to get a clear

36. Cf. John K. Ryan, *The Reputation of St. Thomas Aquinas among English Protestant Thinkers of the Seventeenth Century* (Washington, 1948).

37. The text has been printed several times: Leo XIII, *Epistola encyclica* (Rome, 1879) (title on the cover page: *De philosophia Christiana ad mentem Sancti Thomae Aquinatis doctoris angelici in scholis Catholicis instauranda*); *Acta Sanctae Sedis*, 12 (1879–80), 97–115; Leonis XIII . . . *Litterae Encyclicae duobus primis sui pontificatus annis editae* (Rome, 1880), 33–69; Leonis XIIII . . . *Acta*, I (Rome, 1881), 255–284 (with the same title as the 1879 edition); Leonis XIII *Epistolae Encyclicae*, ser. 1 (Freiburg, 1881), 51 pp.; Sancti Thomae Aquinatis *Opera Omnia*, Editio Leonina, I (Rome, 1882), pp. III–XVI (with the 1879 title on p. I); *Acta Leonis XIII* (Paris, 1885), 40–75 (with the title: *Epistola encyclica de philosophia scholastica*); Leonis Papae XIII *Allocutiones, epistolae, constitutiones aliaque acta praecipua*, I (Bruges and Lille, 1887), 88–108 (with the title: *De colenda S. Thomae philosophia*); *Actes de Léon XIII*, I (Paris, 1925), 42–75; F. Kard. Ehrle, *Zur Enzyklika "Aeterni Patris," Text und Kommentar*, ed. F. Pelster (Rome, 1954), 17–34.

idea of the facts that I have attempted to outline and to distinguish various levels of influence according as this influence has been felt in theology or philosophy within the Dominican Order, outside this order but within the Catholic Church, or outside the Catholic Church itself.

The establishment of the general outline of the history of Thomism, in so far as this can be done in the present state of our knowledge —or rather of my own limited knowledge—has finally prepared us to approach the proper subject of this lecture: the place of Thomism in the Italian thought of the Renaissance. It is fitting to begin this study with the period of Saint Thomas himself, that is, from the second half of the thirteenth century, because even if this period does precede the Italian Renaissance, it nevertheless contains, in Italy, some seeds of that humanism and that Aristotelianism which will be the characteristic aspects of the Renaissance properly so-called.

Saint Thomas was Italian. He was born in Italy, and he also died there, having spent a good part of his life in his native land as student and teacher. But it is no exaggeration to say that the content of his thought and the form of his written work depend essentially upon the intellectual and scholarly traditions of Northern Europe, in particular on those of the Dominican schools of Cologne and also of the University of Paris, where he lived the most important years of his life as a student and professor.[38] He certainly exerted a strong influence in Italy not so much because of his nationality, but rather thanks to the students and friends he left there and to the important work of the schools of his Order. This influence, however, was transformed and limited by the special circumstances which characterized the intellectual and academic situation in Italy and which were very different from those of the other Western countries. The Italian universities were as old as those of the North, but whereas the universities of Paris and Oxford had as their nucleus the faculties of theology, which were composed of numerous secular and regular masters, in Italy the universities of Salerno, Bologna, Padua, and Naples, to name only the oldest, owe their origins to schools of law and medicine. There were no faculties of theology there, and the occasional presence of a course or professor of theology indicated a temporary arrangement and an op-

38. A. Walz, *San Tommaso d'Aquino* (Rome, 1945), (*Saint Thomas Aquinas: A Biographical Study*, trans. S. Bullough, Westminster, Md., 1951). Cf. note 1 above.

tional course for arts students, not a program of studies fit to prepare professional theologians.[39] Without pausing to look for an explanation of this strange but important fact, I am inclined to attribute it to a tendency of the ecclesiastical authority to wish to maintain a monopoly for the faculties of theology of Paris and Oxford, over which it could exert a certain control, rather than to the presence of a lay spirit in the Italian cities—although this lay spirit may be said to have instigated the founding in Italy of schools of medicine and law, instead of theology, during the period of formation of the twelfth century. There thus resulted, as a consequence of this institutional situation, a weakness in theological teaching in the Italian universities which would continue for several centuries. On the other hand, the teaching of philosophy, that is, Aristotelian philosophy, was pursued on a very large scale beginning at least with the thirteenth century. It is important to note that this teaching was connected to that of medicine, not theology, and that it was usually done by laymen interested in medicine.[40] On the other hand, the religious orders, through their schools or *studia*, maintained for a long time the teaching of theology in Italy —teaching that was attended at times both by secular priests and by laymen (as was the case for Dante). But even in university cities these schools did not have the same intimate connection with the university usually enjoyed by those in the North. Accordingly, the Italian theology student, whether secular or regular, often went to the universities of the North in order to pursue advanced studies and obtain the master of theology degree.[41]

39. H. Rashdall, *The Universities of Europe in the Middle Ages*, new ed. by F. M. Powicke and A. B. Emden, I (Oxford, 1936), 250–253. This general judgment is confirmed by documents from Bologna, Padua, Naples, Florence, and Pavia.
40. Rashdall, I, 234–235.
41. Dante, *Convivio*, II, 12, 7 (*ne le scuole de li religiosi*). Paul of Venice studied at Oxford toward the end of the fourteenth century. Giovanni Contarini studied at Oxford and at Paris between 1392 and 1408. Cf. G. Dalla Santa, "Uomini e fatti dell'ultimo Trecento e del primo Quattrocento," in *Nuovo Archivio Veneto*, N.S. 32, pt. I (1916), 5–105; A. Luttrell, "Giovanni Contarini, A Venetian at Oxford: 1392–1399," *Journal of the Warburg and Courtauld Institutes* 29 (1966), 424–436. For an example from the fifteenth century, cf. J. Ruysschaert, "Lorenzo Guglielmo Traversagni de Savone," *Archivum Franciscanum Historicum* 46 (1953), 195–210. For further information on Traversagni, see the third essay in this volume, p. 155. The experts do not agree whether and to what extent Dante was a Thomist (E. Gilson, *Dante et la philosophie*, 2nd ed., Paris, 1953; B. Nardi, *Nel mondo di Dante*, Rome, 1944; idem, *Dante e la cultura medievale*, Bari, 1949; Dante Alighieri, *The Divine Comedy*, translated, with a commentary, by Charles S. Singleton, *Inferno*, 2 vols., Princeton, 1970). He hardly belonged to the Renaissance, but he influenced the Renaissance (M. Barbi, *Dante nel*

This situation was to be modified during the fourteenth century, but the change was not as profound as has been claimed even by those who have written its history. At the time of the foundation of many new universities, such as that of Florence, for example, the popes of Avignon included theology in the charters granted them,[42] which was something completely new for Italy. A little later, they accorded the same rights to the older universities of Bologna and Padua.[43] As a result of these privileges, the *Collegia doctorum theologiae* were immediately established in these cities alongside the universities. These colleges, however, just like the analogous older colleges of law and medicine, did not have faculties composed of university professors but were rather professional corporations that had the right to examine candidates and confer degrees. These corporations were composed both of a certain number of university professors, to the exclusion of others, and also of other members of the liberal professions who were not attached to the university. In the case of the theological colleges established in Florence, Bologna, Padua, and elsewhere, the corporation was composed of professors of theology who resided in these cities and taught either in the local Dominican schools (*studia*) or in those of the other religious orders.[44] The universities themselves never had a separate faculty of theology; the isolated courses and chairs of theology were part of the faculty of arts. The university records of Florence, Bologna, and Pavia indicate that in the fourteenth and fifteenth centuries the teaching of theology was ordinarily limited to only one course that was not even offered every year. The lecturer for the course, who was invited by the government and by the univer-

*Cinquecento, Annali della R. Scuola Normale Superiore di Pisa* 13, 1890, no. 2) and thus acted as an important transmitter of Thomist doctrine during the centuries following him.

42. *Bull* of Clement VI (31 May, 1349) in *Statuti della Università e Studio Fiorentino*, ed. A. Gherardi (Florence, 1881), 116–118.

43. The privilege for Bologna dates from June 30, 1360 (Rashdall, I, p. 252), that for Padua from April 15, 1363. Cf. *I Più antichi statuti della Facoltà Teologica dell'Università di Bologna*, ed. F. Ehrle (Bologna, 1932); G. Brotto and G. Zonta, *La facoltà teologica dell' Università di Padova* (Padua, 1922), 253–254.

44. Cf. Ehrle for Bologna and Brotto and Zonta for Padua. For Florence, cf. G. Cerracchini, *Fasti teologali ovvero Notizie istoriche del Collegio de' teologi della Sacra Università Fiorentina* (Florence, 1738). More reliable, but less complete, information may be found in the volume of Gherardi, cited above in note 42. For Bologna, cf. also C. Piana, "La Facoltà teologica dell'Università di Bologna nel 1444–1458," *Archivum Franciscanum Historicum* 53 (1960), 361–441; idem, *Ricerche su le Università di Bologna e di Parma nel secolo XV* (Quaracchi, 1963); idem, *Nuove ricerche su le Università di Bologna e di Parma* (Quaracchi, 1966).

sity, was always a master of theology from one of the religious orders who taught at the same time in the local *studium* of his order. The subject of his course always was one of the books of the Bible or of the *Sentences*.[45] We should note that, beginning with the middle of the fifteenth century, a special arrangement made it possible for the University of Padua to offer two courses in metaphysics and two courses in theology, one *in via sancti Thomae*, the other *in via Scoti*, in accordance with the Paduan system of competing chairs. The course *in via Thomae* was always given by a Dominican, and the course *in via Scoti* by a Franciscan.[46] Again we should note that at Pavia, during the second half of the fifteenth century, the course in theology was given several times by a Dominican, who was required, according to an explicit clause, to rely on the texts of Saint Thomas.[47] It was only after the middle of the sixteenth century, hence after the Council of Trent, that there was more regularity and variety in the courses of theology offered in the Italian universities; but their number was always restricted to three or four, and they were exclusively a part of the faculty of arts, never of autonomous faculties of theology.[48] Besides, it can be demonstrated that until the end of the eighteenth century, at least at Bologna, the courses in theology were always based on the *Sentences* of Peter Lombard, even when they were given by

45. For Florence, cf. Gherardi, 153–154, 295, 377–378, 476–477. For Bologna, cf. U. Dallari, *I rotuli dei lettori legisti e artisti dello Studio Bolognese dal 1384 al 1799*, 4 vols. (Bologna, 1888–1924). For Pavia, cf. *Memorie e documenti per la storia dell'Università di Pavia*, I (Pavia, 1878), 185–198. For Naples, cf. *Storia dell'Università di Napoli* by F. Torraca and others (Naples, 1924), 27–28, 64–66, 174–175, 186, 255–264, 303–304.

46. The chair of Thomist metaphysics probably dates from 1442, that of Scotist metaphysics was added after 1469. The chair of Scotist theology was established between 1473 and 1490, that of Thomist theology in 1490. See Brotto and Zonta, 93–103, 179–208, who give the list of professors up until 1509. For the professors who taught after 1509, cf. A. Riccobonus, "De Gymnasio Patavino," in *Thesaurus Antiquitatum et Historiarum Italiae*, ed. J. G. Graevius, VI, pt. 4 (Leiden, 1722), 23; J. Facciolati, *Fasti Gymnasii Patavini* (Padua, 1757), I, 94–99; II, 251–272. The Paduan system of Thomist and Scotist chairs is found at Bologna only in 1762 (as early as 1758 for Thomist metaphysics). The two chairs are found at Naples, based on the model of those at Salamanca, beginning in 1614. See *Storia*, 303–304; cf. p. 255.

47. Note 33 above.

48. Cf. Dallari for Bologna, Facciolati for Padua, *Memorie e Documenti* for Pavia, and *Storia* for Naples. For Scotist theology at Naples, cf. D. Scaramuzzi, *Il pensiero di Giovanni Duns Scoto nel Mezzogiorno d'Italia* (Rome, 1927), 293–308. See also A. Poppi, "Il contributo dei formalisti padovani al problema delle distinzioni," in *Problemi e figure della Scuola Scotista del Santo* (Padua, 1966), 601–790. I owe these latter two references and some others to Edward P. Mahoney.

Dominicans and *in via Thomae*.[49] The Jesuits, for their part, established a good number of important colleges and schools in Italy, and even some colleges of university level, but they were rarely if ever found among the theology professors in the faculties of art in the old Italian universities.

If, therefore, we end this examination with the first quarter of the sixteenth century, it must be said that the influence of Thomist theology and philosophy was exerted by means of the teaching in the Dominican schools and the isolated theology courses sometimes, but not always, given by Dominican masters. As we may easily understand, the influence of these masters was limited as a result of the competition created by the teaching of professors from other orders as well as by the teaching of laymen who studied and taught philosophy along with medicine and, later on, along with humanistic subjects or mathematical sciences.

To teaching must be added reading as an important means by which Saint Thomas' influence spread in the milieu of the Italian Renaissance. Along with citations, which have only recently begun to be collected, we lack, just as we do for the preceding period, and as we have already pointed out, a critical census of the manuscripts of Saint Thomas' works. We also lack, for the second half of the fifteenth century and the beginning of the sixteenth, a modern critical bibliography of the early editions. From such a bibliography, we would learn not only their date and place of publication but also the frequency and chronological and geographical distribution of the editions of Saint Thomas' individual works, as well as the identity, importance, and intellectual occupation of the scholars, both within and outside the Dominican order, who took part in their preparation.[50] The compila-

49. Dallari, III, pt. II, 1919.
50. A bibliography is to be found in J. Quétif and J. Echard, *Scriptores Ordinis Praedicatorum*, I (Paris, 1719; repr.: New York, n.d.), 283–345; this work is still indispensable. Another useful, but preliminary, bibliographical essay is to be found in A. Michelitsch, *Thomas-Schriften*, I (Graz, 1913), 60–94 (for the manuscripts) and 197–232 (for the incunabula). I am acquainted with modern bibliographical studies only for the *Opuscula*: B. Kruitwagen, *S. Thomae de Aquino Summa Opusculorum anno circiter 1485 typis edita vulgati opusculorum textus princeps* (Kain, 1924); Giov. Felice Rossi, *Antiche e nuove edizioni degli opuscoli di San Tommaso d'Aquino e il problema della loro autenticità* (Piacenza, 1955). For the other works, we must resort to the general lists of Hain, Copinger, Reichling, Panzer, etc., and to the catalogues of the great libraries. For the mss., see now the works of Dondaine and Shooner, cited above, note 27.

tion of such a bibliography would be an important project involving, to be sure, great obstacles, but it would certainly be of common interest both for the historians of Thomism and the historians of the Renaissance.

Finally, to come to more precise facts, it may be stated, without fear of exaggeration, that the history of Thomism in Italy is identified in its beginnings principally, if not exclusively, with the history of the intellectual activity of the Italian Dominicans. Their writings have been studied in detail, and it has been found that, in theology as well as in philosophy, most of them followed Saint Thomas' fundamental doctrines.[51] Among many others we should mention Remigio de' Girolami, who was important for the range of his teaching at Florence and for perhaps having been one of Dante's masters. He left a vast body of unedited writings that are of interest not only to theologians but also to historians of eloquence and literature.[52] Guido Vernani of Rimini wrote some commentaries on Aristotle, but he is better known for his role as censor of Dante's De monarchia.[53]

In the fifteenth century we find, among Dominican theologians, Saint Antoninus, archbishop of Florence,[54] whose voluminous Summa has attracted above all the attention of historians of economic theory, and also Girolamo Savonarola who, in addition to his celebrated Sermons, left several theological and philosophical treatises of Thomist inspiration.[55] To the Dominican thinkers of the fifteenth century must

51. Besides the general histories of medieval philosophy, one must consult Ehrle, Der Sentenzenkommentar, 262–265, and above all Grabmann, Mittelalterliches Geistesleben, I, 332–391.

52. G. Salvadori and V. Federici, "I sermoni d'occasione, le sequenze e i ritmi di Remigio Girolami fiorentino," in Scritti vari di filologia, A Ernesto Monaci (Rome, 1901), 455–508; S. Orlandi, Necrologio di S. Maria Novella (Florence, 1955), I, 276–307; Charles T. Davis, "An Early Florentine Political Theorist: Fra Remigio de' Girolami," in Proceedings of the American Philosophical Society 104 (1960), 662–676; idem, "Education in Dante's Florence," Speculum 40 (1965), 415–435. Cf. Grabmann, Mittelalterliches Geistesleben, I, 361–369; II, 530–547.

53. T. Kaeppeli, "Der Dantegegner Guido Vernani, O.P. von Rimini," Quellen und Forschungen aus italienischen Archiven und Bibliotheken 28 (1938), 107–146; M. Grabmann, "Methoden und Hilfsmittel des Aristotelesstudiums im Mittelalter," in Sitzungsberichte der philosophisch-historischen Abteilung der Bayerischen Akademie der Wissenschaften (Munich, 1939), no. 5, 84–89.

54. R. Morçay, Saint Antonin, archevêque de Florence (Paris, 1914); R. de Roover, San Bernardino of Siena and Sant 'Antonino of Florence, The Two Great Economic Thinkers of the Middle Ages (Boston, 1967); Thomas Kaeppeli, Scriptores Ordinis Praedicatorum Medii Aevi, I (A–F) (Rome, 1970), 80–100.

55. E. Garin, La cultura filosofica del Rinascimento Italiano (Florence, 1961), 183–212. Cf. P. Villari, La Storia di Girolamo Savonarola e de' suoi tempi, I (Florence, 1910), 95–113; J. Schnitzer, Savonarola, II (Munich, 1924), 762–800; Donald Weinstein, Savonarola and Florence (Princeton, 1970).

be added Dominic of Flanders, who spent a large part of his life in Italy teaching at Bologna and Florence, and who wrote an important commentary on Aristotle's *Metaphysics* that he dedicated to Lorenzo de' Medici.[56] Cardinal Juan Torquemada was more a canonist than a theologian, but one of his important works concerning the controversy over the power of the Pope and the councils is based on a collection of propositions taken from the works of Saint Thomas.[57] Among the Dominican scholars who taught in the Italian schools and universities of the fifteenth century, we must single out Francesco Sicuro of Nardò. He taught metaphysics at Padua for several decades and had numerous lay students, one of whom was Pietro Pomponazzi.[58] Without lingering over the contributions of the Italian Dominicans to general culture, we must mention their important role in the theological debates of the time, especially in those concerning the blood of Christ and the Immaculate Conception, as well as the extensive treatises on the latter question by Vincenzo Bandello.[59] Many of them are also distinguished for their studies of Saint Thomas' works. They composed tables and summaries, copied, translated and later edited his writings, and commented upon them. We should also mention Peter of Bergamo, Paul of Soncino,[60] and above all Thomas de Vio, Cardinal Cajetan, who be-

56. L. Mahieu, *Dominique de Flandres* (Paris, 1942); U. Schikowski, "Dominikus de Flandria O.P.," *Archivum Fratrum Praedicatorum* 10 (1940), 169–221; Kaeppeli, *Scriptores*, I, 315–318. On the Hungarian Dominican, Nicolaus de Mirabilibus, see pp. 90 and 146 below.

57. *Flores sententiarum Beati Thomae de Aquino de auctoritate summi pontificis collecti per Joh. de Turrecremata* (1437), Lyons, 1496 (Hain, 1422). Cf. J. M. Garrastachu, "Los Manuscritos del Cardenal Torquemada en la Biblioteca Vaticana," *La Ciencia Tomista* 41 (1930), 188–217, 291–322.

58. Brotto and Zonta, 195–197; Kaeppeli, I, 390–391; Gargan, 114–115. It should be noted that he published an edition of the Scotist Antonius Andreae (*Quaestiones super XII libros Metaphysicae* [Venice, c. 1473–77]; *Gesamtkatalog der Wiegendrucke* 1656).

59. For the controversy on the Blood of Christ, cf. M.-D. Chenu, in *Dictionnaire de théologie catholique*, 14 (1931), 1094–97; C. Sericoli, *Immaculata B. M. Virginis Conceptio iuxta Xysti IV Constitutiones, Bibliotheca Mariana Medii Aevi*, V (Sibenic and Rome, 1945); G. Roschini and others, "Immacolata Concezione," in *Enciclopedia Cattolica*, 6 (1951), 1651–63; R. Haubst, in *Lexikon fuer Theologie und Kirche*, 2 (1958), 544–545; H. Jedin, "Studien über Domenico de' Domenichi," in *Abhandlungen der Geistes- und Sozialwissenschaftlichen Klasse* (Akademie der Wissenschaften und der Literatur), Mainz, 1957, no. 5, 175–300, at 188–189. For the controversy on the Immaculate Conception, cf. X. Le Bachelet in *Dictionnaire de théologie catholique*, 7 (1922), 845–1218. On Vincenzo Bandello and his two treatises, cf. R. P. Mortier, *Histoire des Maîtres généraux de l'Ordre des Frères Prêcheurs*, V (Paris, 1911), 66–127.

60. Peter of Bergamo is known for his *Tabula Aurea*, printed several times after 1473; cf. G. F. Rossi, 30; Piana, *Ricerche* (1963), 112–114. Peter Maldura of Bergamo O.P. taught for years at Bologna and died in 1482. His *In opera Sancti*

came one of the most important Thomist theologians and philosophers of all time.[61] He taught at Padua and Pavia, and it is probably at Pavia that he began his famous commentary on the *Summa*. There is a tendency to attribute to his stay at Padua the presence in his writings of Scotistic and Averroistic doctrines that he attempted to refute, as well as his behavior at the Lateran Council, where he declared himself fully in favor of a clear distinction between philosophy and theology.[62] His agreement with Pomponazzi on certain details of Aristotle's doctrine of the soul brought on the critique of Bartolomeo Spina, another Dominican theologian of some importance. It has likewise aroused the interest of several recent historians.[63]

The Italian Dominicans of the sixteenth century distinguished themselves as commentators on Saint Thomas and also as polemicists against the Protestant Reformation.[64] I cannot here pass over in silence the name of Crisostomo Javelli who, by his friendly refutation appended to Pomponazzi's *Defensorium*, made its publication possible

---

*Thomae Aquinatis Index seu Tabula Aurea* was recently reprinted (Rome, 1960). Cf. I. Colosio, "La 'Tabula Aurea' di Pietro da Bergamo († 1482)," *Divus Thomas* (Piacenza) 64 (1961), 119–132. Paul of Soncino published forty-nine of Saint Thomas' *Opuscula* at Milan in 1488 with a preface addressed to Cardinal Ascanio Sforza (Hain 1540). Cf. Piana, *Ricerche*, 201–202. Cf. Hain 1328 ff., for the editions of Saint Thomas' works printed before 1500, with information on the editors. Frate Gregorio da Genova translated two opuscula into Italian about 1493. Cf. P. O. Kristeller, *Iter Italicum*, I (Leiden, 1963), 269. For the commentaries on the *De ente*, cf. K. Feckes, "Das Opusculum des hl. Thomas von Aquin 'De ente et essentia' im Lichte seiner Kommentare," in *Aus der Geisteswelt des Mittelalters* (Münster, 1935), I, 677–681. For those on the *Summa*, cf. A. Michelitsch, "De commentariis in summam Theologiae S. Thomae Aquinatis," in *Xenia Thomistica*, III (Rome, 1925), 449–458. Cf. Grabmann's research cited above.

61. "Il Cardinale Tommaso de Vio Gaetano nel quarto centenario della sua morte," *Rivista di filosofia neo-scolastica, Supplemento speciale al vol. 27* (Milan, 1935); C. Giacon, *La seconda scolastica*, I (Milan, 1944); Grabmann, *Mittelalterliches Geistesleben*, II, 602–613; Gargan, 156–157; E. Gilson, "Cajetan et l'humanisme théologique," *Archives d'histoire doctrinale et littéraire du Moyen Age* 30 (1955, published 1956), 113–136.

62. ". . . et R. P. Thomas generalis O.P. dixit quod non placet secunda pars bullae, praecipiens philosophis, ut publice persuadendo doceant veritatem fidei." J. D. Mansi, *Sacrorum Conciliorum . . . collectio*, 32 (Paris, 1902), 843. Cf. C. J. Hefele and I. Card. Hergenroether, *Conciliengeschichte*, VIII (Freiburg, 1887), 587.

63. E. Gilson, "Autour de Pomponazzi," *Archives d'histoire doctrinale et littéraire du Moyen Age* 28 (1961, pub. 1962), 163–279; idem, "L'affaire de l'immortalité de l'âme à Venise au début du XVIe siècle," in *Umanesimo europeo e umanesimo veneziano*, ed. V. Branca (Florence, 1963), 31–61; G. Di Napoli, *L'immortalità dell' anima nel Rinascimento* (Turin, 1963), 214–226.

64. F. Lauchert, *Die italienischen literarischen Gegner Luthers* (Freiburg, 1912).

and saved its reputation. His subsequent writings clearly display the influence of the platonizing current.[65]

On the whole, the Thomism of the Dominican school presented itself during the Italian Renaissance as a current of thought whose solidity and strength were felt in the theological and philosophical debates of the time and which likewise exerted a certain influence outside the framework of the Order, as we shall have occasion to see later. It must be added, however, that it did not play a preponderant role in the philosophical or even the theological thought of the period. It entered into competition with several rival ideas and currents. This rivalry sometimes expressed itself in more or less animated controversies, but more often in a sort of peaceful coexistence and almost always in an exchange of ideas and ways of thought of which the participants were not always conscious. In theology, the strongest rival of the Thomist school was the Scotist school of the Franciscans who, in the course of the Italian Renaissance, perhaps surpassed the Dominican Thomists in literary production and in the influence of their teaching.[66] The rivalry of the two orders likewise expressed itself in the activity of their preachers, whose influence on the political and social life of the period is well attested by the documents, and whose numerous preserved and partially printed sermons constitute an abundant literature. These sermons have been studied from the point of view of their historical content and their literary form, but not yet sufficiently from that of their doctrinal substance.[67] In contrast to what happened in the North, the Occamist current does not seem to have been strong among theologians in Italy, although it exerted a notable influence among lay philosophers.[68] On the other hand, fourteenth-

65. Cf. Gilson and Di Napoli, note 63 above.
66. Brotto and Zonta, loc. cit.; D. Scaramuzzi, *Il pensiero di Giovanni Duns Scoto nel Mezzogiorno d'Italia* (Rome, 1927); A. Poppi, "Per una storia della cultura nel Convento del Santo dal XIII al XIX secolo," *Quaderni per la Storia dell' Università di Padova* 3 (1970), 1–29; idem, "Il contributo dei formalisti" (see above, note 48).
67. For the Franciscan preachers, cf. K. Hefele, *Die franziskanische Wanderpredigt in Italien waehrend des 15. Jahrhunderts* (Freiburg, 1912); V. Rossi, *Il Quattrocento* (Milan, 1933), 157–161. There is a vast body of literature on San Bernardino da Siena. The Franciscan preacher Alberto de Sarteano had very close relations with the humanists of his time.
68. On the Celestine monk Marco da Benevento, editor of William of Occam at Bologna, cf. A. Birkenmajer, "Marco da Benevento und die angebliche Nominalistenakademie zu Bologna," *Philosophisches Jahrbuch* 38 (1925), 336–344. See also the forthcoming book by Herbert S. Matsen, *Alessandro Achillini*

and more particularly fifteenth-century Italy produced an immense literature that was religious in the large sense of the word but was not theological in the more narrow sense of the term. The authors of this literature were members of various religious orders, secular priests, or lay writers who have not yet been sufficiently studied. In its style, its sources, and its ideas, this literature was as strongly permeated with humanism and Platonism as it was with Aristotelianism or Thomism.

If we move from the Dominicans and scholasticism to the broad field of philosophical and lay thought in the Italian Renaissance, it is fitting to speak first of the lay Aristotelianism which dominated philosophical teaching in the faculties of art during the entire period of the Renaissance and which is designated, especially in French works, by the name of Paduan Averroism.[69] This Aristotelianism, which we now know to have existed at Salerno beginning with the twelfth century,[70] and in the other Italian universities beginning with the thirteenth century, flourished in the fifteenth and sixteenth centuries not only at Padua but in all Italian universities and continued to develop until the beginning of the seventeenth century. The abundant and unceasing activity of a large number of professors, who were more or less renowned and productive, reveals itself in the vast number of commentaries, questions, and treatises dedicated to the works of Aristotle and his medieval

---

(1463–1512) and His Doctrine of 'Universals' and 'Transcendentals,' to be published by Bucknell University Press. We possess a nice document for "l'augustinisme avicennisant" in the fifteenth century, whose Italian origin, however, is not certain, in an apocryphal letter from Avicenna to Saint Augustine published by M. T. d'Alverny, Archives d'histoire doctrinale et littéraire du Moyen Age 30 (1963, pub. 1964), 271.

69. E. Renan, Averroès et l'averroïsme (Paris, 1852); L. Mabilleau, Etude historique sur la philosophie de la Renaissance en Italie (Paris, 1881); B. Nardi, Saggi sull'aristotelismo padovano dal secolo XIV al XVI (Florence, 1958); J. H. Randall, Jr., The School of Padua and the Emergence of Modern Science (Padua, 1961); L. Quadri, "Averroismo," Enciclopedia filosofica, 2nd ed., 1 (1967), 660–664; A. Poppi, Introduzione all'Aristotelismo Padovano (Padua, 1970); Charles B. Schmitt, A Critical Survey and Bibliography of Studies on Renaissance Aristotelianism 1958–1969 (Padua, 1971); P. O. Kristeller, La tradizione aristotelica nel Rinascimento (Padua, 1962); idem, "Renaissance Aristotelianism," Greek, Roman, and Byzantine Studies 6 (1965), 157–174; F. E. Cranz, A Bibliography of Aristotle Editions 1501–1600 (Baden-Baden, 1971); Ch. H. Lohr, "Medieval Latin Aristotle Commentaries," Traditio 23 (1967), 313–413; 24 (1968), 149–245; 26 (1970), 135–216; 27 (1971), 251–351; 28 (1972), 281–396; A. Poppi, Causalità e infinità nella Scuola Padovana dal 1480 al 1513 (Padua, 1966).

70. P. O. Kristeller, Studies in Renaissance Thought and Letters (Rome, 1956), 495–551; idem, "Nuove fonti per la medicina salernitana del secolo XII," Rassegna storica Salernitana, 18 (1957), 61–75; idem, La tradizione aristotelica nel Rinascimento (Padua, 1962).

disciples. This literature is only partially printed and still remains very little studied. In the present state of our knowledge, or rather ignorance, of this vast area of Italian thought of the Renaissance, it would be hazardous to make any pronouncements on the influence exercised by Saint Thomas on the lay Aristotelians of the time. Evidently, we cannot expect to discover in them any tendency toward an "orthodox" Thomism as that of the Dominican school, since these philosophers ordinarily did not concern themselves with theological questions and since, in the properly philosophical area, Saint Thomas occupied only the position of one of the numerous commentators on Aristotle. They therefore felt free to follow his opinion on certain points or to reject it on others. Relying on our present limited knowledge, we may, as a matter of fact, observe that Saint Thomas was greatly respected as a commentator on Aristotle without, however, being always followed, and that his commentaries, after those of Averroes and along with others, were often cited and discussed. His properly philosophical writings—the commentaries on Aristotle and the opuscula *De ente et essentia* and *De unitate intellectus contra Averroistas*—were well known and accessible in manuscript copies and printed editions.[71] Moreover, during the second half of the fifteenth century, instruction in Thomism at the University of Padua, which included the teaching of metaphysics along with that of theology, must have left a profound impression on those who followed it.

It suffices for us to cite the case of Pietro Pomponazzi, the best known representative of lay Aristotelianism in the Italian Renaissance. We know that he followed the courses given by the Thomist Francesco of Nardò at Padua and that he often cited, and with great respect, the opinions of Saint Thomas in his published writings as well as in his unedited courses, about which we have greater knowledge today thanks to the research of Bruno Nardi and Antonino Poppi.[72] We now know that in regard to the important problem of the soul and its immortality, the thought of Pomponazzi changed and wavered in an important and complicated manner, dating from his first courses at Padua until his

71. A fairly large number of early editions of Saint Thomas were printed in Italy, particularly at Venice and Padua. This is especially true for his commentaries on Aristotle and his other philosophical works. In order to be more precise, it would be necessary to analyze the references given by Hain, Panzer, and the other bibliographers, which we cannot do here. For the mss., see Dondaine and Shooner (above, note 27). See also Cranz (above, note 69).

72. B. Nardi, *Studi su Pietro Pomponazzi* (Florence, 1965); A. Poppi, *Saggi sul pensiero inedito di Pietro Pomponazzi* (Padua, 1970).

death at Bologna. In this development, his famous treatise of 1516, the *Tractatus de immortalitate animae*, and the two apologetic treatises which followed it occupy a place of primary, but not exclusive, importance.[73] Without now making any pronouncement on the details of this development or on the relative scope of the different texts, it suffices for our purpose to state that Thomist arguments played a decisive role in turning Pomponazzi away from the Averroist position regarding the unity of the intellect that he had seemed to embrace at the beginning of his career, but which he resolutely opposed in his courses and subsequent writings.[74] Moreover, in his treatise of 1516, he seriously examined four positions on the conception of the soul. That of Saint Thomas was discussed alongside those of Averroes, Plato, and Alexander (who is not mentioned by name here, but who was in an earlier work). Of these four positions, that of Saint Thomas is not acknowledged to be identical with that of Aristotle and natural reason, but it is presented with respect as conforming to the position of the Church and to the truth of the faith.[75] I shall not pause over the thorny problem of Pomponazzi's sincerity, which has been delicately and fairly defended recently by Gilson, with whom I am happy to find myself in agreement on this point.[76] But it is important to note that Pomponazzi, a prey to violent attacks from the Dominican Bartolomeo Spina, wrote his work in response to a request of a Dominican student;[77] that he came to an agreement with another Dominican, Crisostomo Javelli, on the joint publication of his own treatise and Javelli's response to it;[78] and that he found himself to be in accord with Cajetan, the greatest Thomist philosopher of his age, on the essential point which formed the prop-

73. Nardi, loc. cit. Cf. P. O. Kristeller, "A New Manuscript Source for Pomponazzi's Theory of the Soul from his Paduan Period," *Revue internationale de Philosophie*, V, 2 (16, 1951), 144–157; idem, "Two Unpublished Questions on the Soul by Pietro Pomponazzi," *Medievalia et Humanistica* 9 (1955), 76–101; 10 (1956), 151; Pomponazzi, *Corsi inediti dell'insegnamento Padovano*, ed. A. Poppi, 2 vols. (Padua, 1966 and 1970).

74. Nardi, *Studi*, 356–357. See also my papers (above, note 73).

75. P. Pomponatius, *Tractatus de immortalitate animae*, ed. G. Morra (Bologna, 1954), ch. 2–9.

76. Cf. note 63 above. Gilson, in "L'affaire . . . ," 59–61, reproduced the correspondence of Pomponazzi and Javelli in which Javelli, with respect to Pomponazzi's adversaries, concluded: "Advertant quod cordium scrutator est solus Deus." Cf. Di Napoli, ch. 5–6. For a different view, see Martin Pine, "Pomponazzi and the Problem of 'Double Truth'," *Journal of the History of Ideas* 29 (1968), 163–176.

77. Ed. Morra, 36. The scene of the ailing Pomponazzi, visited and questioned by students on the problem of immortality, suggests an analogy with the *Phaedo* that appears to me to be more than accidental.

78. Cf. note 76 above.

erly philosophical interpretation of the Aristotelian doctrine of the soul.[79]

In passing from Aristotelianism to the humanism of the Italian Renaissance, we find ourselves in a completely different intellectual climate. In my opinion, it is not so much a question of a group of different philosophical or theological doctrines, as has often been thought, as it is of a group of various studies and preoccupations that touch on philosophical and theological thought in an important but indirect manner and that have other centers of diffusion.[80] In short, the humanism of the Italian Renaissance was a humanism that was neither true nor integral, neither Christian nor scientific in the current sense of the word. It was simply (and this is already a great deal) a cultural orientation bearing on the study of the languages, the literatures, the history and philosophy of Greek and Latin antiquity and on a renewal of poetry and oratorical prose, of historiography and moral thought—all of these finding inspiration, both for their form and content, in the models furnished by the ancient authors. The influence of this movement, which has often been misunderstood in our day, was felt in all areas of Renaissance culture, not only in Italy, but equally in other countries, and especially in France.[81] Our subject does not permit us to penetrate more deeply into Italian humanism, because we must limit ourselves to the contacts which existed between humanism and Thomism, contacts that, in accordance with the very nature of things, could be only marginal and that, moreover, have not yet been fully studied.

It is proper to note, first of all, that the studies of the humanists bearing on the reading of ancient poets and philosophers could not at times help but create anxieties in theologians who had received the traditional scholastic and religious education. We have the documents of a controversy, which continued in Italy at least until the middle of the fifteenth century, on the possibility of studying ancient poetry and Christian religion at the same time. This controversy, which was stirred up by the new vitality of the humanist movement, was similar in several respects to the discussions that took place during the first Christian centuries. We are acquainted with the "defenses of poetry" put forward by Mussato, Boccaccio, and Salutati, to mention only the

79. Gilson and Di Napoli, loc. cit. Cf. G. Heidingsfelder, "Zum Unsterblichkeitstreit in der Renaissance," in *Aus der Geisteswelt des Mittelalters* (Münster, 1935), II, 1265–86; A. C. Pegis, "Some Reflections on *Summa contra Gentiles*, II, 56," in *An Etienne Gilson Tribute*, ed. C. J. O'Neil (Milwaukee, 1959), 169–188.

80. P. O. Kristeller, *Renaissance Thought* (New York, 1961).

81. Idem, *Renaissance Thought II* (New York, 1965), 69–88.

best known witnesses.[82] Among the treatises representing the contrary point of view, which have come down to us, we must note the *Lucula Noctis* of Cardinal Giovanni Dominici, a Florentine Dominican. In this work, Dominici strongly attacked the study of pagan authors, and Salutati planned to prepare a detailed reply to him.[83]

But this effort to resist humanism, interesting though it was in other respects, and not an isolated phenomenon, would not determine the general orientation adopted in literature or science, or even theology. It is not always realized to what extent Italian humanism, a movement of eminently secular origin and content, was able to penetrate the religious literature and thought of the period. This penetration resulted as much from the religious preoccupations of lay humanists as from the active participation of churchmen—priests, monks, and even friars—in this literary and scholarly movement, for which they were ever increasingly prepared by their schools, readings, and personal contacts in their own milieu. There exists a large literature, humanist in form and religious or theological in content, that has not yet been sufficiently studied and that, in addition, should enlighten us on the Florentine and Italian intellectual milieu of the fifteenth century, without our having to discover therein masterpieces of literature or thought. We might mention as representative of this alliance between the humanist and theological cultures Lorenzo Pisano,[84] or Antonio degli Agli, bishop of Fiesole and Volterra,[85] or Domenico de'Domenichi, bishop of Torcello and Brescia, whose writings, recently studied by Jedin, show a strong Thomist orientation.[86] Among French names we can mention that of Guillaume Fichet, who died at Rome.[87] Pietro Barozzi, bishop of Padua, who is known in the history of philosophy for his prohibition of the Averroist doctrine of the unity of the intellect, shows himself in his writings not as a scholastic theologian but

82. K. Vossler, *Poetische Theorien in der italienischen Fruehrenaissance* (Berlin, 1900); A. Buck, *Italienische Dichtungslehren vom Mittelalter bis zum Ausgang der Renaissance* (Tübingen, 1952), 67–87.

83. Iohannis Dominici *Lucula Noctis*, ed. E. Hunt (Notre Dame, 1940). Cf. A. Roesler, *Cardinal Johannes Dominici* (Freiburg, 1893), 63–120. The fragmentary letter of Salutati to Dominici is found in Coluccio Salutati, *Epistolario*, ed. F. Novati, IV, 2 (Rome, 1911), 205–240.

84. Giov. Card. Mercati, *Codici latini Pico Grimani Pio* (Vatican City, 1938), 98–105, 274–286.

85. *Supplementum Ficinianum*, ed. P. O. Kristeller (Florence, 1937), II, 335.

86. Jedin, cf. note 59 above.

87. P. O. Kristeller, "An Unknown Humanist Sermon on St. Stephen by Guillaume Fichet," in *Mélanges Eugène Tisserant*, VI (Vatican City, 1964), 459–497.

as a religious humanist.[88] Many priests and monks, who were humanists themselves or friends of humanists, distinguished themselves with poems, discourses, and historical works written in a rather elegant Latin. On the other hand, the humanists' aversion to scholastic philosophy and theology was often accompanied by an enthusiasm for the original sources of the Christian religion and its thought. The new resources of philological and historical criticism, acquired through the study of the ancient authors, were soon applied to the Bible and the writings of the Fathers, which were considered to be the Christian classics.[89] Along with the Biblical studies of a Valla or a Manetti must be mentioned the immense scholarly activity, in the fifteenth and sixteenth centuries, of laymen and above all of religious that was dedicated to the critical study of the Greek and Latin Fathers and that is found in manuscripts and editions, in Latin and Italian translations, and in commentaries. It is here that we find the true "Christian humanism" of the Italian Renaissance, a fashionable term that we should like to utilize here, while keeping for the word "humanism" its original sense. This was a real and very widespread phenomenon whose historical and intellectual importance has escaped most modern scholars.[90]

In order to discover the role played by Saint Thomas and Thomism in the history of Italian humanism, it is necessary to consider first the part played by the Dominicans. This part was considerable, and although their contributions to humanist studies do not in themselves concern the history of Thomism, one should expect a certain fusion of the two currents, given the role that Saint Thomas played in the schools of his order, where each Dominican had of necessity studied his theology *in via sancti Thomae*. Among the first Italian Thomists, we must again mention Remigio de'Girolami, who taught for many years in Florence at Santa Maria Novella. His classical education, probably fostered by works in the library of his convent, was limited, but among

88. F. Gaeta, *Il vescovo Pietro Barozzi e il trattato "De factionibus extinguendis"* (Venice, 1958). His poems are found in several manuscripts, for example in *Ambr. O 58 sup.* Cf. *Iter Italicum*, I, 336–337.

89. P. O. Kristeller, *Studies* (1956), 362–367.

90. The first representative of this tendency in the fifteenth century was Ambrogio Traversari. For a very important example of the humanist contribution to Patristic studies, see now Sister Agnes Clare Way, "Gregorius Nazianzenus," in *Catalogus Translationum et Commentariorum*, II, ed. P. O. Kristeller and F. E. Cranz (Washington, 1971), 43–192. Cf. also P. Polman, *L'élément historique dans la controverse religieuse du XVIème siècle* (Gembloux, 1932).

his very numerous sermons are to be found a good number delivered during official ceremonies, such as funerals or official visits,[91] a fact which is very important for the subsequent history of eloquence, even of humanistic eloquence. During the first half of the fourteenth century, we find, among the Dominican scholars, Nicholas Trevet (although he was not Italian, he was in contact with Italy through the pontifical court at Avignon), a commentator on Seneca and Titus Livius,[92] and Luca Mannelli, bishop of Osimo, the author of a summary of Seneca.[93] Cardinal Dominici, whom we have met as an adversary of humanist education, was not, after all, devoid of it, and Saint Antoninus, a Thomist theologian, was at least the personal friend of several humanists.[94] Among the Florentine Dominicans of the fifteenth century we find Dominicus Johannis, who dedicated a Latin poem on the Virgin to Piero de'Medici,[95] and Johannes Caroli who, in addition to historical works on his order and his city, was also the author of treatises.[96] Towards the end of the century and the beginning of the sixteenth, there are Vincenzo Mainardi, a Latin poet,[97] and Zanobi Acciaiuoli, a student of Poliziano, who acquired some reputation for his Latin poems and translations from the Greek.[98] Outside Florence, we find Leonardo Mansueti of Perugia, a master general of the Order, whose library has been recently studied,[99] Petrus Ransanus of Sicily, historian and hagiographer,[100] theologians such as Raphael de Pornaxio and Battista de'Giudici,[101] and antiquarians such as Giovanni Nanni

91. Cf. note 52 above.
92. Beryl Smalley, *English Friars and Antiquity in the Early Fourteenth Century* (Oxford, 1960). Maria De Marco, "Un nuovo codice del commento di 'Frater Petrus O.P.' a Valerio Massimo," *Aevum* 30 (1956), 554–558. For Nicolaus Trevet, cf. Ruth J. Dean, in *Medievalia et Humanistica* 14 (1962), 95–105 and her many earlier articles. We know now that Trevet composed his commentary on Boethius' *Consolatio* while in Italy. See Ruth J. Dean, "The Dedication of Nicholas Trevet's Commentary on Boethius," *Studies in Philology* 63 (1966), 593–603.
93. T. Kaeppeli, "Luca Manelli († 1362) e la sua Tabulatio et expositio Senecae," *Archivum Fratrum Praedicatorum* 18 (1948), 237–364.
94. R. Morçay, *Saint Antonin* (Paris, 1914), 296–319.
95. Orlandi, II, 305–315; Kaeppeli, 326-327.
96. Orlandi, II, 353–380. He also wrote a history of Florence (Vat. lat. 5878). See below p. 142.
97. For some poems and letters, cf. *Iter Italicum*, I (1963), 75 and 142.
98. *Supplementum Ficinianum*, II, 334–335.
99. T. Kaeppeli, *Inventari di libri di San Domenico di Perugia* (Rome, 1965).
100. F. A. Termini, *Pietro Ransano* (Palermo, 1915).
101. K. Michel, *Der Liber de consonancia nature et gracie des Raphael von Pornaxio*, in *Beiträge*, XIX, I (Münster, 1915). Battista de Giudici of Finale, bishop of Ventimiglia, wrote a defense of the medieval translation of the *Nicomachean Ethics* against Leonardo Bruni (Bologna, Biblioteca Universitaria, Cod.

and Leandro Alberti.[102] We cannot hope to give here a complete list of Italian Dominicans who contributed either to particular areas of literature and of the sciences which do not relate to humanism or to the historical learning of the later sixteenth century.[103]

Leaving the sphere of theology and the Dominican Order, we should ascertain what traces Saint Thomas' work left in the writings of Italian humanists in general. This is a subject that has not yet been studied, and we shall be able to use as examples only those cases with which we are acquainted, without pretending to give here an exhaustive analysis. In general, it may be said that the foremost humanists of the fourteenth and fifteenth centuries did not care for scholastic philosophy and theology, or at least they were very little interested in these subjects, but that aside, among medieval authors Saint Thomas was one of those whom they most respected. I do not believe that Petrarch had much esteem for Saint Thomas.[104] On the other hand, I know of a manuscript of Saint Thomas copied by Boccaccio,[105] and in

1639; cf. *Iter Italicum*, I, 24); see M. Grabmann, *Mittelalterliches Geistesleben*, I (1926), 440–448; a theological dialogue entitled *Serapion de contemptu mundi* (Mantua, Cod. B IV 16, cf. *Iter*, I, 273; Paris, lat. 8510 and other manuscripts); an *Apologia* in favor of the Jews of Trent who were accused of murdering the child Simon, against Bishop Hinderbach and the humanists of his circle (cf. W. Eckert, in *Studi Trentini di Scienze Storiche* 44 [1965], 217); a funeral oration for Roberto Malatesta (Rimini, Cod. 4 B I 43); the *De migratione Petri Cardinalis S. Sixti*, dedicated to Sixtus IV (Vat lat. 3624 and 5620); and an invective against Platina (Vat. lat. 9020 and Vat. lat. 11761). Kaeppeli, *Scriptores*, I, 139–140. C. Dionisotti, "Una miscellanea umanistica transalpina," *Giornale storico della letteratura italiana* 110 (1937), 253–300, at 276–279.

102. For Giovanni Nanni of Viterbo, known above all for his falsifications of historical texts from antiquity, see R. Weiss, "Traccia per una biografia di Annio da Viterbo," *Italia Medioevale e Umanistica* 5 (1962), 424–451; idem, "An Unknown Epigraphic Tract by Annius of Viterbo," in *Italian Studies Presented to E. R. Vincent* (Cambridge, 1962), 101–120. Leandro Alberti, *De viris illustribus Ordinis Praedicatorum* (Bologna, 1517) (the New York Public Library possesses the personal copy of Cardinal Domenico Grimani); idem, *Descrittione di tutta l'Italia* (Bologna, 1550).

103. We may mention Franciscus Pipinus, Latin translator of Marco Polo; Federico da Venezia, commentator in Italian on the *Apocalypse*; Tommaso Sardi, author of a poem in *terza rima* on the soul; Sante Pagnini, Hebraist scholar; Matteo Bandello; G. B. Bracceschi, scholar of the end of the sixteenth century, and many others.

104. In the *Apologia contra Gallum*, Petrarch mentions Saint Thomas among the Italians who made the University of Paris famous. According to P. De Nolhac, this is the only mention of Saint Thomas in the works of Petrarch. See *Revue des Bibliothèques* 2 (1892), 266. Cf. E. H. Wilkins, *Petrarch's Later Years* (Cambridge, Mass., 1959), 239.

105. *Iter*, I, 280. Cf. E. Franceschini, *Miscellanea Giovanni Galbiati*, III (Milan, 1951), 234. This manuscript was used at Florence in 1472 by G. B. Cambi; cf. *Iter*, I, 225. Vittore Branca doubts that the ms. (Ambr. A 204 inf.) was written by Boccaccio.

the treatises of Salutati we find at least one chapter borrowed from the *Summa Theologiae*.[106] During the fifteenth century, the humanists copied or owned manuscripts of Saint Thomas' works,[107] and the typically humanist libraries that were developed in this period procured, as a matter of course, his most important works.[108] Among the printed editions of his works, there was at least, due to the initiative of a humanist, the very complete collection of opuscula edited by Antonio Pizzamano, who was a friend of Pico della Mirandola and Poliziano, student of Francesco of Nardò and later bishop of Feltre.[109]

This edition contains a life of Saint Thomas written by the very same Pizzamano. Although the editor followed the ancient practice of adding the biography of the author to the collection of his works, in the present case this biography is also a part of hagiographical literature.[110] We have for too long been unaware that the humanists sometimes devoted themselves to the genre of hagiography, which explains why several works in this genre have escaped the attention of the specialists themselves. I know of at least two biographies of Saint Thomas in hagiographical collections written by humanists which have, it seems, remained unknown to the Bollandists. One of these was written by Francesco da Castiglione, secretary to Saint Antoninus,[111] and the other by Giovanni Garzoni, Bolognese physician and humanist.[112]

There is another literary genre that has remained almost unknown to historians in which Renaissance humanism and Thomism meet in a certain manner. This is the literature of the orations or eulogies delivered in honor of the Saint. After the canonization of this great

---

106. Colucii Salutati *De seculo et religione*, ed. B. L. Ullman (Florence, 1957), 94–95, appears to follow the *Summa theologiae*, I, q. 2, a. 3.

107. Cf. *Iter*, I, 187–188 (excerpt of Bartholomaeus Fontius in Ricc. 151); p. 225 (cf. note 105 above).

108. It suffices to cite the collections of the Laurenziana (catalogue of Bandini), the Malatestiana (catalogue of Muccioli) and the Fondo Urbinate Latino (catalogue of Stornaiolo), all established in the fifteenth century, and the bibliographical list compiled by Nicolas V for Cosimo de' Medici. Cf. G. Sforza, "La patria, la famiglia e la giovinezza di papa Niccolò V," *Atti della Reale Accademia Lucchese di Scienze, Lettere ed Arti* 23 (1884), 365 and 370–371.

109. *Opuscula*, Venice, 1490 (Hain, 1541). According to Kruitwagen and Rossi (note 50 above), this edition was copied from another published either in the Low Countries or in Germany about 1485 (Pellechet, 1091). On Antonio Pizzamano, cf. G. Degli Agostini, *Notizie istorico-critiche intorno la vita e le opere degli Scrittori Viniziani*, II (Venice, 1754), 189–200.

110. *Bibliotheca hagiographica latina*, no. 8160.

111. Florence, Biblioteca Nazionale, ms. Magl. XXXVIII 142, f. 100v–116, and Conv. Soppr. J. VII 30, f. 19–35v. Cf. *Iter*, I, 143 and 163.

112. Bologna, Biblioteca Universitaria, ms. 1622, f 209v–219. Cf. *Iter*, I, 24.

theologian, his March 7th feast day was immediately celebrated with a special office.[113] It is to be presumed that after the mass of the feast a sermon was often delivered which sometimes included a eulogy of the Saint. I do not believe that anyone has yet attempted to collect the documents and texts relating to this practice. Nevertheless, I would like to attempt a survey of the accounts, however incomplete, that we have about them from Rome and Padua. The chronicler Burchard states that the Dominicans of Santa Maria sopra Minerva celebrated the feast of March 7th each year with a special mass attended by most of the cardinals and prelates. The mass was followed on each occasion by a sermon containing a eulogy of the Saint, generally given by a layman or religious invited by the Fathers for the occasion, rather than by a Dominican from the convent. Burchard names several of these orators,[114] and there have been preserved, in some ancient editions, several of these speeches, which apparently were delivered on these various occasions.[115] Among the authors of these sermons are to be found some well-known humanists, for example Giovanni Antonio Campano, bishop of Teramo, Lippo Brandolini, and Tommaso Inghirami. These

113. Cf. note 28 above.

114. Johannis Burckardi *Liber notarum*, ed. E. Celani, I (Città di Castello, 1906–42), 184–185 (1487: Martinus de Nimira); 299 (1490: quidam scholaris romanus); 339 (1492: Bernardus Basinus); 405 (1493: Dominicus Crispus Pistoriensis); 460–461 (1494: quidam grecus); 578–579 (1495: Thomas Fedrus Vulterranus); 596–597 (1496: Martinus de Viana); II, 18 (1497: quidam capellanus Hispanus); 74 (1498: Raphael Brandolinus); 130 (1499: quidam Marchianus); 207 (1500: Thomas Fedra); 270–271 (1501: Laur. Sansonius); 321–322 (1502: Camillus Porcarius). Cf. Johannis Burchardi *Diarium*, ed. L. Thuasne, I (Paris, 1883), 243, 397, 448; II (1884), 49, 92, 245, 268–269, 358, 434, 512; III (1885), 23–24, 119, 197. Celani gives some bio-bibliographical notes for most of these orators. I am acquainted with a sermon by Dominicus Crispus, *De ascensione*, that was delivered before Wladislaus II, king of Hungary and Bohemia (Istanbul, Library of the Serail, Ahmet III Collection, ms. 46), and a Latin comedy, *Sirus*, dedicated to Iñigo de Mendoza (Salamanca, University Library, ms. 2648, formerly Madrid, Biblioteca del Palacio, ms. 465).

115. The following speeches are to be found in printed form: Bernardus Basinus (Hain 2705; but according to the *Gesamtkatalog*, III, 570, this would be a part of the 1506 edition); Martinus de Viana (Copinger-Reichling 3900 and 6199); Thomas Phaedra Inghiramus (Hain 9186). There is a printed speech by Lippus Brandolinus (*Gesamtkatalog*, 5016) that has recently been identified as the speech delivered in 1498 by his brother Raphael Brandolinus (cf. note 114 above) by T. Accurti, *Editiones saeculi XV* (Florence, 1930), 170. The speech delivered by Johannes Antonius Campanus between 1467 and 1471 can be found in a printed form in his *Opera* (Venice, c. 1500), f. 86v–90. Cf. Mich. Fernus, "Vita Jo. Ant. Campani," ibid., f. 11; G. Lesca, *Giovanni Antonio Campano* (Pontedera, 1892), 143 and 149. I am acquainted with some speeches on Saint Thomas, which were not necessarily given at Rome, by Petrus de la Hazardière (Ottob. lat. 858), Ant. Puccius (dedicated to Cardinal Oliverius Caraffa; Vat. lat. 3645), Petrus Lazarius, O.P. (Marc. lat. XIV 12), Laur. Gul. Traversagnus, O.M. (Savona, ms. IX B 2–15, f. 66–70) and other anonymous authors (Vat. Chigi. J IV 116 and Marc. lat. XI 80).

compositions are perhaps not very important, but they belong never-theless to what must have constituted Saint Thomas' fortuna during the Italian Renaissance and to a more comprehensive, yet little studied, phenomenon, that of religious eloquence in the era of humanism.[116] It is evident, indeed, that sacred eloquence at Rome and elsewhere felt the influence of humanist rhetoric and that it led to the fusion of clas-sical style and traditional content. This fusion is very interesting from the historical point of view, since it allows one to notice the analogies with what happened at the time in the areas of sacred poetry and the sacred arts, but it has been more frequently and more readily deplored than studied. The transformation of the style of sacred eloquence must evidently be attributed as much to the lay humanists who were invited to bestow the aid of their eloquence on the sacred and traditional do-main as to the religious who were imbued with humanist culture and who were thus inclined to make use of it in their work as preachers.

In the case of Padua, we know that in 1436 Saint Thomas was chosen as the official patron of the faculty of arts and his feast day was celebrated there each year in the Dominican church of Saint Augustine with a mass attended by professors and students that was followed by a sermon.[117] Those sermons given on this occasion which have come down to us in printed editions are relatively late, belonging for the most part to the second half of the sixteenth century or to the seven-teenth,[118] but the tradition of such sermons was older, and perhaps some older example may be found in manuscript. Be that as it may, it is certain that at Padua, as at Rome, these sermons or orations in honor of Saint Thomas were sometimes given by laymen and almost always by individuals who did not belong to the Dominican Order.

---

116. Kristeller, in *Mélanges Tisserant*, VI, 483–484.

117. The feast day had already been established in 1324, but we do not know when the sermon after the mass began to be added. *Del culto di S. Tommaso d'Aquino in Padova* (Padua, 1882); cf. P. Ragnisco, *Della fortuna di S. Tommaso d'Aquino nella Università di Padova durante il Rinascimento* (Padua, 1892). We now know that Gioacchino Castiglioni O.P. delivered a speech in praise of St. Thomas at Padua on March 7, 1435, stating that the long neglected celebration had just been renewed through the effort of his teacher Battista da Fabriano and that he was speaking at the latter's request (Gargan, p. 79).

118. A. Favaro, *Saggio di Bibliografia dello Studio di Padova*, I (Padua, 1922), lists such speeches for 1581 (no. 83: Antonius Riccobonus), 1648 (no. 228), 1658 (no. 275), 1662 (no. 293), etc. Quétif-Echard (I, 312) cities an *Oratio in laudem S. Thomae* by Joh. Ambr. Barbavarius (Venice, 1548). A. Renaudet (*Préréforme et humanisme à Paris*, 1916) cites a eulogy of Saint Thomas delivered in 1512 by Josse Clichtove (p. 617) and a speech by Thomas Radinus O.P. printed at Pavia in 1511 and at Paris in 1514 (p. 659). See also Jacopo Zeno, *In solemnitate Sancti Thomae de Aquino* (a sermon), Ms. Berlin Lat. qu. 469, ff. 140–145. Two speeches

In the case of Rome, we do not know at what time the feast day was established there and when it began to be celebrated by means of orations delivered by invited speakers, who were more or less famous for their eloquence. But we must now examine, among these speeches, the oldest that has come down to us, that of Lorenzo Valla, who delivered in 1457, the very year of his death, a eulogy to Saint Thomas in the church of the Minerva.[119] He states that he had been invited by the Dominicans to deliver this discourse.[120] All the other examples of the genre being later, it is not possible to say whether Valla was the first to deliver a discourse as a "guest speaker." We know from him, however, that others had previously discoursed upon the same subject in the same place.[121]

After having praised the virtues and the doctrine of Saint Thomas, Valla, in contrast to other orators, refuses to place him above the other Doctors of the Church. He particularly refuses to glorify him for his use of logic, metaphysics and the other philosophical disciplines in theology. The example of the Church Fathers shows that these disciplines are not necessary for the knowledge of divine matters. The ancient theologians knew Greek and Latin better than their more recent successors, yet they did not base their theology on philosophy, against which Saint Paul had spoken and which, after all, included nothing firm or certain except the observations of physicians. Furthermore,

were delivered in the sixteenth century at Naples by Paolo Pacelli (cf. *Iter Italicum*, I, 408).

119. J. Vahlen, "Lorenzo Valla über Thomas von Aquin," *Vierteljahrsschrift für Kultur und Litteratur der Renaissance* 1 (1886), 384–396 (reprinted in L. Valla, *Opera omnia*, ed. E. Garin [Turin, 1962], II, 339–352), which follows ms. Paris. lat. 7811. Laurencii e Valle *Encomium S. Thomae Aquinatis*, ed. G. Bertocci (Rome, 1888), which follows ms. Angelica 1500. For a third ms. (Est. lat. 151), cf. *Iter Italicum*, I, 369. There is an Italian translation in Lor. Valla, *Scritti filosofici e religiosi*, ed. G. Radetti (Florence, 1953), 455–469 (cf. pp. XXXVI–XXXVII) and a French translation in P. Mesnard, "Une application curieuse de l'humanisme critique à la théologie: L'Eloge de saint Thomas par Laurent Valla," *Revue Thomiste* 63 (55, 1955), 159–176. Cf. G. Mancini, *Vita di Lorenzo Valla* (Florence, 1891), 307–311; F. Gaeta, *Lorenzo Valla* (Naples, 1955), 11. Cf. Hanna H. Gray, "Valla's Encomium of St. Thomas Aquinas and the Humanist Conception of Christian Antiquity," in *Essays in History and Literature, Presented by Fellows of The Newberry Library to Stanley Pargellis*, ed. H. Bluhm (Chicago, 1965), 37–51. There is also a Harvard Ph.D. dissertation by Brayton Polka, "The Religious Thought of Lorenzo Valla" (1964). Two recent books on Valla are G. Di Napoli, *Lorenzo Valla* (Rome, 1971) and S. I. Camporeale, *Lorenzo Valla* (Florence, 1972).

120. ". . . huc ascendi non mea sponte, sed exoratus a fratribus." Ed. Vahlen, 393.

121. ". . . quosdam, qui de hac re hoc die ex hoc loco orationem habuerunt." Ibid. The Rev. John W. O'Malley is preparing an article on the sermons delivered in praise of St. Thomas.

the theologians of old have avoided this technical terminology which was unknown to the Latin authors but which recent theologians persist in using endlessly. The fact that the ancient theologians did not mix philosophy and theology is no reason for decreasing their merit or for preferring Saint Thomas over them.[122] After this diatribe against Scholastic theology, Valla admits that he prefers Saint Thomas to all other recent theologians and even to most ancient theologians, including Boethius, but excepting Augustine, Ambrose, Jerome, and Gregory among the Latins, and Basil, Gregory Nazianzen, John Chrysostom and Dionysius the Areopagite among the Greeks. Thomas Aquinas thus comes in fifth place after the Latin Fathers named above, just as John Damascene does among the Greeks.[123]

Valla's speech certainly is not lacking in eulogies addressed to Saint Thomas, but it took courage to temper these eulogies by placing him on a level lower than that of the great Church Fathers and by treating as a weakness what the others had praised as his greatest merit, namely, to present philosophy as a support for theology. The aversion to scholasticism and the preference for the Church Fathers reflect a rather widespread tendency among humanists. Valla goes further than most when he denies here that philosophy may contribute something to theology, which he also does in his other writings. We know that he did not respect Saint Thomas as an interpreter of the Bible.[124] From this point on, what he says in Thomas' favor in his speech is evidently proof of his honesty and represents the greatest concession he felt himself able to make to Thomas in front of his Dominican hosts. A historian contemporary with Valla, who was also a humanist, though not very friendly towards him, relates that the speech was poorly received by several in the audience, especially Cardinal d'Estouteville, whom he mentions by name.[125] It must be noted that, in fact, the text of the oration is preserved only in a few manuscript copies and that it was only published comparatively recently.[126]

122. "Quare non est ut illis veteribus vere Pauli discipulis hoc nomine quod ab his philosophia theologiae non (this word is put in square brackets by Vahlen and omitted in the manuscripts) admisceatur aut detrahant novi theologi aut noster Thomas sit praeponendus." Ibid., 394.
123. Ibid., 395.
124. Vahlen, 384–385; Gaeta, 111.
125. Gaspar Veronensis, "De gestis tempore Pauli II, in Le vite di Paolo II di Gaspare da Verona e Michele Canensi, ed. G. Zippel (Città di Castello, 1904), 33.
126. Cf. note 119 above.

Among Saint Thomas' humanist critics should also be included Ermolao Barbaro the younger, who was patriarch of Aquileia at his death. Like Valla, Ermolao did not criticize Saint Thomas for the particular doctrines he had maintained; he includes him only in a more or less general condemnation of scholasticism.[127] But while Valla criticized Thomas Aquinas as an interpreter of the Bible and placed him below the Church Fathers, Ermolao criticizes him as an interpreter of Aristotle and prefers the ancient and contemporary commentators, whom he considers superior because of their knowledge of Greek. This is not the logical criticism of a Pomponazzi, who had been educated in the scholastic tradition and did not know Greek, but it is rather the philosophical criticism of a humanist educated at Padua around the same time, who was attempting to remove Aristotle from the medieval scholastic tradition and to give him a new interpretation by going back to the Greek. We possess the glosses written by Ermolao in his copy of Aristotle's *Ethics* and *Politics*, in which he repeatedly rejects the interpretations of Saint Thomas.[128] Aside from this case, Ermolao cites Thomas rarely, but when, in his celebrated correspondence with Pico della Mirandola, he mounts an attack on medieval authors for their barbaric and inelegant style, we learn from Pico that Saint Thomas was included in this summary condemnation.[129] It is not my intention to suggest here that Ermolao's judgment, or for that matter Valla's, is justified, but it is important to observe that these authors had a conception of letters and study, of Christian theology and Aristotelian philosophy itself, that led them to judge, perhaps unjustly, but in any case not very favorably, the entire scholastic tradition, a judgment in which the works of Saint Thomas were more or less explicitly included.

But the most eloquent and detailed attack against Saint Thomas and the Thomists that has come down to us from the humanist circles of the fifteenth century was, curiously enough, written by a beatified Carmelite friar, Blessed Battista Spagnoli who was called Baptista Mantuanus.[130] Famous for his piety and his efforts on behalf of the

127. Ermolao Barbaro, *Epistolae, orationes et carmina*, ed. V. Branca (Florence, 1943), I, 86, 101–109.
128. Kristeller, *Studies* (1956), 349.
129. *Prosatori latini del Quattrocento*, ed. E. Garin (Milan, 1952), 806.
130. In the very extensive bibliography relating to the Mantuan, a rather clear distinction is to be made between the literary historians, those of the Carmelite Order, and those of Mantua. Several titles from this bibliography have been communicated to me, and the volumes themselves placed at my disposal, by my

reform of his order, of which he was Prior General at his death, he was equally famous for his many Latin poems which gained him the surname of "the second Virgil" and which often served as a school text outside Italy during the sixteenth century. The Mantuan also wrote some moral and theological treatises in prose.[131] The prose opusculum

---

friends, Professors Giuseppe Billanovich and Sesto Prete, by the Rev. Scott Robinson, librarian of the *Carmelitana Collection* at Washington, and by the library of the Catholic University of America at Washington. Only the most important titles are given here: G. Fanucchi, *Della vita del B. P. Battista Spagnoli detto il Mantovano* (Lucca, 1887) (the author gives the decree of beatification of December 17, 1887, pp. 217–218); F. Gabotto, "Un poeta beatificato," *Ateneo Veneto* ser. 16, 1 (1892), 3–19; A. Luzio and R. Renier, in *Giornale storico della letteratura italiana* 34 (1899), 59–70; Benedictus-Maria a S. Cruce (Zimmerman), O.C.D., in *Monumenta historica Carmelitana* (Lirinae, 1907), 483–504; Baptista Mantuanus, *The Eclogues*, ed. W. P. Mustard (Baltimore, 1911); J. Martin, "Un saint de l'humanisme," *Bulletin italien* 14 (1914), 181–193; Gabriel Wessels, O.C., "B. Baptistae Mantuani . . . libri tres 'De calamitate temporum,'" *Analecta Ordinis Carmelitarum* 4 (1916) 1–96; idem, "Excerpta historiae Ordinis, Quartum Centenarium mortis B. Baptistae Mantuani," ibid., 97–105; V. Zabughin, "Un beato poeta," *L'Arcadia* (1917), I (1918), 61–90, and in *Analecta Ordinis Carmelitarum*, 4 (1917–22), 125–157; Bartholomaeus Maria Xiberta, O.C., *De scriptoribus scholasticis saeculi XIV ex ordine Carmelitarum* (Louvain, 1931), 64–65; Benedictus-Maria a S. Cruce, "B. Baptistae Mantuani opera soluta oratione scripta hucusque inedita," *Analecta Ordinis Carmelitarum Discalceatorum*, 7 (1932), 163–208; idem, in *Etudes carmélitaines* 20, 2 (1935), 72–85; Graziano di S. Teresa, O.C.D., "Un carme inedito del B. Batista Mantovano relativo alla S. Casa di Loreto," *Il Monte Carmelo* 28 (1942), 19–20; idem, "Bricciche Lauretane," *L'Osservatore Romano*, January 12–13, 1942; idem, "B. Baptistae Mantuani ineditarum epistolarum fasciculus," *Analecta Ordinis Carmelitarum* 13 (1946–48), 241–264; idem, "Beati Baptistae Mantuani metrorum fasciculus," ibid., 265–267; Ludovico Saggi, O.C., *La Congregazione Mantovana dei Carmelitani* (Rome, 1954), 116–152; Graziano di S. Teresa, "Ramenta Carmelitana 5–11 (Mantuaniana 1–7)" *Ephemerides Carmeliticae* 6 (1955), 192–227; idem, "Ramenta Carmelitana 13 (Mantunaniana 8), Nuova cronologia della vita del b. Battista Mantovano," ibid., 9 (1958), 423–442; L. Rosa, "Un poemetto cristiano della fine del '400: Il 'De calamitatibus temporum' di Battista Mantovano," *Annali della Facoltà di Lettere e Filosofia* (Naples), 8 (1958–59), 139–145; E. Coccia, *Le edizioni delle opere del Mantovano* (Rome, 1960) (cf. *Gesamtkatalog der Wiegendrucke*, nn. 3244–3320); W. E. Painter, "Baptista Mantuanus, Carmelite Humanist," dissertation of the University of Missouri (not seen, cf. *Dissertation Abstracts* 22 [1961], 240–241); Gordon W. Jones, "Baptista Mantuanus—Amateur Physician," *Bulletin of the History of Medicine* 36 (1962), 148–162 (communication from Mr. Philip Weimerskirch); E. Faccioli, in *Mantova, Le lettere*, II (Mantua, 1962), 151–202; P. Clemente Benedettucci, *Gli albori degli scritti intorno al Santuario di Loreto nel territorio di Recanati* (Recanati, 1964) (reprint of an article first published in 1942 and 1943); W. Leonard Grant, *Neo-Latin Literature and the Pastoral* (Chapel Hill, 1965), 125–135 and passim. The most complete edition of the Mantuan's *Opera* is the one printed at Antwerp in four volumes in 1576.

131. *Opera* (1576), IV. The discourse of the Mantuan before Innocent VIII has been published by Gabriel Wessels, O.C., in *Analecta Ordinis Carmelitarum* 6 (1927–29), 129–134; his *Informatio de rebus religionis* by Saggi, loc. cit., 279–284. A manuscript in the Newberry Library (*Wing Ms. ZW 535. B 322*), of which Mr. James M. Wells has sent me a microfilm, contains the following writings, all of which seem to be unedited and unknown: *Contra novam opinionem de loco*

to which we are referring has been mentioned and cited by the bibliographers and historians of the Carmelite Order, but it seems to have remained unknown to the historians of literature who have spoken of the Mantuan; consequently, it will not be wasted effort for us to dwell on it in greater detail. The work is called *Opus aureum in Thomistas*, and it is preserved for us in four manuscripts, only one of which contains the complete text and is at the same time of an ancient date. Two others are fragmentary and the fourth is a more recent copy of the first.[132] The date of the three early manuscripts gives us no reason to question the authenticity of the text. The author is named in all of the manuscripts and in the course of the treatise he relates several episodes from his life that agree with what we know of him from other sources.[133] He also calls Pico della Mirandola his friend[134] and in one

---

*conceptionis Christi* (directed against Petrus Lucensis canonicus regularis); *Ad fratrem Hieronymum Mediolanensem eiusdem ordinis epistola de causa diversitatis inter interpretes sacre scripture; Apologia contra calumniatores ordinis sui.* These writings are dedicated to Cardinal Sigismondo Gonzaga.

132. Vat. lat. 5892, f. 39–61v (s. XVI in.) is complete. It bears on f. 38v the following title written in an old hand: "Carmelitae opus divinum in quo multi errores et priscorum et hodiernorum doctorum insignium ostenduntur." In the old table of contents (f. 2), the following title appears: *F. Baptistae Carmelitae pientissima obiurgatio in fratres praedicatores Divo Thomae Aquinati nimium indulgentes ad Petrum Nubilariensem opus sane aureum.*—Vat. lat. 8105, f. 1–26 (s. XVI); several words are missing at the end.—Ambr. Q 116 sup., f. 13 (370)–18v (377) is the oldest ms. (s. XV ex.), but the most fragmentary.—Bologna, Biblioteca Comunale dell' Archiginnasio, ms. A. 946, f. 1 (185)–18v (202v) is a recent copy (s. XVII) of Vat. lat. 5892. I should like to thank Rev. Alfonso Raes, S.J., of the Vatican Library, Dr. Angelo Paredi, of the Ambrosian Library, and Dr. Gino Nenzioni, director of the Biblioteca Comunale of Bologna, for having sent me microfilms of these manuscripts.—Ms. I 522 of Ferrara, which Xiberta and others cite as containing our opusculum, contains only a description of Vat. lat. 5892 made in the eighteenth century (communication from Dr. Luciano Capra). Cf. C. Piana, *Ricerche su le università di Bologna e di Parma nel sec. XV* (Quaracchi, 1963), 62–65. See now C. Catena, "L'*Opus Aureum in Thomistas* del B. Battista Mantovano O. Carm.," *Carmelus* 14 (1967), 269–278, where the text is fully discussed on the basis of my edition (*Le Thomisme*, 137–185).

133. The author relates a discussion held before Prospero Cafarelli at Bologna (Vat. lat. 5892, f. 46v; ed. P. O. Kristeller, *Le Thomisme et la pensée italienne de la Renaissance*, Montreal, 1967, pp. 149–150); he defended before Sixtus IV the traditional dress of his Order against an attempt to change it (f. 57; ed. Kristeller, p. 173; cf. Saggi, 98–106); he speaks of his experiences at the pontifical court under Sixtus IV and Innocent VIII (ibid.); and he quotes a verse that he wrote himself (f. 53v; ed. Kristeller, p. 166) and that is actually found in the second book of his *Secunda Parthenice* (*Opera*, Bologna, 1502, f. 203v).

134. F. 41v (ed. Kristeller, *Le Thomisme* [1967], p. 141): ". . . astronomiae pars illa quae sibi judicandi artem usurpat, ut Picus noster late disseruit, frivolis argumentis est innixa." Some other passages of the text show what knowledge the author had of the writings of Pico and Ficino. We are acquainted with three letters from Pico to the Mantuan (Johannes Picus, *Opera*, Basel, 1572, 358–359, 369, 375–376), one letter from the Mantuan to Pico (*Opera*, Bologna, 1502, f. a1–

instance very clearly declares that he wrote his text during the pontificate of Innocent VIII.[135] The treatise, which is divided into several unnumbered chapters, is addressed to a certain Petrus, who must be
identified as Pietro Gavasseti da Novellara, O. Carm., a student and
friend of the Mantuan. In the preface, it is connected with another
theological work in which the Mantuan had criticized the doctrine of
Dominican theologians on the blood of Christ. We recall that this
very subtle question had quite frequently been debated between the
Dominicans and the Franciscans during the pontificate of Pius II. It
appears that the controversy continued even after the pope had pro-
nounced his judgment, though in an indecisive manner, and that the
Mantuan dedicated a treatise to it in which he clearly defended the
Franciscan position, criticizing at the same time the position of the
Dominicans not only for their particular opinion on the subject under
debate, but also for their tendency always to wish to defend the opinion
of Saint Thomas.

This treatise by the Mantuan on the blood of Christ, which was
unknown to the historians of the Carmelite Order, and which one
could thus judge was lost, is in fact preserved for us, at least most of
it, in a manuscript at Mantua. This anonymous and fragmentary manuscript was discovered and studied by a local scholar, who correctly
attributed its contents to the Mantuan without, however, publishing it.
The work of this scholar has remained unknown to recent historians
except for a fairly inaccurate note which appeared in a hagiographical
review. Thanks to the courtesy of the director of the library of Mantua,
Professor Ubaldo Meroni, I was able to consult the treatise and the
manuscript in a microfilm copy. I have established that the anonymous
treatise is indeed a work of the Mantuan, corrected in his own hand
and containing in three books a defense of Pietro da Novellara against
the Dominicans on the problem of the blood of Christ and on other
points. I have also verified that the last section of the first book of the
treatise, in its corrected and definitive form, is almost identical to our

---

a1v), and several written by the Mantuan to Gianfrancesco Pico after the death of
his uncle Giovanni (Picus, *Opera*, 386–388, 392–393 and Vat. Capp. 235, f. 148).
Cf. E. Garin, *La cultura filosofica del Rinascimento italiano* (Florence, 1961),
265–266. Two other letters from the Mantuan to Gianfrancesco Pico were ex-
tracted from ms. Bodl. Selden 41 supra by Benedictus Maria a S. Cruce (Zimmerman), *Monumenta historica Carmelitana* (1907), 499–504.

135. F. 57 (ed., p. 173): ". . . praesente Cardinali Malfitensi qui nunc est
Innocentius octavus."

*Opus aureum in Thomistas,* except for the chapter titles. It must therefore be concluded that the Mantuan had first written an elaborate
treatise on the blood of Christ in behalf of his friend, Pietro da Novellara, and that he later decided to transform the section directed
against Thomism into a small, separate treatise and to add to it a
preface to his friend. The treatise written by Pietro on the blood of
Christ has also been preserved in two versions. Since we cannot enter
into detail on the chronological and theological questions concerning
all these treatises, it will have to suffice for us to conclude that this
treatise against the Thomists was evoked by the theological controversy
between the religious Orders on the question of the blood of Christ,
this controversy being connected to the cult of the precious blood,
one of whose principal centers was the Church of Mantua.[136]

To return to our treatise, in his preface the Mantuan, evidently in
response to a letter from his friend, Pietro da Novellara, goes to the
trouble of examining why the Dominicans fancy that Saint Thomas
alone never committed an error when it is known that all men, and
especially all philosophers, have committed some.[137]

In the course of the treatise itself, the Mantuan complains that the
Dominicans always prefer Saint Thomas to all other theologians and
that they scorn the divergent opinions of others, even on questions not
concerning faith.[138] In attempting to impose the Thomist opinion on

---

136. We refer to ms. G II 18 of the Biblioteca Comunale of Mantua, discovered and identified by Filippo Nodari, *Scoperta di un'altra opera del B.
Battista Spagnoli nella Biblioteca Comunale di Mantova scritta nel 1492 e intitolata Tractatus de sanguine Christi* (Mantua, Stab. Tip. Lit. F. Apollonio, 1892),
14 pp.; the author's name appears twice in the opusculum, but not on the title-
page. (A note that appeared in *Analecta Bollandiana* 13 [1894], 69–70, attributes
this opusculum to Ph. Nardi and gives G. 11. 18 as the number of the manuscript).
The Biblioteca Comunale of Mantua possesses, in mss. A I 6 and J IV 94, two
redactions of the treatise on the blood of Christ written in Italian by Pietro da
Novellara (communication from Professor Ubaldo Meroni; cf. Saggi, 112). The
same ms. A I 6 gives on ff. 77v–106, after a preface in Italian by Pietro (f. 76v–
77), a treatise in Latin *De sanguine Christi* (Inc.: *Ignis ille suavissimus*) that was
written, according to the final note, at Weingarten in 1280 by G. de Colonia
Natione Saxonem. The same treatise is to be found in ms. Fulda Aa 48 (which
comes from Weingarten), f. 95-100, the final note of which has been crossed out
(communication from Dr. Eickermann), and in ms. A of S. Domenico of Bologna,
f. 70v–75, which attributes it to Magister Gerardus dictus Saxo natione de Colonia
(communication from P. Abele Redigonda, O.P. through Professor Serafino
Prete). Cf. A. Nagel, "Das Heilige Blut Christi" in *Festschrift der 900-Jahr-Feier
des Klosters* (Weingarten, 1956), 193 and 226, n. 24; for the Bologna manuscript,
M.-H. Laurent, *Analecta Bollandiana* 58 (1940), 32, no. 7.

137. F. 39–39v (ed., pp. 137–138).

138. F. 39v–40v (ed., pp. 138–139).

everyone, they go against nature, which always shows itself to be in favor of variety and diversity.[139] Agreement must exist concerning questions of faith and demonstrable conclusions, such as those of mathematics, but only probable reasons exist in all other sectors of philosophy and knowledge.[140] In matters of faith, the opinion of the Fathers comes after that of scripture, and that of Thomas after that of the Fathers.[141] He does not hold a position superior to that of the other Doctors of the Church. A Dominican is quite capable of maintaining false doctrines, as may be seen in the case of their opinion on the Immaculate Conception of the Virgin. God, the infinite fountain of truth, communicates a part of this truth to all men without reserving it for one school.[142] Just as there was a great diversity of doctrines among the ancient philosophies, so too was Saint Thomas contradicted on several points by other Christian theologians. And while professing admiration for Thomas, the author prefers Duns Scotus in most of the doctrines being disputed.[143] Thomist teaching has never received an approval from the Church as complete as the Dominicans claim. While putting Thomas on the same footing as Saint Augustine, Saint Jerome, Saint Bernard, Peter Lombard, and Gratian does him no injustice, it may be asserted of him no less than of them that he was capable of being mistaken on particular points.

The opusculum of Baptista Mantuanus represents the most virulent attack against Thomism that I have found in the literature of the Italian Renaissance. It was undoubtedly a result of the *furor theologicus* of the times and of the rivalry that existed among the religious orders. The Mantuan, however, was more a humanist than a scholastic theologian and the opusculum reflects perfectly this cultural attitude.

139. F. 40v–41v (ed., pp. 138–142).
140. F. 41v (ed., p. 141): "Velle igitur me rationi probabili tanquam fidei catholice vel quasi demonstrationi subiugare nihil est aliud quam rerum naturam perturbare."
141. F. 41v–44v (ed., pp. 142–147).
142. F. 46v (ed., p. 150): "At spiritus dei multiplex . . . ab infinito fonte veritatis novos assidue rivulos profert, et sapientia quae pro delitiis habet esse cum hominibus omnibus quasdam veritates tanquam commune pabulum communicat . . ."
143. F. 52v–53 (ed., p. 165): ". . . et quanquam Johannis Scoti disciplina me magis a iuventute delectarit, et quod eram a praeceptoribus sic persuasus et quod re vera plus nervorum videbatur habere, nunquam tamen potui Thomam non amare. Placet longe plus Stoici (read: Scoti) sententia de entis univocatione, de intellectus et voluntatis obiecto, de voluntatis praesidentia . . ." Joh. Trithemius (*De scriptoribus ecclesiasticis*, Cologne, 1546, ff. 379–380) attributes to the Mantuan an *Introductorium subtilis Scoti.*

It is more an invective than a treatise. Its style is elegant, if not Ciceronian, and a good number of classical quotations are found in it.[144]
The author frequently speaks of his personal experiences, and he insists, as does Valla, on the superiority of the Bible and the Fathers to
Saint Thomas and the other medieval doctors. While showing a certain
knowledge of scholastic authors and of the doctrines discussed by
them, the Mantuan does not offer us strict reasoning in the scholastic
manner; he presents us, rather, with some rhetorical arguments that
are neither methodical nor systematic, as well as with a large number
of repetitions. He quotes Petrarch[145] and, in mentioning the ancient
theologians from Hermes Trismegistus to Plato,[146] he seems to follow
Ficino without naming him. The central idea of his treatise is that of
the multiplicity of doctrines, all of which derive from the truth of God
and each of which comprises some part of this truth, a theme that he
evidently borrowed from the thought of his friend Pico della Mirandola.[147] But the Mantuan tries to limit this variety by the unity of
religious faith and of demonstrative science. And if I am not mistaken,
he goes further than Pico in the direction of Academic scepticism, when
he accords only the value of simple probability to all other forms of
knowledge.

The reference to Pico della Mirandola and Ficino leads us to the last
intellectual movement of the Renaissance that must be treated in relation to Thomism, namely Platonism. To begin with Pico, it is necessary
to insist on the fact that he was not solely Platonic and that Platonism
represents only one of the numerous elements of a more comprehensive synthesis that he at least outlined, even if he did not complete it.[148]
Pico's formation was not limited to the literary humanism of Ferrara
and the Platonism of Florence; it likewise included the lay Aristotelianism of Padua and the scholastic theology of Paris. To these elements

144. For example, Terence (f. 40, ed., p. 139), Cicero (f. 49v, ed., p. 155), Virgil
(f. 53v, ed., p. 166). There are also the names of many Greek philosophers.

145. F. 59v (ed., p. 178): "Taxatur idem (Bernardus) a Francisco Petrarcha
quod in libro ad Eugenium multa confixerit contra Romanos, quae ipse Franciscus
manifestis rationibus confutavit." Cf. De Nolhac, *Revue des Bibliothèques* 2
(1892), 273–274.

146. F. 52v (ed., p. 164): Hermes Trismegistus, Orpheus, Aglaophemus, Pythagoras, Philolaus, Plato, Cf. f. 54 (ed., p. 167): "Theologiam Plato sibi vindicat."

147. G. Pico della Mirandola, *De hominis dignitate* . . . , ed. E. Garin (Florence,
1942), 138–146; idem, *La cultura* . . . , 238–239; P. O. Kristeller, "Giovanni Pico
della Mirandola and his Sources," in *L'Opera e il pensiero di Giovanni Pico della
Mirandola* (Convegno Internazionale, Mirandola, 1963) (Florence, 1965), I, 84;
G. Di Napoli, *Giovanni Pico della Mirandola* (Rome, 1965).

148. Kristeller, ibid., 35–84.

must also be added the rabbinical theology and the cabalistic specula-
tion that he knew through his quite thorough study of Hebrew. If we
wish to judge the importance of the scholastic element in Pico's
thought, we must state that, more than any other Italian philosopher
of this century, he admired, knew, and utilized the writings and doctrines of medieval thinkers and that, among these, Saint Thomas was
one of his favorite authors. We must add, however, that Pico did not
prefer Saint Thomas to the other medieval thinkers with whom he was
acquainted, nor the scholastic thinkers to the ancient or Oriental philosophers. He was an admirer of Saint Thomas, but not a Thomist. In
his defense of scholastic philosophers against Ermolao Barbaro, what
he says about their value as thinkers, despite their lack of literary elegance, and about the profit that he had gained from prolonged study
of their writings, has reference to Saint Albert, Duns Scotus and
Averroes, as well as to Saint Thomas.[149] Furthermore, some of his
nine hundred theses are borrowed not only from Saint Thomas but
again from Saint Albert, Francis of Meyronnes, Duns Scotus, Henry of
Ghent, and Giles of Rome, to say nothing of his borrowings from numerous Greek and Arabic authors. The most that may be said is that,
among the Latin authors, Saint Thomas is the one from whom he borrows the greatest number of these, forty-five.[150] Moreover, when
thirteen of his theses were condemned by a papal commission, Pico
attempted to defend them in his *Apologia*. In the course of this treatise,
he more than once sets himself in opposition to some Thomist positions
by basing himself on Durandus, on Holcot or on the majority of the
Parisian doctors.[151] This fact is all the more remarkable since Pico was
but slightly acquainted with the doctrines of the nominalist school,
which had temporarily suffered a setback just before his arrival in
Paris. From this it must be concluded that Pico was well-acquainted

149. *Prosatori latini*, ed. Garin, 806; cf. Kristeller, *Giovanni Pico . . .* , 60–61.
150. J. Picus, *Opera* (Basel, 1572), 64–65. The following theses should be
noted: No. 12: "Beatitudo est essentialiter in actu intellectus. Corollarium. Nec
fruitio nec aliquis actus voluntatis est essentialiter beatitudo." No. 22: "Deus in
patria per speciem non videtur, sed ipse per suam essentiam intellectui applicatur
ut species intelligibilis." No. 24: "Subjectum et propria passio realiter distinguuntur." No. 26: "Materia signata est principium individuationis." No. 31: "Essentia et existentia in quolibet creato realiter distinguuntur." No. 42: "Quiditates in
particulari a metaphysico non considerantur." No. 45: "Non sunt ponendae ideae
generum." But he then also gives twenty-two theses taken from Duns Scotus
and accepts *haecceitas* (No. 6) and the univocity of being (No. 7). See my paper
(above, note 147).
151. *Opera*, 128–129, 134–137, 155, 196–198, 238.

with the writings and doctrines of Saint Thomas, which he followed on certain points, but it cannot be said that he was a Thomist, since he utilized a great variety of diverse or contradictory sources, and since he clearly opposed Thomist doctrine on several particular points.[152]

It remains for us to examine the connections to Saint Thomas and Thomism of the other great representative of Italian Platonism—Marsilio Ficino. In this case we have a system of ideas drawn from fewer sources and having more fixed contours than that of Pico, but one that still presents a great many complex problems and questions. We have a testimony according to which Ficino, during his youth and at a moment when his inclination toward Platonism was already evident, was counseled by Saint Antoninus to read the *Summa contra Gentiles* and was thereby protected from the dangers of paganism. This anecdote may contain a kernel of truth, but it is not well attested by the documents, and its importance has been exaggerated.[153] Besides, we are not reduced to this story in order to reveal the influence of Saint Thomas on Ficino's writing and thought. There is to be noted, first of all, a certain number of quotations in his work from Saint Thomas (I have counted twenty-four of them), and while not all these quotations are very precise or explicit, this number is nevertheless greater than the number of quotations present in his writings which are taken from any other Latin medieval thinker. Furthermore, Saint Thomas is always quoted in a favorable way.[154] Except for two opuscula, Ficino quotes only the *Summa contra Gentiles* (four times) among Saint Thomas' writings. One may assume that he knew this work best and that most of the other quotations are given from memory or from an indirect source. Compared with the quotations from classical, patristic, or even Arabic authors, the quotations from Saint Thomas and other scholastic thinkers are not numerous. Their presence simply proves that the

152. Avery Dulles (*Princeps Concordiae*, Cambridge, Mass., 1941) supplies some useful information on Pico's scholastic sources but tends to exaggerate his Thomist orientation. See p. 58: "The fundamentally Thomistic character of Pico's *pax philosophica*." Cf. J. Festugière, "Studia Mirandulana," *Archives d'histoire doctrinale et littéraire du Moyen Age* 7 (1932, pub. 1933), 143–250.

153. P. O. Kristeller, *Studies* (1956), 200–201; R. Marcel, *Marsile Ficin* (Paris, 1958), 207–212 (whose arguments to the contrary do not convince me).

154. Kristeller, *Studies*, 39–41; E. Gilson, "Marsile Ficin et le *Contra Gentiles*," *Archives d'histoire doctrinale et littéraire du Moyen Age* 24 (1957, pub. 1958), 101–113; C. Fabro, "Influenze Tomistiche nella filosofia del Ficino," *Studia Patavina* 3 (1959), 396–413; Ardis B. Collins, "Love and Natural Desire in Ficino's *Platonic Theology*," *Journal of the History of Philosophy* 9 (1971), 435–449; eadem, "The Secular is Sacred: Platonism and Thomism in Ficino's Platonic Theology" (Ph.D. diss., University of Toronto, 1967).

scholastic tradition was not absent from his thought. When we examine in particular the writings of his youth, in which his university studies are reflected, we notice that he knew well the text of Aristotle and Averroes' commentary, but we very rarely find quotations from Saint Thomas or other scholastic thinkers. Evidently from his university studies, which centered on medicine rather than on theology, Ficino derived the lay Aristotelianism of the faculty of arts—the Aristotelianism of Florence that was maintained less by medieval traditions than was that of Paris or even that of Padua. What Ficino added to this Aristotelianism on his own initiative and by his reading was Saint Augustine, Plato and the Neoplatonists, the pseudo-Platonic writings attributed to Zoroaster, Orpheus, Mercurius Trismegistus, and Pythagoras, as well as Lucretius, who made a profound impression on him during a certain phase of his youth. It must be expected that, when his theological preoccupations became more emphasized during the course of his life, he nourished himself on the humanist and literary theology of his Florentine friends, which was scarcely technical or scholastic, and on the reading of Saint Augustine and the Fathers rather than on the teachings of the medieval schools. The reading of Saint Thomas undoubtedly had its place in his development, but on the basis of the facts mentioned above, we would hesitate to accord it a very important place.

But in order to determine what influence Saint Thomas had on Ficino's thought, it does not suffice to be content with the statistics of quotations; we must penetrate to the very heart of his philosophy and search here for the resemblances with Thomist thought that it might contain. These resemblances may result from well-assimilated readings of his youth and extend to those ideas taught in common by Saint Thomas and other scholastic thinkers, since Ficino obviously knew him better than the others. Attempting to construct a system of philosophy that would agree with Christian theology, Ficino relied in pursuit of this goal on Saint Augustine and, for certain points, on Saint Thomas too.

It must be observed, first of all, relative to the very manner of conceiving the relations between reason and faith, philosophy and theology, Ficino was closer to Thomism than were the Aristotelians of his own century, since he proclaimed that there existed at the same time a distinction and a harmony between philosophy and theology.[155]

155. P. O. Kristeller, *Il pensiero filosofico di Marsilio Ficino* (Florence, 1953),

To be sure, he differed with Saint Thomas when he substituted Plato for Aristotle, but this was the Aristotle of the lay disciples of Averroes and Alexander, who were forced to admit a fundamental disagreement between Aristotelian philosophy and Christian theology. In making the immortality of the soul the center of his metaphysical doctrine, Ficino was forced to oppose the Averroist doctrine of the unity of the intellect, and on this point he again found himself on the same ground as Saint Thomas, although the basis of his polemic and the content of his arguments were not entirely the same.[156] But it is in two quite central doctrines in Ficino's thought that his agreement with Saint Thomas is most obviously revealed. These concern the problem of natural desire and the problem of the participation of the members of a genus in the essence of the principle of this genus, two problems that have given rise to lively discussions among the recent interpreters of Saint Thomas. We do not have the time to go into detail on these very interesting problems. We shall limit ourselves, therefore, to several general observations.

When Ficino speaks of the natural appetite of a thing, he does not limit this expression to inanimate things by distinguishing it from the sensible or rational appetite; he gives this expression a very broad meaning that in fact extends to all beings.[157] Each thing is directed by its creator toward a natural goal, and its essence is always accompanied by a desire, love, or appetite for this goal; this appetite cannot be in vain, since it constitutes a necessary element of the very order of the universe. Among the sources of this doctrine, expressed in more or less similar terms not only by Saint Thomas but by most medieval thinkers, we must mention Aristotle's doctrines of final causes, of the natural motions of the elements, and of the unmoved mover. But the more general doctrine of a hierarchy of appetites corresponding to a hierarchy of essences is of Neoplatonic origin and it is to be met again in several well-known texts of Saint Augustine.[158] What connects Ficino with Saint Thomas is that he utilizes the natural appetite of the human soul for God and eternal life as one of the principal arguments in

---

18–20 and 346–349; idem, *The Philosophy of Marsilio Ficino*, trans. V. Conant (New York, 1943), 27–29 and 320–323.

156. *Theologia Platonica*, book XV, in *Opera* (Basel, 1576), 327–367 (ed. R. Marcel, vol. III, Paris, 1970, 8–104). Cf. G. Di Napoli, *L'immortalità dell'anima nel Rinascimento* (Turin, 1963), 121–166.

157. Kristeller, *Pensiero*, 180–212; idem, *The Philosophy*, 171–199.

158. *Confessions*, XIII, 9. Cf. Kristeller, *Pensiero*, 204; idem, *The Philosophy*, 192.

favor of the immortality of the soul, and likewise the natural appetite of the soul for its body as an argument in favor of the resurrection.[159] What is in question here is a rather important point which indicates a fundamental agreement between the two thinkers, apart from the nuances, the emphases on certain points and the labels "Aristotelianism" and "Platonism" that are fastened to their respective systems.

The doctrine of participation presents another case that is even more interesting and complex. The concept of participation comes from Plato, who often utilizes it to indicate the relation of particular things to the universal Idea, a relation denoting a nonreciprocal resemblance. Having rejected the doctrine of Ideas, Aristotle quite naturally makes no positive or technical use of Plato's concept of participation. In Neoplatonism, the term assumes a quite important and enlarged meaning in comparison to that which Plato had given it. In the universal hierarchy of things, each being participates in some way in the essence of the beings that are superior to it. From this there results a generalized principle of participation or communication according to which each principle constituting the essence of a genus causes all the other members of the same genus to participate in this essence, but in a diminished and inferior manner. In St. Thomas, this doctrine of participation has hardly been noted by a good number of his interpreters, since it is mentioned only in the course of his arguments and never appears as the subject of a thesis or proposition which Thomas attempted to defend or to prove. More recently, Father Fabro, Father Geiger, and other scholars, basing themselves on numerous texts, have studied this question in the works of Saint Thomas in all its ramifications and attributed to it a very great importance.[160] It suffices, indeed, to recall among so many other examples, that it is participation in being that characterizes the condition of created things in relation to God. Saint Thomas avails himself of the concept without feeling the need to

159. Kristeller, *Pensiero*, 202–212; idem, *The Philosophy*, 190–199. St. Thomas, *Summa contra Gentiles*, II, 33 and 55; III, 2 and 26; IV, 79. Cf. P. Rousselot, *Pour l'histoire du problème de l'amour au moyen âge*, in *Beiträge zur Geschichte der Philosophie des Mittelalters*, VI, 6 (Münster, 1933); L.-B. Geiger, *Le problème de l'amour chez Saint Thomas d'Aquin* (Montreal, 1952). If I am not mistaken, the criticism directed against Rousselot by Father Geiger does not concern the central problem of which we are speaking here.

160. C. Fabro, *La nozione metafisica di partecipazione secondo S. Tommaso d'Aquino* (Milan, 1939); 2nd ed. (Turin, 1950); 3rd ed. (Turin, 1963); idem, *Participation et causalité selon S. Thomas d'Aquin* (Louvain, 1961); L.B. Geiger, *La participation dans la philosophie de S. Thomas d'Aquin* (Paris, 1942; 2nd ed., 1953). Cf. note 12 above.

justify it or to quote supporting sources. It is very evident, however, that it did not come to him from Aristotle, who did not at all use it, but from Neoplatonism and more particularly from Proclus, several of whose works he knew in Latin translations. Furthermore, it was the same Thomist scholars who, having insisted on the importance of the notion of participation and of certain allied doctrines in his work, have also noticed the importance of the Neoplatonic element not only in his theological thought but also in his metaphysics, the sources of which are not only Saint Augustine but also Proclus, the *Liber de causis*, the pseudo-Dionysius and several Arabic authors.

As to Ficino, his doctrine of participation and of the *Primum in aliquo genere* has likewise remained hidden in his arguments rather than being clearly stated in his central theses; its importance for him has been noticed quite recently, based on a great number of texts.[161] His doctrine approximates that of Saint Thomas, without identifying itself with it, in its Latin terminology as well as in its examples and major applications. Inasmuch as Ficino was well acquainted with the writings of Proclus and other Neoplatonists, it cannot yet be determined whether he borrowed his doctrine or several aspects of it from Saint Thomas or directly from Proclus and the other Neoplatonists. I am inclined to believe that Saint Thomas was one of the sources, but not the only one, of Ficino's doctrine on this point. The agreement and resemblance remain fairly considerable, even if a direct dependence in the case cannot be proven. Moreover, it is altogether logical that the agreement between Ficino and Saint Thomas should especially manifest itself in doctrines of Neoplatonic origin and tendency. We cannot insist on the exclusive Aristotelianism of Saint Thomas and maintain at the same time that he influenced Marsilio Ficino.

The effect that Florentine Platonism was to have on Italian religious thought at the end of the fifteenth century and during the sixteenth century is an important subject that has not yet been very thoroughly studied and it is also one for which we still lack a great deal of the data. In the circle of Ficino and Pico there were several priests and religious, little or not well known, whose writings should provide us with information on the sources and tendencies of their thought and on what they were able to contribute to or receive from the Platonic Academy.[162] The problem of the immortality of the soul, which oc-

161. Kristeller, *Pensiero*, 153–179; idem, *The Philosophy*, 146–170.
162. Kristeller, "Sebastiano Salvini . . . ," in *Didascaliae. Studies in Honor*

cupied a central position in Ficino's philosophy, becomes the subject of a vast literature. Among the authors of treatises written on the subject toward the end of the fifteenth century, we meet several theologians whose connections with the Florentine circle have not been determined. These include two Dominicans—Filippo de'Barbieri the Sicilian, well-known for his treatise on the Sibyls, and Jacopo Camphora, who wrote a treatise in Italian that circulated rather widely both in manuscript copies and also in printed form.[163] The theologians who participated in the controversy against Pomponazzi continued this tradition in a certain measure, and it is quite easy to show that the defenders of immortality against Pomponazzi, including Nifo, continued to use Ficino's *Platonic Theology* as an arsenal of arguments in favor of their cause, since we must not forget that among the principal positions attacked by Pomponazzi there were not only those of Averroes and Saint Thomas, but likewise that of Plato and, consequently, that recently reaffirmed and developed by Ficino.[164] Among Pomponazzi's adversaries there were at least two who underwent the influence of Platonism—the Dominican Crisostomo Javelli[165] and the Augustinian Ambrogio Fiandino.[166] Perhaps we may suppose that the famous decree of the eighth session of the Lateran Council in 1513, which made the immortality of the soul a dogma of the Church,[167] reflects the Platonic current of the philosophy and theology of the period, just as the earlier decree of the Council of Vienne on the soul as the form of the body had reflected the Aristotelian discussions of the time. It may be added that a very celebrated theologian who was present at the Lateran Council, the future Cardinal Egidio da Viterbo, declared himself a disciple of Platonism. He wrote a commentary on the *Sentences* "ad mentem

---

of Anselm M. Albareda (New York, 1961), ed. Sesto Prete, 205–243. Cf. notes 84–88 above.

163. Cf. Di Napoli, 51–120; Garin, *Cultura*, 93–126; D. C. Allen, *Doubt's Boundless Sea* (Baltimore, 1964), 28–74, 150–185. For Filippo de Barberiis, cf. *Gesamtkatalog der Wiegendrucke*, 3388; *Iter Italicum*, I, 427. For Jacopo Camphora's *De immortalitate anime in modum dialogi vulgariter*, cf. *Gesamtkatalog*, 5948–56.

164. *De immortalitate animae*, ch. 5–6, ed. Morra, 70–72; Edward P. Mahoney, "Agostino Nifo's Early Views on Immortality," *Journal of the History of Philosophy* 8 (1970), 451–460.

165. Di Napoli, 326–335.

166. F. Lauchert, *Die italienischen literarischen Gegner Luthers* (Freiburg, 1912), 239–240. For his commentaries on Plato, cf. Kristeller, *Iter*, I, 274–275.

167. Mansi, 32 (1902), 842–843; *Bullarium*, 5 (Turin, 1860), 601–602; cf. Hefele, 8 (1887), 585–587. See Felix Gilbert, "Cristianesimo, umanesimo e la Bolla 'Apostolici Regiminis' del 1513," *Rivista Storica Italiana* 79 (1967), 976–990.

Platonis," and continued the Hebraic and cabalistic studies of Pico della Mirandola.[168] And it was another Catholic theologian—Bishop Agostino Steuco—who in 1540 invented the term *philosophia perennis* to describe the Christian and Platonic tradition that he had studied in the footsteps of Ficino and Pico.[169]

But Florentine Platonism did not meet only approbation on the part of the theologians of its period. We have discovered a document attesting that, at least on the special point of the superiority of the intellect or the will, the doctrine of Marsilio Ficino was subjected to a detailed critique by a contemporary theologian who was a Dominican and a Thomist.[170] The author was a well-known person, Vincenzo Bandello, who was to take an active part in the controversy on the Immaculate Conception and who would die as Master General of the Dominicans.[171] His treatise on the intellect and the will, directed against Ficino and dedicated to Lorenzo de'Medici, was known to the bibliographers of the eighteenth century,[172] but it has remained unknown to recent

168. A Palmieri, in *Dictionnaire de théologie catholique*, 6 (1920), 1365–71; G. Signorelli, *Il Card. Egidio da Viterbo* (Florence, 1929); E. Massa, "L'Anima e l'Uomo in Egidio da Viterbo . . . ," in *Testi umanistici inediti sul "De anima"*: *Archivio di Filosofia* (Padua, 1951), 37–138; Egidio da Viterbo, *Scechina e Libellus de litteris Hebraicis*, ed. F. Secret, 2 vols. (Rome, 1959); F. X. Martin, "The Problem of Giles of Viterbo," *Augustiniana* 9 (1959), 357–379; 10 (1960), 43–60; John W. O'Malley, *Giles of Viterbo on Church and Reform* (Leiden, 1968). Cf. also F. Secret, "Les dominicains et la Kabbale chretienne à la Renaissance," *Archivum Fratrum Praedicatorum* 27 (1957), 319–336.

169. Augustinus Steuchus, *De perenni philosophia* (Lyons, 1540) and several reprintings. Cf. T. Freudenberger, *Augustinus Steuchus* (Münster, 1935); A. S. Ebert, "Agostino Steuco und seine Philosophia perennis," *Philosophisches Jahrbuch* 42 (1929), 342–356, 510–526; 43 (1930), 92–100; Charles B. Schmitt, "Perennial Philosophy from Agostino Steuco to Leibniz," *Journal of the History of Ideas* 27 (1966), 505–532; idem, "Prisca Theologia e Philosophia Perennis: due temi del Rinascimento italiano e la loro fortuna," in *Il pensiero italiano del Rinascimento e il tempo nostro*, ed. G. Tarugi (Florence, 1970), 211–236; G. Di Napoli, "Il concetto di 'Philosophia Perennis' di Agostino Steuco nel quadro della tematica rinascimentale," in *Atti del Quarto Convegno di Studi Umbri* (Gubbio, 1966), 459–489.

170. I treat of this in greater detail in another article: "A Thomist Critique of Marsilio Ficino's Theory of Will and Intellect," in *Harry Austryn Wolfson Jubilee Volume, English Section*, II (Jerusalem, 1965), 463–494.

171. R. P. Mortier, *Histoire des Maîtres généraux de l'Ordre des Frères Prêcheurs*, V (Paris, 1911), 66–127. Cf. C. Piana, *Ricerche* (1963), 268–269 and passim.

172. Quétif and Echard, II (1723), 2: "Extat hoc opus (on the Immaculate Conception) Ms. Florentiae ad S. Marci Arm. III cod. 19, cui et aliud adjunctum eiusdem Vincentii opusculum ad magnificum et generosum virum Laurentium Medicem. Titulus: Quod beatitudo hominis in actu intellectus et non voluntatis essentialiter consistit. Occasio huius scripti fuit sententia Marsilii Ficini ea aetate florentis et aliter opinantis. Idem opusculum item habetur ibidem Arm. IV cod. 89." G. Mazzuchelli, *Gli scrittori d'Italia*, II, 1 (Brescia, 1758), 208; "Fra queste

historians of Renaissance Thomism and Platonism. The text of this treatise is preserved in two manuscripts from the convent of San Marco in Florence. One of them, which also contains one of the treatises by the same author on the Immaculate Conception, has always remained in Florence, having passed by the regular channels to the Fondo San Marco of the Biblioteca Laurenziana.[173] The other manuscript, which contained only our text, was kept at San Marco until the middle of the eighteenth century,[174] and was not included among the manuscripts that passed from the convent to the Biblioteca Laurenziana or to the Biblioteca Nazionale at Florence. It was therefore not included in the inventory of 1768, which still serves today for the *fondo* of the Laurenziana.[175] Not long ago, a manuscript of this text was sold in London by Christie, and later by Maggs,[176] then passed to Witten, the New Haven antiquarian,[177] and was finally repurchased for the Biblioteca Laurenziana.[178] In this manuscript, which contains only the treatise in question, there is a note proving its San Marco provenance,[179]

---

(the unedited works of Bandello) una si conserva in detto Codice della Libreria di S. Marco in Firenze (Armadio III, Cod. 19), ed è intitolata: Quod beatitudo hominis in actu intellectus et non voluntatis essentialiter consistit."

173. Laur. S. Marco 482, 196 folios on parchment. It contains the treatise of Vincentius (Bandellus) de Castronovo on the Immaculate Conception (f. 1–156) and the treatise in question (f. 157–196), copied by two different hands (cf. *Iter*, I, 77). This manuscript is easily identified with the ms. III 19, cited by Quétif and Mazzuchelli. I am indebted to Signora Irma Merolle Tondi, director of the Biblioteca Laurenziana, for a microfilm of this ms.

174. Cf. note 172 above. It is cited by Quétif (but not by Mazzuchelli) with the shelf mark IV 89.

175. These facts were confirmed for me by letters from Signora Merolle, the late Doctor Alberto Giraldi, and the late Professor B. L. Ullman.

176. *Catalogue of Valuable Books and Manuscripts* . . . Christie, Manson & Woods, London, June 22, 1960, p. 30, no. 107 (the manuscript at that time belonged to Sir Kenneth Clark and previously to Henry White and to Noel Frederick Barwell); *Manuscripts, Rare Books, Oriental Miniatures*, Catalogue 871, Maggs Bros. Ltd., London, 1960, p. 90, no. 82 and plate 33. The Maggs catalogue was pointed out to me by my late friend Professor Zofia Ameisenowa of Cracow.

177. Laurence Witten, *Important Books, Manuscripts, Documents & Autographs, Catalogue Five* (New Haven, 1962), 16–17, no. 9. Mr. Witten was kind enough to let me see the manuscript when he had it in his possession.

178. Present shelf mark: Acquisti e Doni 632. The ms. comprises fory-one unnumbered folios; it is written on paper, and the first page bears an ornate margin and the arms of the Medici. I thank Signora Merolle for several communications and for a microfilm of the manuscript.

179. On the back of the fly-leaf is found the following note in an eighteenth century Italian hand: "Codex iste singularis, et quantivis pretii continet opusculum Fratris Vincentii de C. N. cognomento Bandelli qui fuit Prior Generalis. Quod habet singulare est quod conscriptum fuit a Fr. Dominico de Piscia, inter Beatos Ordinis a Benedicto XIII adnumerato, ideoque ut Sacrum Monumentum considerandum."

and on the first page there is the Medici coat of arms, which indicates that it is the copy given Lorenzo by the author, or at least the one intended for him.

Before speaking of the contents of this treatise, it will be useful to outline briefly the history of the problem that it discusses.[180] The Greek philosophers, including Aristotle, had spoken of appetite in opposition to reason and of acts of volition connected with reason. However, the concept of the will as a faculty of the soul distinct from reason or intellect is not found in their texts. We must also discard the rather wide-spread opinion that the problem of the will as a faculty of the soul is connected to that of free will or choice.[181] There are strong indications that it was Saint Augustine who first introduced the idea of will into Western thought by relying on some less explicit precedents from Greek philosophy, but above all by relying on Latin legal terminology and the theological demands of his doctrine of sin.[182] There are several texts of Saint Augustine that connect the will to love and distinguish it plainly from reason. From Saint Augustine, this distinction passed to medieval thought. The question of the superiority of the will or of the intellect is not discussed by Saint Augustine, but Saint Thomas treated this question on several occasions in a rather detailed manner. Basing himself on Aristotle, he tends in general to assert the superiority of the intellect over the will, specifying that the essence of beatitude consists in an act of the intellect; he concedes, however, that from several points of view the will is superior to the intellect, especially during the present life.[183]

This problem represents one of the points upon which Duns Scotus criticized Saint Thomas. While presenting some very detailed arguments, Scotus concluded that in the present life and in the future life the will is superior to the intellect and that beatitude consists essentially in an act of the will. In the course of his argumentation, he points

180. For more details, cf. my article referred to above in note 170.

181. This error comes from the fact that English usage does not clearly distinguish between "will" and "free will" as Latin does. For those who use English usage as the sole criterion of truth, therefore, the distinction does not exist, as I have had occasion to remark during more than one discussion on the subject.

182. Neal W. Gilbert, "The Concept of Will in Early Latin Philosophy," *Journal of the History of Philosophy* 1 (1963), 17–35.

183. *Contra Gentiles*, III, 26; *Quaestiones disputatae, De veritate*, q. 22, a. 11; *Summa Theologiae*, Ia, q. 12, a. 12; q. 26, a. 2; q. 82, a. 3; I–IIae, q. 3–5; *In III Sent.*, dist. 27, q. 1, a. 4; *In IV Sent.*, dist. 49, q. 1, a. 1. Cf. E. Gilson, *Le Thomisme*, (1945), 341–342; *The Christian Philosophy*, 243–244; J. Durantel, *Le retour à Dieu par l'intelligence et la volonté dans la philosophie de Saint-Thomas* (thesis, Paris, 1918).

out that the doctrine of the will is not solidly established in Aristotle.[184]

It is to be presumed that this question was dealt with again by others in the course of the discussions between the Thomist and Scotist schools during the fourteenth and fifteenth centuries, but I know of no modern study that has been made of it. On the other hand, it is interesting to find echoes of this discussion in the writings of the humanists who, in other respects, manifested such little interest in the questions of scholastic theology and philosophy. The question is entered upon, for example, by Petrarch and Salutati, who both decide in favor of the superiority of the will.[185]

Ficino discussed the theory of the intellect and the will in great detail in several of his writings. The importance he attributes to this question is one of the most notable examples enabling us to determine the role of medieval thought in his system. He always maintains the distinction between these two faculties, and he shows a tendency throughout his work to establish a sort of parallelism between them.[186] The interest this question aroused in the discussions of the Florentine academy is also revealed in a little treatise written by one of his students, Alamanno Donati. This treatise collects a great number of arguments relative to the problem of the intellect and the will, but it does not decide the question of the superiority of one of these faculties over the other.[187] This problem preoccupied Marsilio Ficino repeatedly during the various periods of his life. Indeed, it is one of the points regarding which some oscillations and changes in his thought may be observed. In his commentary on Plato's *Philebus*, which resulted from a course given in 1468, he maintains, while citing several supporting arguments, that the intellect is superior to the will.[188] But in his *Platonic Theology*, written between 1469 and 1475, he emphasizes strongly the superiority of the will and of love, and the same position

184. *Opus Oxoniense*, IV, 49; *Reportata Parisiensia*, IV, 69. Cf. Gilson, *Jean Duns Scot* (Paris, 1952), 600–602. "Posset aliter dici, quod Philosophus communiter non distinxit intellectum a voluntate in ratione principii operativi sive operatione ad extra." Duns Scotus, *Opera omnia*, XXI (Paris, 1894), 141.

185. Petrarch, *Le traité De sui ipsius et multorum ignorantia*, ed. L. M. Capelli (Paris, 1906), 70; Coluccio Salutati, *De nobilitate legum et medicinae*, ed. E. Garin (Florence, 1947), 182–196. The Thomist Giovanni Dominici places the intellect above the will (*Lucula Noctis*, ed. E. Hunt, Notre Dame, 1940, 314–318).

186. Kristeller, *Pensiero*, 289–291; idem, *The Philosophy*, 270–271.

187. Alamannus Donati, *De intellectus voluntatisque excellentia*, ed. L. Borghi, in *La Bibliofilia* 42 (1940), 108–115.

188. Ficinus, *Opera* (1576), II, 1251–52. Cf. Kristeller, *Pensiero*, 291–292; idem, *The Philosophy*, 271–272. Cf. Michael J. B. Allen, *Ficino's Commentary on the Philebus* (Ph.D. diss., University of Michigan, 1970).

is found in several of his letters.[189] Near the end of his career, however, he again appears undecided. When preparing his commentary on the *Philebus* for publication, he adds, at an appropriate point of the commentary, that he had elsewhere resolved the question in an opposite sense, and he attempts to propose a compromise, distinguishing between the will in the sense of a distinct faculty and the will as a part of the intellect.[190] In a letter of 1496, Ficino attempts to explain to a friend the apparent contradiction between his commentary on the *Philebus* and his subsequent letters. He proposes here the distinction between the natural activity and the supernatural activity of the soul, maintaining that the intellect is superior in the former and the will in the latter.[191] This solution is neither very clear nor very convincing, but it shows us that the problem continued to preoccupy him and that he had not at all succeeded in arriving at a firm or categorical opinion on this particular question. Could these hesitations of the last period have been stirred up by Vincenzo Bandello's treatise? We cannot assert this with confidence, since Ficino never quotes it.

The text of Ficino that provided Bandello with the opportunity to compose his opusculum was a little treatise entitled *Epistola de felicitate*, written in the form of a letter and sent to Lorenzo de'Medici, probably in 1473.[192] The letter claims to summarize a discussion held between Ficino and Lorenzo several days earlier. The same discussion was taken up again by Lorenzo himself in a fairly well-known poem entitled *L'Altercazione*. Ficino's letter contains three parts. In the first, he presents a hierarchy of goods and concludes that the final beatitude of man is found in God. In the second, he asserts that, in final beatitude,

---

189. Kristeller, *Pensiero*, 292–294; idem, *The Philosophy*, 272–274.

190. Ibid., 294–295; idem, *The Philosophy*, 274–275.

191. Ibid., 295–296; idem, *The Philosophy*, 275–276. In a letter to Colet written towards the end of his life, Ficino again seems to place the intellect above the will, but he discusses the problem in somewhat different terms. See Sears Jayne, *John Colet and Marsilio Ficino* (Oxford, 1963), 82–83, cf. 56–76; Kristeller, "The European Significance of Florentine Platonism" (*Medieval and Renaissance Studies*, ed. John M. Headley, Chapel Hill, 1968, 206–229), 228, n. 69. Cf. James A. Devereux, "The Object of Love in Ficino's Philosophy," *Journal of the History of Ideas* 30 (1969), 161–170.

192. Ficinus, *Opera*, 662–665. I am now inclined to date the letter of Ficino and the poem of Lorenzo de'Medici to 1473 instead of 1475, relying on a letter from Naldo to Niccolò Michelozzi that bears the date "pridie idus septembris 1473." Cf. Kristeller, in *Studi di Bibliografia e di Storia in onore di Tammaro De Marinis*, III (Verona, 1964), 13. The same date is proposed for different reasons by A. Rochon, *La jeunesse de Laurent de Médicis* (Paris, 1963), 476. The letter has now been published: *Nuovi Documenti per la Storia del Rinascimento*, ed. T. De Marinis and A. Perosa (Florence, 1970), 56.

the act of the will is superior to the act of the intellect, and he presents a series of arguments in favor of this proposition. In the third, he touches upon some related questions and concludes by referring the reader to his commentary on the *Symposium* and to his *Platonic Theology* for a more complete discussion.

Bandello's opusculum opens with a preface in the form of a letter addressed to Lorenzo de'Medici. Several days earlier he had read by chance a letter by Marsilio Ficino in which the author, with his usual clarity and elegance, relates the outcome of a disputation on the final beatitude of rational creatures which he had pursued with Lorenzo at Careggi. Bandello believes that in this disputation it was Ficino who upheld the superiority of the will and that Lorenzo defended that of the intellect. He addresses some compliments to Lorenzo for the interest that he shows in theological questions along with his public and private occupations and to Ficino for his skill in handling the argument and in convincing others. But since his conclusion in favor of the will is opposed to that of Saint Thomas and many other eminent theologians, Bandello has decided to present his own opinion, which is contrary to that of Ficino, in an opusculum that he dedicates to Lorenzo. At the same time, he says he is sure that this difference of opinion will not disturb the friendship that binds him to Ficino, and he begs Lorenzo to be good enough to excuse the lack of literary elegance in his work, since he has adopted the simple style of theologians for the benefit of the clarity of his account. He hopes that Lorenzo will be willing to examine the arguments put forward in favor of the two opposed solutions and to choose the one that seems to him the most certain.[193]

This preface contains all the historical facts we possess on the composition of the opusculum. Evidently Bandello had visited Florence and met Lorenzo and Ficino (the polite and friendly tone of the preface should be noted), and he read Ficino's letter, *De felicitate*, of which we have just spoken. It is probable that this letter passed through the hands of the members of the Florentine circle before being inserted into the collection of Ficino's letters. Bandello's opusculum was probably written around 1474–75, this date being suggested by a curious detail. As we have seen, Bandello pretends to believe that in the course of the dispute recounted by Ficino it was Lorenzo who maintained the superiority of the intellect, and that the decision in favor of the will was

193. Laur. Acquisti 632, f. 1–2 (ed. Kristeller, *Le Thomisme* [1967], 105–106).

the result of the arguments proposed by Ficino. This remark contradicts two statements of Ficino's letter which assert that it was Lorenzo who brought to the discussion several new arguments in favor of the will.[194] Now these statements are omitted in one of the oldest manuscripts and are found in the margins of several others.[195] Consequently, I believe that Bandello had read Ficino's letter without this assertion and that Ficino added it after having seen Bandello's opusculum, which he does not otherwise mention.

It is easy to understand Bandello's intervention in this question. He was certainly accustomed to defending the Thomist and Dominican positions against the Scotist and Franciscan positions, as is seen in his subsequent treatises on the Immaculate Conception. The question of the primacy of the intellect or the will was one of the points debated between the two schools. At the time that he read Ficino's letter, Bandello must have been unaware that Ficino had supported the Thomist position several years earlier. He noticed that Ficino seemed to adopt the Scotist position in his letter, without using, however, any of Duns Scotus's characteristic arguments, but giving instead some arguments that were either new or drawn from the text itself of Saint Thomas. Let us add that on the point in question Bandello's position is simpler and more categorical than that of Saint Thomas himself, of which he omits many subtle details, even though he knew his texts and his arguments very well. The importance which Bandello attributed to the superiority of the intellect is confirmed by the preface of one of his treatises on the Immaculate Conception.[196]

There is no reason to believe that the discussion between Ficino and Lorenzo took the rigid form of a scholastic disputation with arguments *pro* or *contra*, responses to the arguments, and a determination of the question. But Bandello credits them with the utilization of this type of disputation to which he was accustomed. He thus treats the central part of Ficino's letter (it is this part alone that deals with the problem) as a scholastic *quaestio*, although an incomplete one, since the arguments in the opposite direction and the replies to the arguments have been omitted. Bandello begins his opusculum with a for-

194. ". . . ubi tu novas quasdam rationes quod felicitas in voluntatis potius quam intellectus actu consistat subtiliter invenisti." *Opera*, 662. ". . . magna ex parte a te inventa." *Opera*, 665.

195. *Supplementum Ficinianum*, ed P. O. Kristeller (Florence, 1937), I, 28.

196. *Libellus recollectorius de veritate conceptionis Beate Virginis Marie* (Milan, 1475) (*Gesamtkatalog* 3237) f. 1.

mal presentation of Ficino's position and his eighteen arguments.[197] Except for several slight differences, this presentation is faithful enough. In the second part of his treatise, Bandello presents eighteen arguments in favor of the intellect opposed to those of Ficino.[198] The third part is entitled *Determinatio questionis* and it contains fifteen conclusions with their respective arguments.[199] The fourth part contains a detailed refutation of the arguments of Ficino which were presented in the first part.[200] In a short epilogue addressed to Lorenzo, Bandello excuses himself for having omitted many other arguments. Besides, those he has discussed should suffice, since the arguments presented by Ficino are the most effective and the most commonly advanced.[201]

Since we cannot devote ourselves to a detailed analysis of the arguments in this treatise, which we have, nevertheless, attempted elsewhere,[202] we shall content ourselves with several general observations. The opusculum of Bandello has the well-defined structure of the scholastic *quaestio*. There is a thesis proposed at the beginning and repeated at the end as having been demonstrated, a series of arguments drawn up in order to sustain and refute the thesis (the second and first parts), and a detailed refutation of the opposed arguments (the fourth part). Inasmuch as Bandello is attempting to refute the central part of Ficino's letter, which he treats as a question, the arguments opposed to his thesis precede the arguments maintaining it. The third part, with its independent conclusions and their proofs, abandons the ordinary scheme of the *quaestio*, but it serves as the foundation of the fourth part. The preface and the epilogue follow humanistic literary conventions. The Latin style is ordinary and simple, and the terminology is not exceedingly technical. His arguments sometimes smack of pedantry and are repetitious, but they are most often well thought out. The presentation of Ficino's opinions is always objective, although it seems to me that he does not always understand what Ficino is driving at. The texts most frequently quoted, and literally, come from the Bible, Aristotle, and Saint Thomas. There are less frequent quotations from

197. Laur. Acquisti 632, f. 2–5 (ed. Kristeller, pp. 197–203).
198. Ibid., f. 5v–12v (ed. Kristeller, pp. 203–217).
199. Ibid., f. 12v–22. Ms. S. Marco 482 offers here a longer text and includes sixteen arguments (ed. Kristeller, pp. 217–243).
200. Ibid., f. 22–41 (ed. Kristeller, pp. 243–278).
201. Ibid., f. 41 (ed. Kristeller, p. 278).
202. Cf. note 170 above.

Saint Augustine, Boethius, Dionysius, Cicero, Saint Gregory the Great, and Hugh of Saint-Victor. Those of Origen and the Platonists probably come from indirect sources.

Concerning the numerous and detailed arguments that are presented, the following points may be noted. Bandello introduces a certain number of precise distinctions, absent from Ficino's exposition, which allow him to restate the problem in somewhat different terms. The most important is one Bandello borrows from Saint Thomas according to which the final end of man can be understood in the sense of an internal or external end, the latter being God, the former being the possession of beatitude.[203] Another important distinction concerns the theory of pleasure. Bandello follows the Aristotelian theory that makes of pleasure a perfection which accompanies an activity and which therefore cannot constitute the principal object of a desire.[204] Ficino, on the other hand, had been influenced in his youth by the hedonism of Epicurus and Lucretius,[205] and his orientation toward Neoplatonism must have promoted the idea that the good and the appetite directed toward the good receive a more elevated and extensive place in the universe than does the order of truth and intellect.[206] Evidently Bandello was not in a position to know and appreciate Ficino's ideas and their sources. But the most profound difference between the two positions concerns the analysis of the acts of knowledge and of love. According to Ficino, on its own level the intellect comprehends its object through images or species. When this object is God, the intellect finds itself reducing and limiting Him by adapting Him to its own capacities. Love, on the contrary, moves the soul toward its object in accordance with what it is in itself. When this object is God, love can then elevate the soul and lead it to open itself to the divine infinity.[207] These eloquent assertions of Marsilio Ficino, repeated in Italian verses by Lorenzo de'Medici, are not only the reflection of Neoplatonic and medieval theories, but also of the spiritual and personal ex-

203. Section 3, arguments 3–8 (ed. Kristeller, pp. 218–232).
204. Section 2, argument 10 (ed., pp. 207–208), and section 3, argument 9 (ed., pp. 232–235).
205. Kristeller, *Pensiero*, 14; idem, *The Philosophy*, 24. Cf. *Supplementum Ficinianum*, II, 81–87.
206. Kristeller, *Pensiero*, 292–294; idem, *The Philosophy*, 272–274.
207. "Proinde cognoscendo Deum ejus amplitudinem contrahimus ad mentis nostrae capacitatem atque conceptum, amando vero mentem amplificamus ad latitudinem divinae bonitatis immensam . . ." *Opera*, 664. Cf. *Pensiero*, 293; *The Philosophy*, 273.

periences of their author. Indeed, the historian Jacob Burckhardt saw in them one of the most noble expressions of Renaissance thought.[208] Bandello's response to this argument is characteristic: the distinction between acts of the will and of the intellect as Ficino presents it is true for the present life, but in the future life knowledge will be reinforced by the *lumen gloriae*. The soul will then know God directly and in His essence, and will be open to the divine infinity by means of the vision of God, not by means of the enjoyment of God.[209] For Bandello there is a radical difference between the present life and the future life, and also between the knowledge of God in this life and in the other. The highest beatitude possible in this life, of which Aristotle and other philosophers have spoken, resembles only remotely the real beatitude of the future life. The future knowledge of God will include certain characteristic traits that cannot be found in the experience of the present life. On his side, Ficino, heir of the Neoplatonic tradition, does not admit that the difference between the present life and the future life is so radical. He is convinced that the highest contemplative experience that the Platonic philosopher may attain in this life is an authentic anticipation of the future life and that the future life may be described through analogies derived from this experience. He is far from denying the importance of Christian faith, of grace, and of the *lumen gloriae*, but he insists on the fact that the experiences of the present and future lives are profoundly similar. Their difference is a relative, not an absolute difference: the perfect knowledge of God in this life is accessible only to a very small number and for a very short time, but in the future life it will be granted to all saved souls and for all eternity.[210] A final observation may be added. Bandello treats the problem of the will and the intellect as if it were a theological question, in other words, a question of Christian theology. He considers above all the state of the saved soul and follows the texts relative to this question in the theological works of Saint Thomas. For Ficino, who is chiefly concerned with the interpretation of the experience available to philosophers in the present life, it is a question of philosophy, meta-

208. J. Burckhardt, *Die Kultur der Renaissance in Italien*, 13th edition (Stuttgart, 1921), 415. Cf. Lorenzo de'Medici, *Altercazione*, Capitolo V, verses 49–54, in *Scritti scelti*, ed. E. Bigi (Turin, 1955), 76: "Avvien all'alma nostra, Dio intendendo, / che a sua capacità tanta amplitudine / contrae, e Dio in se vien ristrignendo. / Amando, alla sua immensa latitudine / amplifichiamo e dilatiam la mente: / questo par sia vera beatitudine."

209. Section 4, arguments 7 and 15 (ed. Kristeller, pp. 259–261 and 270–271).

210. *Pensiero*, 238–239, 360–364; idem, *The Philosophy*, 224–225, 332–336.

physics, or, if you will, of Platonic theology. It must therefore be admitted that there are questions that theology and philosophy dispute between themselves, even in those thinkers who attempt to establish the clearest possible distinction between the two spheres. But even if the problem of the intellect and the will is considered a theological question, it is not a problem that touches upon religious orthodoxy, although it does touch upon Thomist orthodoxy in theology, and perhaps also in philosophy. In his letter, the *De felicitate*, Ficino certainly defended a position on this point that was contrary to that advanced by Thomism and he thus provoked the detailed criticism of a very learned and acute Thomist. Although he never quotes the opusculum of Bandello, it is possible that Ficino read it and that his subsequent hesitations were aroused in part by this critique. However courteous, that critique must at least have warned him that in respect to the doctrine of the will and love he was moving away from Saint Thomas, whom he admired and followed on many other important points.

Bandello's opusculum against Ficino and the variety of opinions that it reveals to us have an historical interest that is quite exceptional not only on account of certain details of the discussion and the arguments proposed, but also because of the problem itself and the general framework of intellectual currents in which it must be situated. We have a new Quattrocento text on a problem that is most important for the philosophy of the Middle Ages and the Renaissance, and for the whole history of Western thought. We also have here, if I may use a fashionable word, a precious testimony of a serious and friendly "dialogue" held in the fifteenth century between important representatives of Thomism and Platonism. It is an example that has not been much followed in the twentieth century. This episode furnishes us with proof, if one is still necessary, both that the Platonism of the Renaissance was a very serious philosophical and metaphysical movement that attempted to resolve in part the same problems which had preoccupied medieval thinkers and also that a detailed discussion between a theologian, who was a disciple of Saint Thomas, and the leader of the Platonic Academy in Florence, at least on the precise points we have mentioned, was possible and even useful. The intervention of Lorenzo de'Medici, to whom Ficino's letter and Bandello's opusculum are dedicated, confirms that he was more than superficially interested in philosophical and theological questions.[211] Finally, Ban-

211. Dominic of Flanders dedicated his commentary on the *Metaphysics* to

dello's treatise fills a serious gap in the history of Thomism in Italy during the fifteenth century.[212] We were already acquainted with the teaching of Francesco of Nardò, which had borne fruit among his students rather than in writings from his own hand; with Cajetan's important activity, which had scarcely begun at the end of the century; and with the treatises by Saint Antoninus and other Dominicans which bore on theological questions in the narrow sense of the word. The opusculum of Bandello furnishes us with the most notable example (I hope that I am not exaggerating) of a fifteenth-century Thomist treatise on a question involving a clearly philosophical interest or, at least, an interest common to philosophy and theology.

To conclude this survey, which is still quite superficial and full of gaps, of a very interesting but little studied subject, we may assert that Thomism occupied an important place in the thought of the Italian Renaissance. It did not dominate the scene, even in theology, but it did contribute to the intellectual activity and to the literature of the period, thanks above all to the work of Dominican theologians, but thanks also to the diffusion of Saint Thomas' ideas, through teaching and reading, in the work of lay thinkers who showed themselves ready to adopt his ideas on certain points even while criticizing or ignoring him on many others. On the other hand, if we extend our gaze to the sixteenth century and to the rest of Europe, it must be said that the Renaissance occupies a very important, though often unacknowledged, place in the history of Thomism. If the position occupied by Thomism at the end of the sixteenth century is compared to the actual, and not imaginary, situation in which it found itself at the beginning of the fourteenth or even fifteenth century, it is apparent that things have changed in a very notable and surprising manner. The *Summa Theologiae* succeeded in replacing Peter Lombard's *Sentences* as the theological text for teaching, first of all in the Dominican

Lorenzo (cf. n. 56 above). In 1477, Lorenzo asked Giovanni Bentivoglio to lend him Buridan's questions on Aristotle's *Ethics* (Rochon, 309 and 340). In 1489, a theological dispute between Nicolas de Mirabilibus, O.P. (Hain 11221) and George Benignus, O.M. (*Gesamtkatalog* 3842) was held in Lorenzo's house; cf. C. Dionisotti, in *Italia Medioevale e Umanistica* 4 (1961), 305.

212. "Noch immer ist das ausgehende 15. Jahrhundert problemgeschichtlich eine Landkarte mit grossen weissen Flecken." Jedin, *Studien ueber Domenico de' Domenichi* (1957), 300. Cf. 298: "Es wird Aufgabe einer kuenftigen dogmengeschichtlichen Untersuchung sein, ihn in die Geschichte des Thomismus einzuordnen." For the *Corona aurea* (ed. Venice, 1496) of Jacobus Brutus, a layman, and its Thomist orientation, see Leonard A Kennedy, "A Fifteenth-Century Thomist," *The Modern Schoolman* 42 (1964–65), 193–197.

schools, and then in many universities and other schools. Within the Church and outside the Dominican Order, the authority of Saint Thomas grew considerably and his prestige markedly increased among lay philosophers and scholars who were at work outside the theological sphere and even outside the Catholic Church. Many thinkers—and we have seen examples of this in Ficino, Pico, and Pomponazzi— without being orthodox or even eclectic Thomists, borrowed important ideas from him. Moreover, for the typical thinkers and readers of modern times since the second half of the sixteenth century, he became what he has remained up until the most recent upsurge of medieval studies, namely, the representative thinker of the Middle Ages, almost the only one whom they have been prepared to read or to quote or whom they have known at least by name. The history of Thomism during the Renaissance is a very vast subject that cannot be limited to Cajetan or the school of Salamanca. We have hardly been able to scratch its surface, and detailed study of it in its manuscript and printed sources may yet occupy a large number of scholars and still yield results that will be interesting and not lacking in surprises.

# THE CONTRIBUTION OF RELIGIOUS ORDERS TO RENAISSANCE THOUGHT AND LEARNING

The subject of this paper, which was suggested to me by the project of the Monastic Manuscript Microfilm Library in Collegeville,[1] has to my knowledge not yet received much attention. There are scattered contributions that deal with particular orders, places or persons,[2] but there is no comprehensive treatment of Renaissance monasticism, although so much has been written both on monasticism and on the Renaissance. What is worse, the very problem which I shall try to discuss does not seem to exist if we accept as correct some widespread historical notions. Nobody questions the fundamental contribution of

This paper is based on a lecture given on October 15, 1968, at St. John's University, Collegeville, Minnesota, under the auspices of its Monastic Manuscript Microfilm Library. The lecture was repeated before the University Seminar on the Renaissance at Columbia University on October 7, 1969. I wish to thank the Rt. Rev. Baldwin Dworschak O.S.B. of St. John's University, Collegeville, and Prof. Julian G. Plante, Curator of its Monastic Manuscript Microfilm Library, for their kind invitation to deliver the lecture and for their generous hospitality during my visit. I am also indebted for some of my references to the following scholars: Klaus Arnold (Würzburg), Marshall Clagett (Institute for Advanced Study, Princeton), Carlo Dionisotti (University of London), Norman Dukes (Provincetown), Luciano Gargan (Università Cattolica, Milan), Rabbi David Geffen (Wilmington), the Rev. Thomas Kaeppeli, O.P. (Santa Sabina, Rome), Julius Kirshner (University of Chicago), Edward P. Mahoney (Duke University), Herbert Matsen (University of South Carolina), Otto Meyer (Würzburg), the Rev. Francis X. Roth O.E.S.A. (formerly of the Augustinian Historical Institute, New York), Eugene Sheehy (Columbia University Library), Nancy Siraisi (Hunter College), Josef Soudek (Queens College), Charles Trinkaus (University of Michigan), Donald Weinstein (Rutgers University), Helene Wieruszowski (formerly of City University, New York), Ronald Witt (Duke University), and the librarians of St. John's University.

1. See *Monastic Manuscript Microfilm Project, Progress Reports 1–5*, 1965–68, by the Rev. Oliver L. Kapsner, O.S.B.; *Checklist of Manuscripts Microfilmed for the Monastic Manuscript Microfilm Library*, Saint John's University, Collegeville, Minnesota, by Prof. Julian G. Plante, 1967.

2. For the contributions of various religious orders to Renaissance humanism, see the studies by Arbesmann, Kaeppeli, Mariani, Smalley, Vonschott and Zimmerman, and Kristeller, *Le Thomisme*, listed below in the Bibliography. Bio-bibliographical data for the individual religious orders, though often antiquated or incomplete, are found in the works listed in the Bibliography: Ossinger, Perini, Zumkeller (Augustinians); Ziegelbauer, Kapsner (Benedictines); Ziegelbauer, Mittarelli-Costadoni (Camaldulensians); de Villiers, Xiberta (Carmelites); Quétif-Echard, Orlandi (Dominicans); Wadding, Sbaralea (Franciscans); De Backer-Sommervogel (Jesuits); Giani (Servites). I rarely cite contributions made after 1530, and hence the Jesuit scholars and the Spanish scholastics are not covered by this study. For a general history and bibliography of the religious orders, see Heimbucher. Individual contributions are scattered in the periodicals devoted to the individual orders and their history. They can best be followed through the bibliographies appended to the *Revue d'histoire ecclésiastique*. The book by Angeleri, useful in many other ways, does not contain a separate treatment of monasticism and its problems. See now also Denys Hay, *Italian Clergy and Italian Culture in the Fifteenth Century* (London, 1973).

the religious orders to the civilization of the Middle Ages, and it is no exaggeration if we say that the monastic orders and their monasteries provided the chief centers for certain periods and aspects of medieval civilization. If we were to take away the Benedictine and Cistercian monasteries, not only the theological but nearly the entire intellectual movement of the Carolingian age and of the centuries following it would seem to disappear. And without the contribution of the mendicant orders, the scholasticism of the thirteenth and early fourteenth century would lose much of its vigor and significance. On the other hand, Renaissance culture is generally considered as a lay culture, a period in which the major contributions were due to laymen, whereas the monks and friars were at best confined to fighting a rearguard action and to preserving a part of the medieval heritage.

Now I am not prepared, out of an inborn spirit of contradiction, or in compliance with my theme today, completely to reverse the historical view which I have briefly indicated. I am convinced, and I have stated this on more than one occasion, that Renaissance culture, and especially Renaissance humanism, is in important ways a lay culture.[3] There can be no doubt that during our period the share of the layman in the intellectual life steadily and greatly increased, and that in comparison with theology and other religious studies, the lay subjects vastly expanded both in quantity and in relative importance. This trend which began already in the later medieval centuries may be observed in all areas of study, in law and medicine, mathematics and philosophy, grammar and rhetoric as well as in classical and literary studies. What I hope to show is merely this: the contribution of the monks and friars to Renaissance culture was much greater than is usually realized. This contribution lay partly in the vigorous continuation of medieval traditions—a rearguard action, to be sure, but an important one—and partly in the active participation of the religious in the new intellectual movements of the period. For they competed with contemporary laymen in the secular studies of the period—a perfectly honorable activity if we attach any genuine value to these secular studies. Moreover, the monks utilized for their own religious studies, learning and thought the new knowledge and method supplied by the humanists. Thus we may talk with some justification of a monastic culture of the Renaissance that was also humanistic and hence different in style, if not in ultimate purpose, from the monastic

3. See my *Renaissance Thought*, 2 vols. (New York, 1961–65).

culture of the Middle Ages. We may thus hope to modify, if not to reverse, the prevalent view of which we spoke before, and at least to formulate, if not to solve, a problem whose very existence has been concealed by too literal and narrow a historical perspective.

Since my topic is very large, and my allotted space and knowledge are limited, I can only attempt a kind of outline, hoping that future research will add substance and content to it, and will confirm at least a part of the observations that I shall try to make on the basis of my own impressions and readings. Let me first define the limits of my subject. When I speak of the Renaissance, I mean to include most of the period from 1300 to 1600, and although I have a special interest in the fifteenth century, I do include much that others would exclude from the Renaissance and prefer to call the late Middle Ages or the Reformation. I should like to keep all of Western Europe in perspective, but it is inevitable to pay special attention to Italy and the Low Countries, and in the case of our theme, to the German speaking countries. When I speak of thought and learning, I include all areas of study as they were then defined and classified, with a special emphasis on the philosophical disciplines and on the literary and classical studies then called *studia humanitatis*. I must exclude the arts, although a thought of Fra Angelico or Fra Filippo Lippi is sufficient to envisage the importance of the contribution of the religious orders to Renaissance art. More important, I cannot deal with the vast subject of religious thought, learning and literature during the Renaissance, for the simple reason that many important contributions to that literature were made by laymen.[4] I must also omit the important contributions made to the religious as well as secular culture of the period by the secular clergy, by popes, bishops and canons, by priests and clerics. We must limit our survey to the contributions of the religious orders. This is in itself a vast field, especially since I have been encouraged not to limit my survey to the Benedictines, Cistercians and their affiliates, but to include also the canons regular,

4. P. O. Kristeller, "Lay Religious Traditions and Renaissance Platonism," in my *Studies in Renaissance Thought and Letters* (Rome, 1956), 99–122. The same, "Sebastiano Salvini . . . ," in *Didascaliae, Studies in Honor of Anselm M. Albareda*, ed. Sesto Prete (New York, 1961), 207–243. The same, "An Unknown Humanist Sermon on St. Stephen by Guillaume Fichet," in *Mélanges Eugène Tisserant, VI, Studi e Testi*, CCXXXVI (Vatican City, 1964), 459–497. The humanist contribution to religious thought has been treated by Charles Trinkaus in his recent book, *In Our Image and Likeness: Humanity and Divinity in Italian Humanist Thought* (London and Chicago, 1970).

the mendicant orders, and even the new orders founded during the Reformation period.[5] I shall mainly focus on two facets of my subject: monastic libraries, and monastic scholars.

The wealth and importance of medieval monastic libraries is too well known to require much elaboration.[6] Some of them have been preserved intact on the spot or as compact units within larger public libraries; others have been, or can be, reconstructed from scattered remains or from old inventories.[7] Apart from the Bible and the Church Fathers, monastic rules and liturgical books that one would naturally expect to find in a monastic library, there were also works of classical and medieval secular literature and learning,[8] and each generation of monks added the books that interested them, that were given to them, or that were useful for study and for teaching. For most monasteries were not only centers of learning, but also had schools attached to them that were attended by novices and younger monks, but also by lay pupils. The monastic libraries reflect the intellectual life of the community in that they would naturally absorb the works composed or copied by its members. In the earlier Middle Ages, the art of calligraphy had its chief centers in the Benedictine monasteries, and a number of them were the leading *scriptoria* that would supply not only their own library but also others, a function later shared or taken over by the cathedrals, the courts, the universities and the professional book dealers.

In the period after 1300, most of the older monastic libraries survived and were in active use.[9] Lay scholars in the various urban cen-

5. For the bibliography, see above, note 2.

6. For printed inventories, see the works by Becker, Gottlieb and Lehmann, noted below in the Bibliography.

7. See the list of monastic libraries in Appendix A. Monastic libraries have been preserved intact in Austria. In Italy, Cava, Grottaferrata, Monte Cassino, Subiaco, the Antoniana in Padua and some others have been preserved, whereas the others have been absorbed by the public libraries of the region or scattered. In Switzerland, Beromuenster, Einsiedeln, Engelberg, Sarnen and St. Gallen are preserved. In Catholic Germany, the only old library that survives is Ottobeuren, whereas all other Bavarian monastic collections were absorbed by the Staats-bibliothek in Munich. In Holland, Cuyk survives, and in Belgium Averbode. In France and Portugal all monastic collections were absorbed by the public libraries, and the same may be said about Spain, except for the Escorial, San Domingo de Silos and a few smaller collections. In Protestant Germany and in England the monastic libraries were secularized and scattered.

8. See Manitius. For an example, see L. D. Reynolds, *The Medieval Tradition of Seneca's Letters* (Oxford, 1965), 100–111.

9. See Sabbadini, *Le scoperte*, and the literature cited in Appendix A under Florence.

ters would normally have access to the books of local monasteries, and when the humanists tried to rediscover some of the classical Latin texts that were not commonly known and survived only in one or two manuscripts, they made many of their finds in such places as Monte Cassino or St. Gall, Bobbio and perhaps Fulda.[10] In the late fifteenth and early sixteenth century when humanists and other scholars prepared printed editions of classical and also of patristic and other religious texts, we often learn from their prefaces that they were permitted to copy or even to loan the manuscripts owned by various monasteries.[11] Many monks and friars of our period continued the old practice of copying books for themselves or for their library,[12] and when the new art of printing spread from Germany to Italy and the rest of Europe, we find significant if not numerous cases where a monastery offered its hospitality and some service to a newly established printing press. This happened in Augsburg, but it is especially notable that the first printing press in Italy was established in Subiaco, and that one of the chief early presses in Florence was housed in the convent of S. Jacopo di Ripoli.[13] It is this press which produced the first edition of Marsilio Ficino's Plato in 1484.[14]

Yet the medieval monastic libraries not only preserved their old holdings, but also increased them through the acquisition of new manuscripts, and for that matter, of printed books. When we scan the lists of manuscripts found in monastic collections, preserved or reconstructed, we shall invariably find some religious literature of the Renaissance period, but also some typically humanistic texts, and although it is not always possible to determine the precise date when a manuscript entered the collection, it is safe to assume in many cases that the manuscripts have been in the collection ever since the

10. See Sabbadini, Billanovich, and the literature cited under Bobbio.

11. This is apparent from the editorial prefaces of Jacobus Faber Stapulensis that have been published by Eugene Rice. See now *The Prefatory Epistles of Jacques Lefèvre d'Etaples and Related Texts*, ed. Eugene F. Rice, Jr. (New York, 1972).

12. See Bénédictins du Bouveret, Lieftinck, Samaran and my *Iter Italicum*. See also Appendix B under Strada.

13. For Ripoli, see Emilia Nesi, *Il diario della stamperia di Ripoli* (Florence, 1903). For Subiaco and other monastic presses in Italy and Germany, see Hirsch, 17 and 54–55. Some of the earliest printed editions in England were produced in the monasteries of Westminster and St. Albans. See E. G. Duff, *Fifteenth Century English Books* (Oxford, 1917); Leo Gourde, O.S.B., "Early Benedictine Printing in England," a paper read before a meeting of the Library Section of the American Benedictine Academy at St. Martin's Abbey, Olympia, Washington, 1962 (typed).

14. Nesi; and Kristeller, *Supplementum Ficianum* (1937), II, 108–109.

time when they were written. This is true of Monte Cassino and of many of the Austrian collections represented in the Monastic Manuscript Microfilm Library, such as Klosterneuburg, Kremsmuenster or Melk.[15] I remember a particular manuscript at St. Paul in Carinthia, a rich miscellany of humanist letters and speeches connected with Padua and written by a Northern hand of the fifteenth century, probably the commonplace book of a Northern student at Padua who left it to the monastery of which he may have been a member or at least a friend.[16] If we consider collections that are no longer extant but can be reconstructed, we know that the Benedictine libraries of Polirone near Mantua and of S. Giustina in Padua came to contain some interesting humanistic manuscripts.[17] The library of S. Giovanni in Verdara in Padua received the books of two bibliophile scholars of the fifteenth century, Pietro da Montagnana and Giovanni Marcanova, many of which are now in the Marciana in Venice.[18] The library of the Camaldulensians in S. Michele di Murano is now scattered, but we have its eighteenth-century catalogue that shows a remarkable wealth in humanistic manuscripts many of which can still be identified.[19] And if we go outside of Italy, we find some humanistic manuscripts in the Abbaye des Dunes near Bruges, in Cuyk near Nijmegen, in S. Maria de Ripoll and S. Cugat del Valles near Barcelona.[20] S. Miguel de los Reyes near Valencia acquired early in the sixteenth century a sizable share of the Aragon library from Naples,[21] whereas S. Giovanni in

15. See Appendix A and Kristeller, *Latin Manuscript Books*. Many manuscripts in Austrian monasteries are described in *Xenia Bernardina*. For Monte Cassino, see Kristeller, *Iter Italicum*, I, 393–395. Cf. above, note 7.
16. St. Paul im Lavanttal, ms. 28.4.9 (D 79).
17. See Appendix A.
18. Frati, 331–333; Kristeller, *Iter Italicum*, II (indices).
19. J. B. Mittarellius, *Bibliotheca codicum manuscriptorum Monasterii S. Michaelis Venetiarum prope Murianum* (Venice, 1779). Some of the mss. are in the Marciana, others in Camaldoli; others are scattered as far as Berlin, Moscow and New York. Father Giuseppe Cacciamani, O.Cam. (Camaldoli), and Father Vittorino Meneghin, O.F.M. (Venice), have been preparing different checklists of these manuscripts.
20. Bruges, Groote Seminarie, ms. 15/76 contains a humanist translation of St. John Chrysostom; ms. 113/78 several works by Petrarch. Both are from the Abbaye des Dunes. Cuyk ms. 50 contains another humanist translation of John Chrysostom copied on the spot in 1465. Fiecht ms. 183 contains Boccaccio, *De montibus*, copied in Pavia, 1466, and a collection of epigrams by Petrarch that is known from only one or two other mss. For San Cugat del Valles and S. Maria de Ripoll, both now in the Archivo de la Corona de Aragón in Barcelona, see the printed catalogues.
21. See M. Repullés, "Catálogo de los códices procedentes del Monasterio de S. Miguel de los Reyes," *Revista de Archivos, Bibliotecas y Museos* 5 (1875),

Carbonara in Naples acquired the libraries of Giano Parrasio and of the Cardinal Girolamo Seripando.[22] Some Northern monastic libraries that otherwise show no interest in secular Renaissance literature may contain an occasional manuscript of one of Petrarch's moral treatises.[23]

The Renaissance period did not merely witness the increase of some of the older monastic libraries, but a number of collections were newly founded, and they thus fully reflect the intellectual interests and perspectives of their own time rather than those of the preceding centuries. The library of S. Marco in Florence was founded by Cosimo de'Medici and increased by his successors and others. It received the books of the humanist Niccolò Niccoli, and came to be known by its wealth in classical and humanistic as well as medieval and religious manuscripts. It is for this library and for Cosimo that a young scholar who was to become Pope Nicolaus V compiled a library canon or guide that has come down to us. This list comprises the chief texts and authors that should be found in a well supplied library, and the subjects include, not only theology, but all other disciplines of learning, and especially the *studia humanitatis* (as a matter of fact, this is one of the earliest documents that helps us to establish the meaning of the *studia humanitatis* in the Renaissance).[24] The famous library of Cardinal Domenico Grimani, which included many of Pico's books, went to S. Antonio di Castello in Venice.[25] This monastery was destroyed by fire in the seventeenth century, and hence it is widely believed that the library was completely lost. Fortunately, this is not the case, for numerous manuscripts and printed books that belonged to Grimani are preserved in many places including New York,[26] and we must assume that they were stolen or sold some

---

9–13, 52–55, 68–72, 87–91, 103–105. M. Gutiérrez del Caño, *Catálogo de los manuscritos existentes en la Biblioteca Universitaria de Valencia,* 3 vols. (Valencia, c. 1913–14). T. De Marinis, *La biblioteca napoletana dei Re d'Aragona,* II (Milan, 1947), 3–179.

22. Frati, 438–439 and 516. Cf. also Appendix B under Raphael de Marcatel and Petrus de Nigrono.

23. Rottenburg, Priesterseminar, ms. H 25 (from Ehingen) contains Petrarch's *De remediis.* Brno ms. A 100 (from the Augustinians) contains rhetorical treatises by Johannes Serra with an important biographical note on Jacobus Publicius.

24. G. Sforza, "La patria, la famiglia ed i parenti di Papa Niccolò V," *Atti della Reale Accademia Lucchese di Scienze, Lettere ed Arti* 23 (1884), 1–400, at 359–381. Kristeller, *Studies,* 573; *Renaissance Thought* (1961), 162.

25. Jac. Phil. Tomasinus, *Bibliothecae Venetae manuscriptae* (Udine, 1650), 1–19.

26. Frati, 269–270. Giovanni Card. Mercati, *Codici Latini Pico Grimani Pio . . . , Studi e Testi,* LXXV (Vatican City, 1938). Grimani mss. are now found all over Italy, in Paris, Stockholm and elsewhere. For a printed book owned by

time before the fire. The largest monastic library founded during the Renaissance also suffered some losses through fire in the seventeenth century, but most of its riches survive to the present day. I am speaking of the Escorial, founded by Philip II. Although entrusted to the care of a monastery, it is in fact a typical princely collection of the Renaissance in which all branches of learning and of literature are represented, and in which classical and humanistic manuscripts occupy a very prominent place indeed. Actually Philip II acquired for the Escorial the private libraries of many Spanish and Italian scholars including Francesco Patrizi.[27]

I have much less to say on a topic which is somehow connected with the libraries and in a sense of equal importance for intellectual history: the role of the religious houses as centers of instruction. We know that Dante acquired some of his learning at the schools of the friars, at a time when Florence was not yet the seat of a university.[28] In spite of the gradual rise of secular instruction, through private and public schools as well as the practice of tutoring, there is every reason to believe that the schools attached to the religious houses continued to function throughout the fifteenth century and served not merely the members of the monastic community, but also a number of lay pupils. In fifteenth-century Florence, some religious houses such as S. Spirito and S. Maria degli Angeli were the centers of scholarly discussions between their learned members and their lay friends, and thus may have served as precedents and models for the later more formally organized Academies.[29] In the sixteenth century, the new order of the Jesuits made it its specialty to set up numerous secondary schools that followed the best standards of instruction in all subjects including the classics and mathematics, and that were widely attended by lay students of intellectual and social distinction.

---

him and now by the New York Public Library, see Appendix B under Leander Albertus.

27. G. Antolín, *Catálogo de los códices latinos de la Real Biblioteca del Escorial*, 5 vols. (Madrid, 1910–23). See also Appendix A under Escorial. Father H. D. Saffrey in reviewing the first version of this paper (*Bibliothèque d'Humanisme et Renaissance* 33 [1971], 232–234) makes a valuable additional point: Several scholars who belonged to religious orders had important private libraries that were later absorbed by institutional or public libraries, e.g., Johannes de Ragusa and Johannes Cono.

28. Dante, *Convivio*, II, 12, 7. Charles T. Davies, "Education in Dante's Florence," *Speculum* 40 (1965), 415–435.

29. A. Della Torre, *Storia dell'Accademia Platonica di Firenze* (Florence, 1902), 184–190, 200–202, 226–228.

The relation of the religious orders to the universities was more complicated. The leading medieval universities drew some of their teachers of theology from the mendicant orders, to be sure, but a large part of their theologians belonged to the secular clergy, and most of the teachers in the other disciplines such as law and medicine, philosophy and the arts were laymen.[30] On the other hand, the mendicant orders especially organized their own school system for the members of their respective orders, and this system culminated in the *studia generalia* of the order which gave advanced training in theology and were usually located in university towns, often sending some of their students and teachers to the university.[31] The monastic university, that is, the university controlled and staffed by an order, is unknown to the Middle Ages and seems to be an invention of the sixteenth century, that is, of the Catholic Reformation. The Jesuits and also some other orders obtained papal privileges authorizing them to open a university especially in places which had no older university, including the Spanish colonies in America. Occasionally an order was authorized to reopen or to take over one of the older universities.[32]

I have mentioned the monastic schools and universities because they represent an important aspect of the monastic contribution to Renaissance learning, and because the libraries of the various monasteries often derived some of their importance from the fact that they supplied the intellectual needs of a teaching institution. Yet I cannot go any further into this important subject with which I am but superficially acquainted, and should rather proceed to the second major part of my lecture that will discuss the monks and friars as scholars during the Renaissance. I shall try to illustrate the contributions made by individual monks and friars to Renaissance thought and learning. Since it would be tedious to give a list of names that could be easily extended, I shall merely survey the various disciplines and traditions that are relevant to our topic, and illustrate each of them with one or a few examples. I cannot hope to be complete even as far as famous figures are concerned, and I gladly admit that my selection depends very much on my own interests and recent research.

30. See Rashdall, and U. Dallari, *I Rotuli dei lettori legisti e artisti dello Studio Bolognese*, 4 vols. (Bologna, 1888–1924).
31. See the studies by Douais and Felder.
32. This appears from the documents of the newly founded universities, and it would require a more detailed study than we can pursue here. Rashdall does not cover the sixteenth century, and D'Irsay does not seem to clarify this point.

I should like to mention in passing that some of the greatest figures of the sixteenth century began their careers as monks and friars although their later work would hardly remind us of these beginnings: Erasmus, Luther and Bruno. During the Reformation period the monk or friar turned layman became a frequent phenomenon, and his peculiar contribution to scholarship might be worth investigating. We might mention, as examples, the Franciscan Bernardino Ochino, who became an influential Protestant theologian and preacher, and the Carmelite John Bale, who began as a historian of his religious order and ended as a literary historian of his native country.[33]

Our attention must naturally focus on those scholars who remained faithful to the religious ideal until the end of their lives. If we look at the history of the universities during the Renaissance period, at their curriculum and text books, and at the learned literature that grew out of their instruction, it is quite evident that the tradition of scholastic learning as it had developed during the thirteenth century underwent a number of changes during the next few centuries, but continued to maintain some of its fundamental characteristics. The same may be said even more strongly of the monastic schools and their *studia*. The mendicant orders had played a leading part in the development of scholastic theology during the thirteenth and early fourteenth century (and it is sufficient to think of St. Albert and St. Bonaventura, St. Thomas, Aegidius Romanus, Duns Scotus and William of Occam) and this predominance, easily explained by the training offered in the schools of these orders, continued through the subsequent centuries. The large literature of commentaries on the Bible and on Peter Lombard's *Sentences* that has come down to us from this period was to a considerable extent the work of friars,[34] as was the important change in theological instruction that took place during the late fifteenth and early sixteenth century and that led to the adoption of Thomas' *Summa Theologiae* in the place of Peter Lombard's *Sentences* as the main text of theology.[35] The leading theological commen-

---

33. Roland H. Bainton, *Bernardino Ochino* (Florence, 1940). W. T. Davies, "A Bibliography of John Bale," in *Oxford Bibliographical Society, Proceedings and Papers* 5 (1940), 201–279. For Erasmus, see now Roland H. Bainton, *Erasmus of Christendom* (New York, 1969).

34. See the Repertoria of Stegmueller.

35. Ricardo G. Villoslada, *La Universidad de Paris durante los estudios de Francisco de Vitoria* (Rome, 1938), 279–307. M. Grabmann, *Mittelalterliches Geistesleben*, III (1956), 411–448. Kristeller, *Le Thomisme*, 36–38. See above, pp. 40–41.

tators of the fifteenth and sixteenth century belonged to the Dominican order or to the other mendicant orders that were soon joined by the new order of the Jesuits whose members also took a very active part in the study and teaching of theology. It is enough to mention Thomas de Vio, Cardinal Cajetan, the leading commentator of St. Thomas in the early sixteenth century, and the school of Salamanca that began with Francis of Vitoria and flourished to the early seventeenth century with the Jesuits Suarez and Mariana.[36] Also the systematic theological texts of the fifteenth century were due to friars such as the Dominicans S. Antonino or Savonarola.

In the field of polemical theology it is again the friars who made the most numerous contributions. In the fifteenth-century controversies about the Blood of Christ and the Immaculate Conception, we encounter the Franciscan Francis of Savona who became Pope Sixtus IV, the Dominican Vincenzo Bandello who became the general of his order, and the Carmelite Baptista Mantuanus.[37] In the sixteenth century, when Catholic theologians were engaged in refuting Luther and other Protestant Reformers, it was again the friars, and significantly the Augustinians, who played a leading role.[38]

The literature on asceticism and mysticism was very extensive and important in our period, and it is sufficient to think of the German, Dutch and Spanish schools of mysticism. Many of the authors were laymen or secular clerics, but Master Eckhart and some of his followers were Dominicans, and Dionysius Rykel, the prolific fifteenth-century theologian, was a Carthusian.[39] The great Cusanus, who was not a monk and who derived most of the mystical and contemplative elements of his thought from Neoplatonic sources, was engaged in a lively discussion with the Benedictines of Tegernsee and of other monasteries about some points of his doctrine.[40]

Another branch of religious activity and literature that had been much cultivated by the friars was preaching. As from the twelfth and thirteenth century, so there has come to us from the following cen-

36. See Giacon, and Grabmann, *Geschichte der katholischen Theologie.*
37. Kristeller, *Thomisme,* passim, and the references given there. (See chapter 2 of this volume.) See also Appendix B under Philippus de Barberiis, Georgius Benignus, Arnoldus Bostius, Eusebius Corradus, Ambrosius Massarius, Nicolaus de Mirabilibus, Nicolaus Palmerius, Petrus de Nubilaria, Raphael de Pornasio, Johannes de Turrecremata.
38. See Lauchert, and Appendix B under Ambrosius Flandinus and Augustinus Steuchus.
39. See Appendix B.
40. See Vansteenberghe, *Autour de la docte ignorance.*

turies a vast body of sermons, many of them anonymous, but many composed by individual preachers, most of whom belonged to one of the religious orders. In the fifteenth century, the type of the preacher who often speaks in the vernacular and takes an active part in the social and political problems of the day became very common in Italy and elsewhere. We might cite as examples S. Bernardino of Siena, who traveled through most of Italy, and Girolamo Savonarola, who for a few years became a leading political force in Florence.[41]

If we pass from theology to the other academic disciplines, it is worth noticing that the monks and friars made almost no contribution to the vast literature on law and on medicine that was produced during the Renaissance period. This is easily understandable, for the clerics were excluded from the medical and notarial profession, and even the lawyers and legal professors were for the most part laymen. Also most of the professors of canon law were laymen or secular clerics, and the contribution of the friars to canonistic literature, at least during the later period, is limited for the most part to monographs or specific questions that were of interest to the friars, such as usury or the Monti di Pietà.[42]

The religious were more active in the mathematical disciplines. Fra Luca Pacioli wrote important treatises on mathematics, and among the astronomers of the sixteenth century we find the Jesuits, Clavius and Scheiner. One of the closest pupils of Galileo was the Benedictine, Benedetto Castelli, who also wrote a number of important letters and treatises.[43] In the fifteenth century, when musical theory was still a part of the Quadrivium, we find a number of writers on music who were members of religious orders: Johannes Hothby, Johannes Gallicus and Johannes Bonadies.[44]

More closely associated with theology, but distinct from it in its subject matter, was the field of Aristotelian philosophy. In the four-

41. See also Appendix B under Roberto Caraccioli and S. Giacomo della Marca.

42. See De Roover, Schulte and Appendix B under Nicolaus Tedescus. For various treatises written by several friars on the city debt in Florence and elsewhere, see J. Kirshner, "A Document on the Meeting of the Chapter General in Florence (1365)," *Archivum Franciscanum Historicum* 62 (1969), 392–399. For a medical treatise, see Appendix B under Jacobus Soldus.

43. See Appendix B, also under Augustinus de Tridento, Gulielmus Becchius, Bonaventura Cavalieri, Jacobus de S. Cassiano, Johannes de Casali, Leonardus Cremonensis, Marcus de Benevento, Franciscus Paduanus, Johannes Maria Tolosanus. See also under Franciscus Wiler for his *Cosmographia*.

44. G Reese, 178. Kristeller, *Studies*, 458–462. See also Appendix B under Raphael Brandolinus, Rutgerus Sycamber, and Thomas Walsingham.

teenth and fifteenth centuries, not to speak of the sixteenth, most of the professors of Aristotelian philosophy were laymen. Yet I should like to mention a few exceptions with which I am familiar and that might be supplemented by others. When the traditions of logic and physics that had flourished at Paris and Oxford during the fourteenth century were brought to Italy, a very important part was played by the Augustinian Paul of Venice, who had studied at Oxford. He taught for many years at Padua, and his text books of logic and physics were in wide use to the end of the century.[45]

In Padua and elsewhere the teaching of metaphysics was often combined with that of theology, and hence we find a number of philosophical treatises composed by friars, such as the Franciscan Antonio Trombetta.[46] In the controversy on Averroism, which involved the relations between philosophy and theology, it is significant to note that within the Dominican order Thomas de Vio opposed the Lateran decree of 1512,[47] and was no less sharply attacked by his fellow Dominican Bartolomeo Spina than was Pietro Pomponazzi.[48]

I have so far been largely concerned with that sector of Renaissance learning that was most closely connected with the medieval tradition and that might be labeled as scholasticism. I am now going to discuss another sector that may be considered more typical of the later period and may be roughly called humanism. I shall try to show that the monastic contribution to this area was considerable, and far greater than is usually realized by historians. When I speak of humanism, I mean the scholarly, literary and intellectual activity that centers around the *studia humanitatis*, that is, the study of the classical languages and literature, and the fields then labeled grammar, rhetoric, poetry, history and moral philosophy. When these studies began to rise again after some decline towards the end of the thirteenth century,

45. See Appendix B under Paulus Venetus, and also under Baptista de Fabriano, Georgius Benignus, Leoninus de Padua, Marinus de Castignano, Bernardinus Landuccius, Ambrosius Massarius, Stephanus de Flandria, Franciscus Titelmannus for logic; under Gulielmus Becchius and Dominicus de Flandria for commentaries on Aristotle. See also under Montaldus for a stylistic revision of the medieval Latin version of pseudo-Aristotle's *Secretum Secretorum.*

46. See Appendix B under Trombetta, and also under Vincentius Bandellus, Philippus de Barberiis, Dominicus de Flandria, Johannes Ferrariensis, Petrus Galatinus, Hieronymus Lucensis, Chrysostomus Javellus, Ambrosius Massarius, Paulus Orlandinus, Raphael de Pornasio, Bartholomaeus Spina.

47. J. D. Mansi, *Sacrorum Conciliorum . . . Collectio,* XXXII (Paris, 1902), 843.

48. Barth. Spina, *Propugnaculum Aristotelis de immortalitate animae contra Thomam Caietanum* (ed. 1519).

and to acquire great prominence in the fourteenth and fifteenth century, they met with some resistance from the theologians. We should not be surprised to learn that Albertino Mussato had to defend poetry against Fra Giovanni da Mantova,[49] and that a hundred years later, after the efforts of Petrarch and Boccaccio, Salutati felt compelled to answer the criticisms of Fra Giovanni da S. Miniato and of the Dominican cardinal Giovanni Dominici.[50] These friars were obviously opposed to the ideal of humanist learning, and the best we can say is that they opposed only some excesses, and were themselves not completely devoid of humanist knowledge or interests. Yet by the middle of the fifteenth century, the climate seems to have changed, and it is no coincidence that this was the time when two humanists ascended the papal throne, Nicolaus V and Pius II. When the bishop of Verona, Ermolao Barbaro the Elder, published his orations against the poets,[51] a polite defense of the poets, addressed to Nicolaus V and entitled *In sanctam rusticitatem*, was written by a regular canon, Timoteo Maffei of Verona.[52] By this time the monks and friars were by no means solidly aligned against the humanists, but were taking an active part in humanist scholarship. It is this phenomenon, often overlooked, to which we must now turn our main attention, and it will be easiest to survey some of the main branches of humanist literature, although individual scholars naturally were apt to contribute to more than one of them.

I should like to begin with oratory, which played such a large role in Italian humanism. Aside from the medieval tradition of preaching of which we spoke before and which had its theory in many treatises on the art of preaching,[53] early Italian humanism developed its own theory and practice of secular oratory that were based on ancient Roman theories and models, mainly Cicero, and adapted to the particular occasion on which a speech was to be delivered. During the later fifteenth century, and especially in Rome, the influence of humanist oratory

49. See Appendix B under Johanninus de Mantua.
50. For Giovanni de San Miniato, see Coluccio Salutati, *Epistolario*, ed. F. Novati, IV (Rome, 1905), 170–205. Salutati's letter to Giovanni Dominici is given, ibid., 205–240.
51. For Ermolao Barbaro the Elder, bishop of Verona (c. 1410–71), see Giovanni degli Agostini, *Scrittori Viniziani*, I, 229–256. *Dizionario Biografico degli Italiani*, VI (1964), 95–96 (by E. Bigi). For some mss. of his *Contra poetas*, see V. Branca, *Lettere Italiane* 8 (1956), 67–68. See now Ermolao Barbaro il Vecchio, *Orationes contra Poetas, Epistolae*, ed. G. Ronconi (Florence, 1972).
52. For mss. of Timoteo's treatise, see *Iter Italicum*, I–II (index).
53. See Caplan and Charland.

began to be felt also by the preachers. There is a whole literature of Latin sermons preached before the pope and cardinals on religious holidays or public celebrations, some of them preserved in manuscripts or early editions, others attested to by contemporary chronists, which follow in their arrangement, style and quotations the humanist rather than the medieval pattern.[54] This adaptation of sacred art to contemporary taste, which has its parallels in the painting and sculpture of the time, seemed perfectly natural to its audience, but it has been shocking and displeasing to most modern historians who hence have paid little attention to the phenomenon. The authors of these sermons are partly obscure, and the more famous ones include laymen and secular clerics, but among the monks and friars we notice the Augustinian Aurelio Brandolini, a well known Florentine humanist who also was the author of important religious, rhetorical and political treatises.[55] Rhetoric and oratory, along with poetry, were also the main interest of a Franciscan who has been recently studied, Lorenzo Guglielmo Traversagni, and who attracts additional interest because his studies and travels took him to England, France and Austria.[56]

Perhaps the most extensive branch of humanist literature is that of epistolography. The formal letter, edited and collected for publication, is not merely a personal document, but also the carrier of news, and often the medium of short literary expression for scholarly or philosophical subjects. The humanist letters and letter collections vary greatly in content and purpose, but they share a common style and literary function. The author of letters in the humanist style must for that reason alone be counted among the humanists, especially if his correspondents include humanists of unquestioned literary and scholarly merit. Among the humanist letter-writers of the fifteenth century, we find the Camaldulensian Ambrogio Traversari, a prominent member of the Florentine circle, the Benedictine Girolamo Aliotti of Arezzo, and the Franciscan Alberto da Sarteano.[57] Later in the century, the

54. On humanist sermons, see Kristeller, *Fichet* (see above note 4). Galletti, *L'Eloquenza*.

55. See also Appendix B under Apollonius Bianchus, Andreas Bilia, Matthaeus Bossus, Aurelius and Raphael Brandolinus, Giovacchino Castiglioni, Johannes Gattus, Marianus de Genazzano, Ambrosius Massarius, Filippo Mucagalla, Nicolaus Palmerius, Petrus de Castelletto, Bartholomaeus Sibylla, Ambrosius Traversarius, Johannes Trithemius.

56. See Appendix B, also under Antonius Raudensis, Aurelius Brandolinus.

57. See also Appendix B under Aegidius Viterbiensis, Matthaeus Bossus, Isidorus Clarius, Hilarion Corbetta, Gregorius Cortesius, Bernardinus Gadolus, Paulus Justinianus, Franciscus Paduanus, Petrus Quirinus.

Camaldulensian Pietro Dolfin presents himself as a prolific letter-writer.[58] When the humanist Mario Filelfo composed a large collection of model letters, a kind of updated *ars dictaminis*, the work was dedicated to, and posthumously edited by, a Franciscan friar, Ludovico Mondello, and must have attained a great popularity also in monastic circles.[59] The art of letter writing in the humanist sense was cultivated by monks and friars not only in Italy but also in the North. We may mention Robert Gaguin in France, Arnoldus Bostius in the Low Countries, and especially in Germany Nicolaus Ellenbog, Johannes Butzbach, Rutgerus Sycamber, and above all Johannes Trithemius.[60]

Of the huge body of Latin and vernacular poetry that was produced during the Renaissance, only a small part even of the religious poetry was due to monastic authors, but some of them deserve mention for their influence, if not for their quality. Dominicus Johannis de Corella wrote a poem on the life of the Virgin,[61] and many other monks and friars composed Latin poems.[62] The Carmelite Baptista Mantuanus, a prolific author of Latin poetry, was one of the most famous writers of his age, and his works were even more widely known in the North than they were in Italy, and often were used as readings in schools.[63] We might mention another Florentine Dominican, Tommaso Sardi, for a large vernacular poem written after the formal pattern of Dante's *Divine Comedy*.[64]

The humanists were much concerned with historiography, and works of history and biography occupied an important place in their literary production. It is quite understandable that monastic scholars

58. See Appendix B for editions and mss.
59. See Appendix B under Mondellus.
60. See Appendix B, also under Vitus Bild, Henricus Cranebrooke and Jacobus Siberti.
61. See Appendix B.
62. See Appendix B under Zenobius Acciaiolus, Bernardus Andreae, Theophilus Bona, Matthaeus Bossus, Arnoldus Bostius, Johannes Butzbach, Benedictus Chelidonius, Christophorus Fanensis, Dionysius Faucherius, Johannes Andreas Ferabos, Vincentius Mainardus, Marianus Vulterranus, Adam Montaldus, Leonardus Oddus, Paulus Orlandinus, Paracletus Cornetanus, Raphael Placentinus, Rutgerus Sycamber, Angelus Sangrinus, Jacobus Siberti, Philippus Strada, Laurentius Gulielmus Traversagnus, Johannes Trithemius, Mapheus Vegius.
63. See Kristeller, *Thomisme*, 80–82 and the literature cited there. (See above pp. 65–66.)
64. See Appendix B, also under Matteo Bandello, Francesco Colonna, Federico da Venezia, Marcello Filosseno, Teofilo Folengo, Evangelista Fossa, Federico Frezzi, Lazzaro Gallineta, Guido Pisanus, Julianus de Istria, Filippo Strada, Thomas Ferrariensis for contributions to Italian and Maccheronic literature. We may also mention Joh. de Serravalle and Matthaeus Rontus who both attempted to translate Dante into Latin.

imbued with humanist training and interests would turn their attention to such subjects as ecclesiastic history or hagiography, in addition to general or local history. Jacopo Filippo of Bergamo is well known for his world chronicle. Paolo Attavanti of Florence wrote a history of Mantua for one of its princes. Johannes Caroli wrote on Florentine history as well as on the lives of prominent members of his convent of S. Maria Novella. Antonio da Barga wrote on the history of Monte Oliveto as well as on famous Tuscans. Just as Bale wrote on famous Englishmen after having studied the history of his Carmelite order, so Trithemius is known for his works both on ecclesiastic writers and on famous Germans.[65]

The branch of humanist literature that may not be the largest but that has attracted greatest interest among students of intellectual history is that of the prose treatises and dialogues dealing with moral, educational, political and religious problems. The monastic humanists, if I may be allowed to use this term, made their contribution also to this significant branch of literature. Lippo Brandolini, whom we mentioned as an orator (and whom we might have mentioned as an improviser of poetry and music), also composed a number of treatises. Baptista de Judicibus, the bishop of Ventimiglia, who defended the Jews of Trent against the bishop of Trent and against his humanist flatterers, also wrote a dialogue *De contemptu mundi*, and Thomas of Ferrara composed a lengthy dialogue in his local dialect on religious subjects. Also Baptista Mantuanus wrote prose treatises on moral subjects, and the list could be easily expanded.[66] Especially interesting is the case of Antonio da Barga. He was in contact with Fazio and Manetti, and when Fazio composed his treatise on the excellence and dignity of man, the first humanist treatise specifically devoted to this subject, we know that he acted upon a request from Antonio da Barga, who not only urged him to supplement the famous treatise of Pope Innocent III on the misery of man, but also supplied him with an outline for the content of his treatise.[67] And when Pier Candido Decembrio wrote his

65. For other historical works, see Appendix B under Leander Albertus, Philippus de Barberiis, Bernardus Andreae, Andreas Bilja, Arnoldus Bostius, Joh. Butzbach, Giovanni Colonna, Felix Fabri, Thomas Fazellus, Augustinus Justinianus, Maurus Lapius, Ambrosius Massarius, Sigismund Meisterlin, Petrus de Castelletto, Petrus Ransanus and Johannes Whethamstede.

66. For other treatises and dialogues, see Appendix B under Hieronymus Aliottus, Apollonius Bianchus, Matthaeus Bossus, Raphael Brandolinus, Jacobus Camphora, Petrus Galatinus, Leonardus Chiensis, Franciscus Paduanus, Ludovicus de Strassoldo.

67. Kristeller, "The Humanist Bartolomeo Facio and his Unknown Corre-

treatise on immortality, we know that his chief source was a work often attributed to St. Augustine, but actually composed by a Cistercian scholar of the twelfth century.[68]

Apart from their interest in literature and in moral thought, the humanists were especially noted for their classical scholarship, and it is important to note that we find a number of monks and friars among the Latin and Greek scholars of the Renaissance period. Dionysius de Burgo composed a very influential commentary on Valerius Maximus,[69] and Bernardus Andreae, a French Augustinian active in England, composed not only a good deal of Latin poetry and oratory, but also a bulky commentary on St. Augustine's City of God.[70] For the humanists, the study of the Church Fathers belonged to the study of classical antiquity, and was conducted with the same methods of grammatical and historical scholarship and of textual criticism. Naturally, a monk with a humanist training would apply himself most eagerly to copying, editing and expounding the Latin Fathers, and the writings of these Fathers occupy a large and important place, in manuscript and in print, in the monastic and other libraries of the period.[71]

Greek as distinct from Latin scholarship experienced a tremendous increase during the Renaissance, although even at that time the number of Greek scholars remained much smaller than that of humanists who had a command of classical Latin literature. We encounter also some monks and friars among the leading Greek scholars of the Renaissance, and we may again expect that most, though not all, of their attention was concentrated on Biblical and patristic studies. Traversari,

---

spondence," in From the Renaissance to the Counter-Reformation: Essays in Honor of Garrett Mattingly, ed. Charles H. Carter (New York, 1965), 56–74, at 68.

68. Kristeller, "Pier Candido Decembrio and His Unpublished Treatise on the Immortality of the Soul," in The Classical Tradition, Literary and Historical Studies in Honor of Harry Caplan, ed. L. Wallach (Ithaca, 1966), 536–558, at 548–549. Giles Constable, "The Popularity of Twelfth-Century Spiritual Writers in the Late Middle Ages," in Renaissance Studies in Honor of Hans Baron, ed. A. Molho and J. A. Tedeschi (Florence, 1971), 3–28.

69. For the study of Latin classical authors, see also Appendix B under Petrus Berchorius, Aurelius Brandolinus, Fra Giocondo, Giunta da S. Gimignano, Lucas Mannellus, Petrus O.P., Philippus Bergomensis, Thomas Schifaldus, Nicolaus Trevet, Thomas Walsingham.

70. For the study of the Latin Church Fathers, see Appendix B under Antonius Raudensis, Bartholomaeus de Urbino, Nicolaus Trevet.

71. We might also mention Calepinus for his Latin dictionary, Fra Giocondo for his collection of inscriptions, Fra Mariano da Firenze for his topography of Rome, and Annius of Viterbo for his classical forgeries. For the humanist attitude towards the Church Fathers, see Kristeller, Studies (1956), 355–372. For Calligraphy, see Appendix B under Leonhard Wagner.

whom we have mentioned for his letters, was also a prominent Greek scholar to whom we owe the standard translation of Diogenes Laertius as well as of several Greek Fathers such as Basil and Gregory Nazianzene. Andrea Biglia, a less famous Augustinian friar, translated Plutarch, Isocrates and also Aristotle. Around the turn of the century, Johannes Cono, a German Dominican trained in Italy, was active in Basel where Beatus Rhenanus was his pupil, and did extensive work on the Greek dramatists and some Church Fathers, as we can see from several of his preserved manuscripts.[72] In the sixteenth century, also Hebrew studies were cultivated by monastic scholars such as Sante Pagnini,[73] as they had been in the fourteenth by Nicolaus of Lyra.

I should like to conclude my survey with the philosophical currents of the fifteenth and sixteenth century that were indebted to both scholasticism and humanism but are not entirely reducible to either. In the circle of the Platonic Academy of Florence, we find a number of monks and friars who showed interest in the work of Ficino, of Pico and of Diacceto, even if we hesitate to attach excessive significance to the fact that Landino's famous dialogue on the active and contemplative life has its setting in Camaldoli.[74] The famous and learned Camaldulensians, Paolo Giustiniani and Pietro Querini, had many personal contacts among the Platonists and other scholars, but their primary concern was with religious reform rather than with any particular brand of philosophy or scholarship.[75] Yet the famous Augustinian Hermit, Cardinal Giles of Viterbo, was definitely influenced by Ficino's Platonism, as we learn from his own words, and even wrote a commentary on the Sentences *ad mentem Platonis* which has not yet been studied with sufficient care.[76] Moreover, he emulated Pico as a student of Hebrew and of Cabalism, and became one of the most

---

72. See Appendix B, also under Zenobius Acciaiolus, Jacobus Billius, Gregorius Cortesius, Ambrosius Ferrarius, Jacobus de S. Cassiano, Johannes Franciscus Brixianus, Johannes de Ragusa, Matthias Monachus, Jacobus Perionius, Christophorus Persona, Nicolaus Scutellius, Constantius Sebastianus, William Selling, Severus Varinus. Note also Johannes Crastonus for his Greek dictionaries.

73. See also Appendix B under Augustinus Justinianus, Petrus Galatinus, Ludovicus S. Francisci.

74. Landino's *Disputationes Camaldulenses* were first printed in 1478 (Hain-Reichling 9852). For members of Ficino's Academy, see Appendix B under Paulus Florentinus and Paulus Orlandinus.

75. See Appendix B under Paulus Justinianus and Petrus Quirinus.

76. For the influence of Platonism, see Appendix B under Aegidius Viterbiensis, Nicolaus Ellenbog, Ambrosius Flandinus, Franciscus Georgius, Chrysostomus Javellus, Paulus Orlandinus, Hannibal Rosselius, Nicolaus Scutellius, Hieronymus Seripandus, Augustinus Steuchus.

learned scholars of his age.[77] Another Augustinian, Ambrosius Flandinus, is known for his attacks on Pomponazzi and on Luther, but we know from his bulky commentaries preserved in manuscript that he was an enthusiastic and diligent Platonic scholar. The Franciscan, Franciscus Georgius, contributed a significant treatise, *De harmonia mundi*, to the extensive cosmological literature of Renaissance Platonism. And we might appropriately conclude with a prolific major thinker of the late Renaissance, a theologian and philosopher influenced both by Platonism and by the new empiricism of Telesio, who happened to be a Dominican and in spite of many persecutions remained a member of his order to the last: Tommaso Campanella.

The purpose of this sketchy survey has been to redress a balance, but not to propose a new exaggeration in contrast to another. It remains true that the civilization of the Renaissance was in many of its prevalent and characteristic traits a lay rather than a religious culture, and that even its religious culture was to a large extent supported by laymen and by secular clerics rather than by monks and friars. On the other hand, I have tried to show that scholars of the religious orders made significant contributions to the religious culture of the period, both to its traditional and to its novel aspects, and even to some aspects of its secular culture. This contribution of the religious orders to Renaissance culture should not be forgotten, and it goes a long way to explain the transition from the monastic culture of the Middle Ages to the monastic and Catholic culture of the modern age.

77. For the influence of Cabalism, see Appendix B under Archangelus de Burgonovo, and the studies by Blau and Secret.

# GENERAL BIBLIOGRAPHY

Angeleri, C. *Il problema religioso del Rinascimento*. Florence, 1952.

Arbesmann, R. *Der Augustiner-Eremitenorden und der Beginn der humanistischen Bewegung*. Würzburg, 1965. First published in *Augustiniana* 14 (1964), 250–314, 603–639; 15 (1965), 259–293.

De Backer, A. and Sommervogel, C. *Bibliothèque des écrivains de la Compagnie de Jésus*, 3 vols. Liége and Paris, 1869–76.

Becker, G. *Catalogi bibliothecarum antiqui*. Bonn, 1885.

Bénédictins du Bouveret. *Colophons de Manuscrits occidentaux des origines au XVIᵉ siècle*, vols. 1–3. Fribourg, 1965–73.

Besutti, G. M. and Serra, A. M. *Bibliografia dell'Ordine dei Servi*, vol. 1. Bologna, 1971.

Billanovich, G. *I primi umanisti e le tradizioni dei classici latini*. Fribourg, 1953.

———. "Dall'antica Ravenna alle biblioteche umanistiche," *Aevum*, 30 (1956), 319–353; second edition in *Università Cattolica del S. Cuore, Annuario 1955–57* (Milan, 1958), 71–107.

Blau, Joseph. *The Christian Interpretation of the Cabala in the Renaissance*. New York, 1944.

Brotto, G. and Zonta, G. *La facoltà teologica dell'Università di Padova*. Padua, 1922.

Bühler, Curt F. *The Fifteenth-Century Book*. Philadelphia, 1960.

Cantimori, D. *Eretici italiani del Cinquecento*. Florence, 1939.

Caplan, H. *Mediaeval Artes Praedicandi*, 2 pts. Ithaca, 1934–36.

Cattana, V. M. "Un trattato sugli studi dei monaci della seconda metà del sec. XV," *Benedictina* 14 (1967), 234–253.

Charland, Th. M. *Artes Praedicandi*. Ottawa and Paris, 1936.

Chevalier, U. *Répertoire des Sources Historiques du Moyen Age, Bio-Bibliographie*, 2 vols. Repr. New York, 1960.

———. *Topo-Bibliographie*, 2 vols. Repr. New York, 1959.

Church, F. C. *The Italian Reformers*. New York, 1932.

Cottineau, L. *Répertoire topo-bibliographique des abbayes et prieurés*, 3 vols. Mâcon, 1935–70.

Della Torre, A. *Storia dell'Accademia Platonica di Firenze*. Florence, 1902.

Douais, C. *Essai sur l'organisation des études dans l'ordre des Frères*

*Prêcheurs au treizième et au quartorzième siècle.* Paris and Toulouse, 1884.

Duhem, P. *Etudes sur Léonard de Vinci,* 3 vols. Repr. Paris, 1955.

Fabricius, J. A. *Bibliotheca Latina Mediae et Infimae Aetatis,* ed. J. D. Mansi. 6 vols. in 3. Florence, 1858–59; repr. Graz, 1962.

Felder, H. *Geschichte der wissenschaftlichen Studien im Franziskanerorden bis um die Mitte des 13. Jahrhunderts.* Freiburg, 1904.

Ferrari, Luigi. *Onomasticon.* Milan, 1947.

Frati, Carlo. *Dizionario bio-bibliografico dei Bibliotecari e Bibliofili italiani.* Florence, 1933.

Galletti, A. *L'Eloquenza.* Milan, 1904–38.

Gargan, L. *Lo Studio Teologico e la Biblioteca dei Domenicani a Padova nel Tre e Quattrocento.* Padua, 1971.

Garin, E. *La cultura filosofica del Rinascimento italiano.* Florence, 1961.

Giacon, C. *La seconda scolastica,* 3 vols. Milan, 1944–50.

Giani, A. *Annalium sacri ordinis fratrum servorum B. Mariae Virginis . . . centuriae quatuor,* 2nd ed., 3 vols. Lucca, 1719–25.

Gilson, E. "Autour de Pomponazzi," *Archives d'histoire doctrinale et littéraire du Moyen Age* 28 (1961, pub. 1962), 163–279.

——. "L'affaire de l'immortalité de l'âme à Venise au debut du XVIᵉ siècle," in *Umanesimo europeo e umanesimo veneziano,* ed. V. Branca, Florence, 1963, 31–61.

Gottlieb, Th. *Über mittelalterliche Bibliotheken.* Leipzig, 1890.

——, and others. *Mittelalterliche Bibliothekskataloge Oesterreichs,* vols. 1–3. Vienna, 1915–61.

Grabmann, M. *Die Geschichte der katholischen Theologie.* Freiburg, 1933, repr. Darmstadt, 1961.

Harbison, E. H. *The Christian Scholar in the Age of the Reformation.* New York, 1956.

Heimbucher, M. *Die Orden und Kongregationen der katholischen Kirche,* 2 vols. Repr. Paderborn, 1965.

Hirsch, Rudolph. *Printing, Selling and Reading, 1450–1550.* Wiesbaden, 1967.

Humphreys, K. W. *The Book Provisions of the Medieval Friars, 1215–1400.* Amsterdam, 1964.

Hurter, H. *Nomenclator literarius theologiae catholicae,* 5 vols. in 6. Innsbruck, 1906–26; repr. New York, 1962.

D'Irsay, S. *Histoire des universités françaises et étrangères,* 2 vols. Paris, 1933–35.

Joachimsen, P. *Geschichtsauffassung und Geschichtsschreibung in Deutschland unter dem Einfluss des Humanismus*, vol. 1 (no more published). Leipzig and Berlin, 1910.

Joecher, C. G. *Allgemeines Gelehrten-Lexicon*, 4 vols. Leipzig, 1750–51, and supplements.

Kaeppeli, T. *Scriptores Ordinis Praedicatorum Medii Aevi*, vol. 1 (A-F). Rome, 1970.

Kapsner, Oliver L. *A Benedictine Bibliography*, 2nd ed., 2 vols. Collegeville, Minn., 1962.

Kramm, H. *Deutsche Bibliotheken unter dem Einfluss von Humanismus und Reformation.* Leipzig, 1938; repr. Nendeln, 1968.

Kristeller, P. O. *Iter Italicum*, 2 vols. Leiden, 1963–67.

————. *Latin Manuscript Books before 1600.* 3rd ed., New York, 1965.

————. *Renaissance Thought*, 2 vols. New York, 1961–65.

————. *Studies in Renaissance Thought and Letters.* Rome, 1956; repr. 1969.

————. *Le Thomisme et la pensée italienne de la Renaissance.* Montreal, 1967.

Lanning, John Tate. *Academic Culture in the Spanish Colonies.* New York and London, 1940; repr. Folcroft, Pa., 1969.

Lauchert, F. *Die italienischen literarischen Gegner Luthers.* Freiburg, 1912.

Lehmann, P. *Mittelalterliche Bibliothekskataloge Deutschlands und der Schweiz*, 3 vols. in 5. Munich, 1918–39.

Lieftinck, G. I. *Manuscrits datés conservés dans les Pays-Bas*, vol. 1–2, Amsterdam, 1964.

Manitius, M. *Handschriften antiker Autoren in mittelalterlichen Bibliothekskatalogen.* Leipzig, 1935; repr. Wiesbaden, 1968.

Mariani, U. *Il Petrarca e gli Agostiniani.* Rome, 1946; repr. 1959.

Mittarelli, J. B. and Costadoni, A. *Annales Camaldulenses.* 9 vols. Venice, 1755–73.

di Napoli, G. *L'immortalità dell'anima nel Rinascimento.* Turin, 1963.

Orlandi, S., O.P.,*Necrologio di S. Maria Novella.* 2 vols. Florence, 1955.

Ossinger, J. F. *Bibliotheca Augustiniana Historica.* Ingolstadt and Augsburg, 1768; repr. Turin, 1963.

Perini, D. A. *Bibliographia Augustiniana, Scriptores Itali*, 4 vols. in 1. Florence, 1929–37.

Piana, C. *Ricerche su le Università di Bologna e di Parma nel sec. XV.* Quaracchi, 1963.

―――. *Nuove ricerche su le Università di Bologna e di Parma.* Quaracchi, 1966.

Poppi, A. "Il contributo dei formalisti padovani al problema delle distinzioni," in *Problemi e figure della Scuola Scotista del Santo,* Padua, 1966, 601–790.

Prantl, K. *Geschichte der Logik im Abendlande.* 4 vols. Leipzig, 1855–70; repr. Graz, 1955.

Puliatti, P. *La letteratura ascetica e mistica del Quattrocento.* Catania, 1953 (not seen).

Quétif, J. and Echard, J. *Scriptores ordinis Praedicatorum.* 2 vols. Paris, 1719–23; repr. New York (ca. 1959).

Rashdall, H. *The Universities of Europe in the Middle Ages.* Ed. F. M. Powicke and A. B. Emden, 3 vols. Oxford, 1936.

Reese, G. *Music in the Middle Ages.* New York, 1940.

―――. *Music in the Renaissance,* rev. ed. New York, 1959.

Renaudet, A. *Préréforme et humanisme à Paris pendant les premières guerres d'Italie (1494–1517).* Paris, 1916 and 1953.

de Roover, R. *San Bernardino of Siena and Sant' Antonino of Florence: the Two Great Economic Thinkers of the Middle Ages.* Boston, 1967.

Rossi, V. *Il Quattrocento.* Milan, 1933; 8th ed. by A. Vallone, Milan, 1964.

Sabbadini, R. *Le scoperte dei codici latini e greci ne' secoli XIV e XV.* 2 vols. Florence, 1905–14; repr. with additions, ed. E. Garin, Florence, 1967.

Samaran, C. and Marichal, R., ed. *Catalogue des manuscrits en écriture latine, portant des indications de date, de lieu ou de copiste,* vols. 1–2 and 5–6. Paris, 1959–68.

Sbaralea, J. H. *Supplementum et Castigatio ad scriptores trium ordinum S. Francisci,* 3 parts. Rome, 1908–36.

Schirmer, W. F. *Der englische Fruehhumanismus.* Leipzig, 1931; 2nd ed. Tübingen, 1963.

von Schulte, J. F. *Die Geschichte der Quellen und Literatur des Canonischen Rechts,* vol. 2. Stuttgart, 1877.

Secret, F. *Les Kabbalistes Chrétiens de la Renaissance.* Paris, 1964.

―――. "Les dominicains et la Kabbale chrétienne de la Renaissance," *Archivum Fratrum Praedictorum* 27 (1957), 319–336.

Smalley, Beryl. *English Friars and Antiquity in the Early Fourteenth Century*. Oxford, 1960.

Stegmueller, F. *Repertorium commentariorum in Sententias Petri Lombardi*, 2 vols. Würzburg, 1947.

——. *Repertorium Biblicum Medii Aevi*, vols. 1–7. Madrid, 1950–61.

Thorndike, L. *A History of Magic and Experimental Science*, vols. 3–6. New York, 1934–41.

Tiraboschi, G. *Storia della letteratura italiana*, 9 vols. in 27. Venice, 1823.

Trinkaus, Ch. *Adversity's Noblemen*. New York, 1940; repr. 1965.

——. *In Our Image and Likeness: Humanity and Divinity in Italian Humanist Thought*, 2 vols. London and Chicago, 1970.

Vansteenberghe, E. *Autour de la docte ignorance, Beiträge zur Geschichte der Philosophie des Mittelalters*, XIV, pts. 2–4, Münster, 1915.

de Villiers, C. *Bibliotheca Carmelitana*, ed. G. Wessels, 2 vols. in 1. Rome, 1927.

Voigt, G. *Die Wiederbelebung des classischen Alterthums*. 3rd ed. by M. Lehnerdt, 2 vols. Berlin, 1893.

Vonschott, H. *Geistiges Leben im Augustinerorden am Ende des Mittelalters und zu Beginn der Neuzeit, Historische Studien*, CXXIX. Berlin, 1915.

Wadding, L. *Scriptores Ordinis Minorum*. Rome, 1906.

Way, Sister Agnes Clare, "S. Gregorius Nazianzenus," in *Catalogus Translationum et Commentariorum*, vol. 2, ed. P. O. Kristeller and F. E. Cranz. Washington, 1971, 43–198.

Weiss, R. *Humanism in England during the Fifteenth Century*. 2nd ed., Oxford, 1957; 3rd ed., 1967.

——. *The Dawn of Humanism in Italy*. London, 1947. New ed. (with a bibliographical appendix) in *Bulletin of the Institute of Historical Research* 42 (1969), 1–16.

——. *Il primo secolo dell'umanesimo*. Rome, 1949.

Wormald, F. and Wright, C. E. *The English Library before 1700*. London, 1958.

*Xenia Bernardina*, pt. II in 2 vols. Vienna, 1891.

Xiberta, Bartholomaeus. *De scriptoribus scholasticis saeculi XIV ex Ordine Carmelitarum*. Louvain, 1931.

Ziegelbauer, M. *Centifolium Camaldulense*. Venice, 1750; repr. Farnborough, 1967.

————. *Historia rei literariae Ordinis S. Benedicti,* 4 vols. Augsburg and Würzburg, 1754; repr. Farnborough, 1967.

Zimmerman, Benedictus-Maria de S. Cruce, "Les Carmes Humanistes," *Etudes Carmélitaines* 20, 2 (1935), 19–93.

————. *Monumenta historica Carmelitana,* vol. 1. Lirinae, 1907.

Zumkeller, A. "Manuskripte von Werken der Autoren des Augustiner-Eremiten-Ordens in mitteleuropaeischen Bibliotheken," *Augustiniana,* 11 (1961), 27–86, 261–319, 478–532; 12 (1962), 27–92, 299–357; 13 (1963), 418–473; 14 (1964), 105–162.

# APPENDIX A: LIBRARIES OF RELIGIOUS ORDERS

Selective list of (monastic) libraries, especially in Austria and Italy. For the printed and handwritten lists of extant collections, see P. O. Kristeller, *Latin Manuscript Books before 1600* (3rd ed., New York, 1965). I add an asterisk to the libraries no longer extant.

Admont, Austria.

*Alcobaça, Portugal. Now in the Biblioteca Nacional, Lisbon.

Altenburg, Austria.

Assisi, Italy, S. Francesco. Intact in the Biblioteca Comunale. L. Alessandri, *Inventario dell'Antica Biblioteca del S. Convento di S. Francesco in Assisi compilato nel 1381* (Assisi, 1906).

Averbode, Belgium.

Basel, Switzerland. Dominikanerkloster. See P. Schmidt, "Die Bibliothek des ehemaligen Dominikanerklosters in Basel," *Basler Zeitschrift für Geschichte und Altertumskunde* 18 (1919), 160–254.

Beromünster, Switzerland.

*Bobbio, Italy. See Sabbadini, *Le scoperte*. G. card. Mercati, "Prolegomena de fatis bibliothecae monasterii S. Columbani Bobiensis . . . " in M. Tulli Ciceronis *De re publica libri e codice rescripto Vaticano latino 5757 phototypice expressi* (Vatican City, 1934). G. Ottino, *Codici Bobbiesi nella Biblioteca Nazionale di Torino* (Turin, 1890).

*Bologna, Italy, S. Salvatore. The mss. are now in the Biblioteca Universitaria.

Bolzano-Bozen, Italy, Benediktinerabtei Muri Gries.

*Brno, Czechoslovakia. Several monastic collections are now in the Universitni knihovna. See the catalogues by V. Dokoupil.

Brugge, Belgium. Abbaye des Dunes. Now in the Groot Seminarie. See *Tentoonstelling van Miniaturen en Boekbanden, Catalogus* (Bruges, 1927).

Camaldoli, Italy.

Cava, Italy.

Cesena, Italy. Biblioteca Malatestiana. It was once annexed to S. Francesco.

Cuyk-Sint Agatha, Netherlands.

*Ehingen, Germany. The mss. are now in Rottenburg, Priesterseminar.

Einsiedeln, Switzerland.

Engelberg, Switzerland.

Escorial, Spain. See also E. Jacobs, "Francesco Patrizi und seine Samm-
lung griechischer Handschriften in der Bibliothek des Escorial,"
*Zentralblatt für Bibliothekswesen* 25 (1908), 19–47. R. Beer, "Die
Handschriftenschenkung Philipp II. an den Escorial vom Jahre
1576," *Jahrbuch der Kunsthistorischen Sammlungen des Aller-
hoechsten Kaiserhauses* 23 (1903), pt. I.

Fiecht, Austria.

Firenze, Italy. The former monastic libraries are now divided between
the Biblioteca Medicea Laurenziana and the Biblioteca Nazionale
Centrale.

—*Badia, R. Blum, *La biblioteca della Badia fiorentina e i codici di
Antonio Corbinelli, Studi e Testi*, CLV (Vatican City, 1951).

—S. Croce. C. Mazzi, "L'inventario quattrocentistico della biblioteca
di S. Croce in Firenze," *Rivista delle biblioteche e degli archivi* 8
(1897), 99–113. Charles T. Davis, "The Early Collection of Books
of S. Croce in Florence," *Proceedings of the American Philosophical
Society* 107 (1963), 399–414.

—S. Marco. The library received the manuscripts of Niccolò Niccoli.
A few mss. are kept in the Museo. B. L. Ullman and P. A. Stadter,
*The Public Library of Renaissance Florence: Niccolò Niccoli, Cosi-
mo de'Medici and the Library of San Marco* (Padua, 1972).

—*S. Maria del Carmine. K. W. Humphreys, *The Library of the Carmelites at Florence at the End of the Fifteenth Century* (Amsterdam, 1964).

—S. Maria Novella. S. Orlandi, *La Biblioteca di S. Maria Novella in
Firenze dal secolo XIV al secolo XVI* (Florence, 1952). A few mss.
are kept in the Archivio.

—*S. Spirito. A. Mazza, "L'inventario della 'Parva Libraria' di Santo
Spirito e la biblioteca del Boccaccio," *Italia Medioevale e Umanistica*, 9 (1966), 1–74.

Fonte Avellana, Italy.

*Gent, Belgium. Abbey of St. Bavo. It once had the library of Raphael
de Marcatel whose mss. are now found in Gent as well as in
Bruges, Haarlem, Seville and in several English libraries. See K. G.
Van Acker in *National Biografisch Woordenboek*, II (1966), 507–
512.

Geras, Austria.

Goettweig, Austria.

Grottaferrata, Italy.

Hall, Austria. Franziskaner.

Heiligenkreuz, Austria.

Herzogenburg, Austria.

Innsbruck, Austria. Serviten.

Klosterneuburg, Austria. B. Černik, "Die Anfaenge des Humanismus im Chorherrenstift Klosterneuburg," *Jahrbuch des Stiftes Klosterneuburg* 1 (1908), 57–94; A. Lhotsky, "Studia Neuburgensia . . . ," ibid. N.F., 1 (10, 1961), 69–103.

Kremsmuenster, Austria.

Lambach, Austria.

Lilienfeld, Austria.

Melk, Austria.

Michaelbeuern, Austria.

Monte Cassino, Italy.

Monte Oliveto, Italy.

Monteprandone, Italy. Intact in the Biblioteca Civica. A. Crivellucci, *I codici della Libreria raccolta da S. Giacomo della Marca nel Convento di S. Maria delle Grazie presso Monteprandone* (Livorno, 1889); *Atti del III Convegno di studi celebrato a Loreto (Ancona) il 28 dicembre 1970 e dedicato alla Libreria di S. Giacomo della Marca (Picenum Seraphicum 8, 1971).*

Montevergine, Italy.

Montserrat, Spain.

*Napoli, Italy. S. Giovanni in Carbonara. It received the books of Giano Parrasio and Girolamo Seripando. Most mss. are now in the Biblioteca Nazionale.

*Nonantola, Italy. G. Gullotta, *Gli antichi cataloghi e i codici della Abbazia di Nonantola, Studi e Testi,* CLXXXII; J. Ruysschaert, *Les manuscrits de l'Abbaye de Nonantola, Studi e Testi,* CLXXXII (bis), Vatican City, 1955.

*Nova Riša, Czechoslovakia. Now in Brno, Universitni knihovna.

*Osek (Ossegg), Czechoslovakia. Now in Praha, Narodni Museum.

Ottobeuren, Germany.

Padova, Italy. Biblioteca Antoniana. K. W. Humphreys, *The Library of the Franciscans of the Convent of St. Antony, Padua at the Beginning of the Fifteenth century* (Amsterdam, 1966).

—*S. Giovanni in Verdara. It received the manuscripts of Pietro Montagnana and Giovanni Marcanova. Many mss. are now in Venice, Biblioteca Marciana, but many are scattered. See Jac. Phil. Tomasinus, *Bibliothecae Patavinae Manuscriptae* (Udine, 1639), 9–40. P. Sambin, "La formazione quattrocentesca della biblioteca di S. Giovanni di Verdara in Padova," *Istituto Veneto di Scienze, Lettere ed Arti, Atti, Classe di Scienze Morali e Lettere* 114 (1956), 263–280.

—*S. Giustina. See G. Mazzatinti, *Inventario dei manoscritti italiani delle biblioteche di Francia*, II (Rome, 1887), 549–661. R. Sabbadini, "Frammenti di poesie volgari musicate," *Giornale storico della letteratura italiana* 40 (1902), 270–272. G. Soranzo, "Preziosi codici già del Convento di Santa Giustina di Padova nella Rosminiana di Stresa," *Atti e Memoire dell'Accademia Patavina di Scienze, Lettere ed Arti* 73 (1960–61), pt. 3, 43–54.

*Polirone, Italy. The mss. are now in Mantova, Biblioteca Comunale. See B. Benedini, "I manoscritti Polironiani della Biblioteca Comunale di Mantova," in *Accademia Virgiliana di Mantova, Atti e Memorie*, N.S. XXX, 1958. There is also a typed catalogue by U. Meroni (1962).

*Pomposa, Italy. Giov. Mercati, "Il catalogo della biblioteca di Pomposa," in his *Opere Minori*, I, *Studi e Testi*, LXXVI (Vatican City, 1937), 358–388.

*Raijhrad (Raigern), Czechoslovakia. Now in Brno, Universitni knihovna.

*Reichenau, Germany. Now in Karlsruhe, Landesbibliothek.

Reichersberg, Austria.

Reun (Rein), Austria.

Rimini, San Francesco. G. Mazzatinti, "La Biblioteca di San Francesco (Tempio Malatestiano) in Rimini," in *Scritti vari di Filologia (A Ernesto Monaci gli scolari)* (Rome, 1901), 345–352.

*Ripoll, S. Marie de, Spain. Now in Barcelona, Archivo de la Corona de Aragón.

Rome, S. Gregorio Magno.

—S. Isidoro.

Salzburg, Austria. Abtei Nonnberg.

—Stiftsbibliothek St. Peter.

*San Cugat del Valles, Spain. Now in Barcelona, Archivo de la Corona de Aragón.

Sankt Florian, Austria.

Sankt Gallen, Switzerland.

Sankt Paul im Lavanttal, Austria. The collections come from St. Blasien and from the Hospitalstift am Pyrhn.

*Sankt Wolfgang, Austria. Now in Linz, Priesterseminar.

Sarnen, Switzerland.

Schlaegl, Austria.

Schlierbach, Austria.

Schwaz, Austria. Franziskaner.

Seitenstetten, Austria.

Silos, San Domingo de, Spain.

Stams, Austria.

Subiaco, Italy.

*Tegernsee, Germany. Now in München, Staatsbibliothek.

*Valencia, Spain. S. Miguel de los Reyes. Now in the Biblioteca Universitaria. See note 21.

*Venezia, Italy. S. Antonio di Castello. It received the books of Card. Domenico Grimani. The library was burned in the seventeenth century. See Jac. Phil. Tomasinus, *Bibliothecae Venetae manuscriptae* (Udine, 1650), 1–19. Many mss. are now scattered. T. Freudenberger, "Die Bibliothek des Kardinals Domenico Grimani," *Historisches Jahrbuch* 56 (1936), 15–45.

*—S. Michele di Murano. The mss. are now scattered, and some of them are in Camaldoli. See note 15. E. Mioni, "I manoscritti greci di S. Michele di Murano," *Italia Medioevale e Umanistica* 1 (1958), 317–343.

Vorau, Austria.

Vyšší Brod (Hohenfurt), Czechoslovakia.

*Weingarten, Germany. The mss. are scattered, many of them are now in Fulda and Stuttgart. See K. Loeffler, *Die Handschriften des Klosters Weingarten* (Leipzig, 1912).

*Wiblingen, Germany. The mss. are now in Tübingen, Wilhelmsstift.

Wien, Austria. Dominikaner.

Wien, Austria. Schottenkloster.

Wiener-Neustadt, Austria. Neukloster.

Wilhering, Austria.

Zwettl, Austria.

*Zwiefalten, Germany. The mss. are now in Stuttgart, Landesbibliothek. K. Loeffler, *Die Handschriften des Klosters Zwiefalten* (Linz, 1931).

# APPENDIX B: HUMANISTS AND SCHOLARS OF THE RELIGIOUS ORDERS

Selective list of humanists and other scholars, most of them active in Italy and Germany between 1400 and 1530, who were members of religious orders or congregations. The emphasis will be on their contributions to fields other than theology, and on data not found in the standard bio-bibliographical sources. Manuscripts will usually be cited from printed catalogues or from my *Iter Italicum* and unpublished notes, rather than from old bibliographies.

Acciaiolus, Zenobius O.P. (1461–1519). He translated Eusebius, Olympiodorus and Theodoretus, and composed many poems and letters. Kristeller, *Supplementum Ficinianum* (Florence, 1937), II, 334–335. Cf. Quétif, II, 44–46.

Adam Genuensis, see Montaldus.

Aegidius Viterbiensis O.E.S.A. (1470–1532). Wrote many letters and a few poems, a commentary on the Sentences *ad mentem Platonis,* a *Historia viginti saeculorum,* and a cabalistic work entitled *Scechina.* Ossinger, 190–198. Perini, I, 177–186. Zumkeller (1961), 67–68. E. Massa, "L'anima e l'uomo in Egidio da Viterbo," in *Testi umanistici inediti sul 'De anima,'* *Archivio di Filosofia* (Padua, 1951), 37–138. F. X. Martin, "The Problem of Giles of Viterbo," *Augustiniana* 9 (1959), 357–379; 10 (1960), 43–60. John W. O'Malley, *Giles of Viterbo on Church and Reform* (Leiden, 1968). C. Astruc and J. Monfrin, "Livres latins et hébreux du Cardinal Gilles de Viterbe," *Bibliothèque d'Humanisme et Renaissance* 23 (1961), 551–554.

Aindorffer, Caspar O.S.B. (s. XV). Cf. E. Vansteenberghe, *Autour de la docte ignorance, Beiträge zur Geschichte der Philosophie des Mittelalters,* XIV, pts. 2–4 (Münster, 1915).

B. Albertus de Sarteano O.F.M. (1385–1450). Composed letters and orations. Sbaralea, I, 8–9. S. Albertus a Sarthiano, *Vita et opera,* ed. F. Haroldus (Rome, 1688).

Albertus, Leander O.P. (1479–1553). Quétif, II, 137 and 825. *Descrittione di tutta l'Italia* (Bologna, 1550). *De viris illustribus Ordinis Praedicatorum* (Bologna, 1517); the New York Public Library copy,

Spencer Collection, Ital. 1517, carries the note (f. 2): Liber D. Grimani Car. lis S. Marci.

Aliottus, Hieronymus O.S.B. (1412–1480). *Epistolae et opuscula*, ed. G. M. Scarmalius, 2 vols. (Arezzo, 1769). G. M. Mazzuchelli, *Gli scrittori d'Italia*, I, 1, 1753, 497. P. O. Kristeller, "An Unknown Correspondence of Alessandro Braccesi . . . , " *Classical Mediaeval and Renaissance Studies in Honor of Berthold Louis Ullman*, ed C. Henderson (Rome, 1964), II, 326–327, 346 and plates 1–2.

Ambrosius de Cora or Coranus, see Massarius.

Ambrosius Parthenopaeus, see Flandinus.

Amidei, see Hieronymus Lucensis.

Annius Viterbiensis O.P. (Johannes Nannius, 1432–1502). Quétif, II, 4–7. *De imperio Turcorum*, ed. 1471. *De futuris Christianorum triumphis in Saracenos*, ed. 1480. etc. *Antiquitatum variarum volumina XVII*, ed. 1498 etc. The last work contains many texts attributed to ancient authors that are now generally considered to be forgeries. Cf. R. Weiss, "Traccia per una biografia di Annio da Viterbo," *Italia Medioevale e Umanistica* 5 (1962), 424–451. The same, "An Unknown Epigraphic Tract by Annius of Viterbo," in *Italian Studies Presented to E. R. Vincent* (Cambridge, 1962), 101–120. The same, *The Renaissance Discovery of Classical Antiquity* (Oxford, 1969), 94 and passim.

S. Antoninus O.P. (1389–1459). S. Orlandi, *Bibliografia Antoniniana* (Vatican City, 1961). De Roover. Kaeppeli, 80–104.

Antonius Bargensis O.S.B. Congr. Olivet. (d. 1452). *Chronicon Montis Oliveti*, ed. Placidus M. Lugano (Florence, 1901). A manuscript in Monte Oliveto also contains *De magistratibus et prelatis* (a fragment), *De illustribus Tuscis*, and *De dignitate hominis et de excellentia humane vite* (to Barth. Facius). Cf. Kristeller, *Iter Italicum*, II, (Leiden, 1967), 543–544.

Antonius de Luca O. Serv. (s. XV). Author of a musical treatise. See E. de Coussemaker, *Scriptorum de musica medii aevi nova series*, IV (Paris, 1869), 421 ff. Kristeller, *Studies*, 459, n. 35.

Antonius de Pera O.P. (ca. 1400). Translated several works on medicine and veterinary art from Latin into Italian. Kaeppeli, 117.

Antonius Raudensis O.F.M. (Antonio da Rho, d. ca. 1450). He wrote letters and poems, *Lactantii errores* in three books (many mss.) and a *Dictionarium elegantiarum* (Paris. lat. 7636–37). Sbaralea, I, 93–94. Voigt, passim.

Archangelus (Puteus) de Burgonovo O.F.M. (d. 1571). *Apologia pro defensione cabalae contra Petrum Garziam* (defending Pico), ed. Bologna, 1564. *Interpretationes in Cabalistarum selectiora dogmata Jo. Pici*, ed. Venice 1569. Sbaralea, I, 101. Secret, p. 137 and passim.

Attavanti, see Paulus Florentinus.

Augustinus de Tridento O.E.S.A. (ca. 1360). *Epistola astrologica ad Nicolaum episcopum Tridentinum.* Zumkeller (1961), 279.

Bale, John O. Carm. (1495–1563). A Protestant after 1530. Several works on Carmelite history are preserved in manuscript. *Illustrium Maioris Britanniae scriptorum . . . summarium*, ed. 1548. *Scriptorum illustrium Maioris Britanniae . . . catalogus*, ed. 1557. W(illiam) T. Davis, "Bibliography of John Bale" in *Oxford Bibliographical Society, Proceedings and Papers* 5 (1940), 201–279.

Bandello, Matteo O.P. (1485–1561). He wrote letters and poems, an oration and a biography of G. B. Cattaneo and turned one of Boccaccio's stories (*Decam. X 8*) into Latin (ed. 1509). He is famous for his *Novelle*, ed. 1554 and (pt. 4) 1573. C. Godi, "Per la biografia di Matteo Bandello," *Italia Medioevale e Umanistica* 11 (1968), 257–292; C. Dionisotti, "Una canzone sacra del periodo mantovano del Bandello," ibid., 293–307.

Bandellus, Vincentius, de Castronovo O.P. (1435–1506). He wrote two treatises on the Immaculate Conception, and a treatise entitled *Quod beatitudo hominis in actu intellectus et non voluntatis essentialiter consistit*, dedicated to Lorenzo de' Medici and directed against Marsilio Ficino. P. O. Kristeller, "A Thomist Critique of Marsilio Ficino's Theory of Will and Intellect," in *Harry Austryn Wolfson Jubilee Volume, English Section*, II (Jerusalem, 1965), 463–494. The same, *Le Thomisme*, 104–106, 111–123, 195–278. (See above pp. 79–81 and 83–90.)

Baptista de Fabriano O.P. (d. 1446). His explanation was printed with Gulielmus Hentisberus (Heytesbury), *De sensu composito et diviso* (Venice 1500, Hain 8438). His questions on Aristotle's *Organum* are preserved in Turin, Biblioteca Nazionale, ms. F. III 5, f. 251–260 (Kristeller, *Iter*, II, 573). Gargan, 70–73. Kaeppeli, 138–139.

Baptista Ferrariensis, see Panetius.

Baptista de Judicibus Finariensis O.P., bishop of Ventimiglia (d. 1484). In the trial following the death of Simon of Trent, he tried to defend the Jews against the charge of ritual murder raised by Bishop Johannes Hinderbach. See W. P. Eckert, "Il Beato Simonino negli

'Atti' del Processo di Trento contro gli Ebrei," *Studi Trentini di Scienze Storiche* 44 (1965), 193–221 (at pp. 217–219). The same, "Beatus Simoninus, Aus den Akten des Trienter Judenprozesses," in *Judenhass-Schuld der Christen*, ed. W. P. Eckert and E. L. Ehrlich (Essen, 1964), 329–357. Baptista defended the medieval Latin version of the *Nicomachean Ethics* against Leonardo Bruni, wrote a letter, a poem, an oration, *De migratione Petri Card. S. Sixti* (to Sixtus IV), *De canonizatione B. Bonaventurae libri II*, and a dialogue entitled *Serapion de contemptu mundi* (also in ms. Canon. lat. eccl. 211, f. 101–121 of the Bodleian Library). See Kristeller, *Le Thomisme*, 68. See above pp. 58–59. C. Dionisotti, "Una miscellanea umanistica transalpina." *Giornale storico della letteratura italiana* 110 (1937), 253–300, at pp. 276–279. Kaeppeli, 139–141; Piana, *Ricerche*, 283–284.

Baptista Mantuanus O. Carm. (1448–1516). His collected works (ed. 1576) include several moral treatises and numerous Latin poems for which he was famous. See Kristeller, *Le Thomisme*, pp. 81–90, 127–185, where his invective against the Thomists is published and his unpublished treatise on the blood of Christ is discussed. See above pp. 65–71. De Villiers, I, 217–240. E. Coccia, *Le edizioni delle opere del Mantovano* (Rome, 1960). Piana, *Ricerche*, 130–133.

Barberiis, Philippus de, O.P. (s. XV). Quétif, I, 873–874. He published *Chronica virorum illustrium, Discordantiae Hieronymi et Augustini, Sibyllarum de Christo vaticinia, De animorum immortalitate*, and *De providentia* (*Gesamtkatalog der Wiegendrucke* 3384–88).

Bartholomaeus de Urbino O.E.S.A. (d. 1350). His *Milleloquium S. Ambrosii* and *Milleloquium S. Augustini* appear in many mss. Arbesmann 36–55. Zumkeller (1961), 281–283.

Becchius, Gulielmus O.E.S.A., bishop of Fiesole (d. 1491 ?). He wrote commentaries on the Aristotelian *Economics, Ethics* and *Politics* (Laur. Aedil. 152–154), a *Protesto* (Laur. 61, 38, f. 76v–79), *De cometa* to Piero di Cosimo de'Medici (Magl. XI 40), a commentary on Porphyry's *Isagoge* (Ricc. 574, f. 50–64), *De falso dogmate Maumethi* (Marc. lat. III 130), *De potestate spirituum* (Vat. lat. 4593), *De potestate papae et concilii* (Vat. lat. 3673). Ossinger, 112–114. Perini, I, 103–105. Kristeller, "An Unknown Correspondence of Alessandro Braccesi," in *Classical, Mediaeval and Renaissance Studies in Honor of Berthold Louis Ullman*, II, (Rome, 1956), 319, 322, 347.

Benignus de Salviatis, Georgius O.F.M., bishop of Cagli and archbishop of Nazareth (d. 1520). *Dialectica nova* (ed. 1489, GW 3841), *Mirabilia LXXVII in opusculo Nicolai de Mirabilibus* (ed. ca. 1489, GW 3842), *De natura angelica* (ed. 1499, GW 3843), *Oratio funebris pro Junio Georgio* (GW 3844), *Propheticae solutiones* (ed. 1497, GW 3845), *An Judaeorum libri quos Thalmud appellant sint potius supprimendi quam tenendi et conservandi* (ed. 1518, BM), *De libertate et immutabilitate Dei ad Bessarionem* (Vat. lat. 1056), *De reformatione calendarii ad Leonem X* (Vat. lat. 8226), *Federicus de anima regni principe* (Urb. lat. 995), *Quaestiones septem in rhythmum Laurentii Medicis ad Leonem X* (Laur. 83, 18), *De gratia* (Ricc. 317), *Apologeticon ad Julium II* (Magl. XXX 215), *De assumptione B. V. Mariae* (Ambros. A 30 sup.), *Contemplationes vexilli Christianae fidei* (Vindob. 4797 and Milan, Cappuccini 16, [59]), *Contemplationes de B. V. Maria* (Brussels ms. 10783), and some letters. Kristeller, *Supplementum Ficinianum* (1937), II, 350–351; *Le Thomisme*, p. 122. C. Dionisotti, *Italia Medioevale e Umanistica* 4 (1961), 305. C. Vasoli, "Notizie su Giorgio Benigno Salviati (Jurai Dragišic)," *Studi storici in onore di Gabriele Pepe* (Bari, 1970; not seen).

Berchorius (Bersuire), Petrus O.S.B. (d. 1362). *Reductorium morale* in 16 books (book 15 is the *Ovidius moralizatus*). *Repertorium morale*. French translation of Livy. C. Samaran (and J. Monfrin), *Histoire littéraire de la France*, XXXIX (1962), 259–450. K. V. Sinclair, *The Melbourne Livy* (Melbourne, 1961). *Reductorium morale, Liber XV: Ovidius moralizatus,* ed. J. Engels (Utrecht, 1960–66). J. Engels, "La lettre-dédicace de Bersuire à Pierre des Prés," *Vivarium* 7 (1969), 62–72.

B. Bernardinus (Tomitanus) Feltrensis O.F.M. (1439–94). *Sermoni,* ed. C. Varischi, 3 vols. (Milan, 1964). Sbaralea, I, 140.

S. Bernardinus Senensis O.F.M. (1380–1444). Many sermons and treatises. *Opera omnia,* 8 vols. (Quaracchi, 1950–63). Sbaralea, I, 137–140. See De Roover.

Bernardus Andreae O.E.S.A. (d. ca. 1521). He wrote poems and orations, a history of Henry VII, and a commentary on Augustine's *De civitate Dei.* Ossinger, 124–125. *Dictionary of National Biography*, I, 398–399. William Nelson, *John Skelton Laureate* (New York, 1939; repr. 1964), 239–242 and passim. A study of this author is being prepared by Mrs. Constance Blackwell.

Bernardus de Waging O.S.B. See Vansteenberghe, *Autour de la docte ignorance, Beiträge,* XIV (1915), 204.

Bianchus, Apollonius O.F.M. (s. XV). Sbaralea, I, 99–100. He wrote letters, orations, *De vitae pauperis praestantia* (Ricc. 771, f. 334–344, and Venice Museo Correr, ms. Cicogna 797, f. 27–41), *De virtute colenda* (Palermo, Nazionale I C 5, f. 1–28).

Bild, Vitus O.S.B. (1481–1529). Knew Greek and Hebrew, was interested in music and mathematics, in history and theology. His letters and other writings are in Augsburg, Bischöfliches Ordinariatsarchiv, ms. 81 (3 vols.) and 81 a, and some of his letters have been published. Alfred Schroeder, "Der Humanist Veit Bild, Moench bei St. Ulrich, sein Leben und sein Briefwechsel," *Zeitschrift des Historischen Vereins für Schwaben und Neuburg* 20 (1893), 173–227; A. Bigelmair, "Der Briefwechsel von Oekolampadius mit Veit Bild," *Reformations geschichtliche Studien und Texte* 40 (1922), 117–135; *Neue Deutsche Biographie,* II (1955), 235; *Lexikon für Theologie und Kirche,* II (1958), 457–458.

Bilia (Biglia, de Biliis), Andreas Mediolanensis O.E.S.A. (c. 1395–1435). Ossinger, 130–134. Perini, I, 127–131. Arbesmann, 120–141. He wrote historical works and orations, and translated Plutarch's *Timoleon* (Macerata, 5, 3 C 26, f. 89–119), Aristotle's *Physics* (Budapest, Academy of Sciences 4° 36) and *De anima* (Bodleian Library, ms. Bywater 10). R. Sabbadini, "Andrea Biglia (Milanese) Frate Agostiniano del sec. XV," *Rendiconti del R. Istituto Lombardo,* ser. 2, XXXIX (1906), 1087–1102. F. Novati, "Di un codice originale del 'Liber rerum mediolanensium' di frate Andrea Billia esistente nella Nazionale di Madrid," *Archivio Storico Lombardo,* ser. 4, VII (anno 34, 1907), 217–224.

Billius (Billy), Jacobus O.S.B. (1535–81). Ziegelbauer, III, 353–357. Kapsner, I, 79. He translated Gregory Nazianzen and other patristic authors. See Sister Agnes Clare Way in *Catalogus Translationum,* II, ed. P. O. Kristeller and F. E. Cranz (Washington, 1971), 77–85, 104–105, 118–121, 158–164, and 176–177.

Bona, Theophilus O.S.B. (d. 1512). Author of Latin poems, including one in praise of St. Bernard, which was repeatedly printed, and a verse dialogue entitled *De vita solitaria et civili,* dedicated to Guidubaldo da Montefeltro. Mazzuchelli, *Scrittori,* II, 3 (1762), 1525–28; *Dizionario Biografico degli Italiani* 11 (1969), 447–448 (by R. Negri).

Bonadies (Godendach), Johannes O. Carm. (s. XV). Composer and teacher. Chiefly known as the teacher of Franchino Gafori (Reese, *Renaissance*, p. 178) and as the copyist of ms. Faenza 117 in 1473–74 (Kristeller, *Iter*, I, 52).

Borro, Gasparino O. Serv. (d. 1498). Published a commentary on Sacrobosco's *Sphaera* and religious poems in Italian. Besutti, 115–128.

Bossus, Matthaeus Can. Reg. (1427–1502). His collected works (Bologna, 1627) include moral treatises, orations and many letters. A manuscript in the British Museum (Add. 24072) contains a collection of epigrams by M. B. and the catalogue identifies the author with Bossus, but another attribution (Marinus Becichemus) seems more probable. G. Soranzo, *Matteo Bosso di Verona* (Padua, 1965).

Bostius, Arnoldus O.Carm. (d. 1499). De Villiers, I, 198–200. Zimmerman, "Les Carmes humanistes," 33–38. He wrote religious poems and treatises, including a treatise on the Immaculate Conception against Vincenzo Bandello, and several works on the history of the Carmelite and of the Carthusian orders. He was in correspondence with Ermolao Barbaro, Robert Gaguin and Erasmus. A few of his letters have been published: Bened. Zimmerman, *Monumenta historica Carmelitana* (Lirinae, 1907), 511–522; P. S. Allen, "Letters of Arnold Bostius," *English Historical Review* 34 (1919), 225–236.

Bracceschi, Giov. Battista O.P. (d. 1612). He wrote poems, orations, sermons and antiquarian collections, for the most part unpublished. Quétif, II, 381–382. Mazzuchelli, II, 4 (1763), 1952–53; Kristeller, *Iter*, I (see index).

Brandolinus, Aurelius Lippus O.E.S.A. (c. 1440–1497). He wrote poems, orations and letters, *Paradoxa Christiana* (ed. 1531 etc.), *De humanae vitae conditione* (ed. 1543 etc.), *De ratione scribendi* (ed. 1549), *De comparatione rei publicae et regni* (ed. 1890), *Epithoma in sacram Judeorum historiam* (Ottob. 121 and 438), *Rudimenta grammaticae* (Regin. lat. 1558). He commented on Vergil's *Georgica* (Vat. lat. 2740) and translated Pliny's *Panegyricus* into Italian (Paris. ital. 616). Elisabetta Mayer, *Un umanista italiano della corte di Mattia Corvino, Aurelio Brandolini Lippo* (Rome, 1938). L. Thorndike, "Lippus Brandolinus *De comparatione Reipublicae et Regni* . . . ," in *Science and Thought in the Fifteenth Century* (New York, 1929), 233–260.

Brandolinus, Raphael O.E.S.A. (?) (d. 1515). He wrote letters and orations, a dialogue *Leo* (ed. 1753), *De musica et poetica* (Casanat. 805), and *De quatuor belli rationibus in Turcas suscipiendi* (Berlin Hamilton 116). M. Quartana, "Un umanista minore della corte di Leone X, Raphael Brandolinus," *Atti della Società Italiana per il progresso delle Scienze* 20, 2 (1932), 464–472.

Bulengerus, Julius Caesar S.J. (1558–1628). De Backer, I, 945–948. Classical scholar. Wrote antiquarian works and commentaries on Latin poets.

Buratellus, Gabriel O.E.S.A. (s. XVI). *Praecipuarum controversiarum Aristotelis et Platonis conciliatio* (ed. 1573).

Burellus (Bureau), Laurentius O. Carm. (c. 1448–1504). Latin poet. Zimmerman, "Les Carmes humanistes," 85–88.

Butzbach, Johannes O.S.B. (1476–1526). He wrote poems and letters, an *Auctarium* to Trithemius' *De scriptoribus ecclesiasticis*, an *Odeporicon*, and a *Libellus de praeclaris picturae professoribus* (ed. 1925). Ziegelbauer, III, 335–338. *Allgemeine deutsche Biographie*, III (1876), 663–664 (Geiger). *Neue Deutsche Biographie*, III (1956), 82 (R. Newald). K. S. Schottenloher, *Bibliographie zur deutschen Geschichte*, I (1933), nos. 2219–28. Bonn, Universitätsbibliothek, mss. S 355–358.

Caccia, Bartholomaeus O.P. (d. after 1412). Composed theological works, and a commentary on Dante's *Paradiso* which is now lost. Kaeppeli, I, p. 146. Julius Kirshner, article in *Dizionario Biografico degli Italiani* (forthcoming).

Caietanus, Thomas de Vio O.P. (1469–1534). He wrote many theological and philosophical treatises as well as commentaries on Aristotle and on Thomas Aquinas. *Opuscula omnia* (Antwerp, 1576); *Scripta philosophica* (Rome, 1934–39); *Opuscula oeconomico-socialia* (Rome, 1934). *Il cardinale Tommaso de Vio Gaetano nel quarto centenario della sua morte, Rivista di filosofia neoscolastica*, Supplement to 27 (Milan, 1935); C. Giacon, *La seconda scolastica*, I (Milan, 1944); *Enciclopedia Cattolica*, IV, 1506–9. Gargan, 156–157.

Calepinus, Ambrosius O.E.S.A. (d. c. 1510). *Dictionarium* (Latinum, ed. 1505, etc.).

Campanella, Tommaso O.P. (1568–1639). L. Firpo, *Bibliografia degli scritti di Tommaso Campanella* (Turin, 1940). Campanella, *Theologica*, ed. R. Amerio (Florence, 1955–69).

Camphora (Campora), Jacopo O.P. (d. 1478). *Dell'immortalità dell' anima*, ed. 1472 etc. (GW 5948–56). Quétif, I, 856. The treatise also appears in several mss.

Canals, Antonius O.P. (d. 1419). Made Catalan translations of Seneca and Valerius Maximus. Kaeppeli, 105–108.

Capgrave, John O.E.S.A. (d. 1464). Theological and historical writings. A. de Meijer, "John Capgrave," *Augustiniana* 7 (1957), 118–148, 531–575. Ossinger, 200–202. Zumkeller (1962), 67–68.

Caraccioli da Lecce, Roberto O.F.M. (1425–95). Famous preacher whose sermons were frequently printed (GW 6039–6115). Wadding, 204–205. Sbaralea, III, 49–54.

Castelli, Benedetto O.S.B. (1577–1643). Famous scientist, pupil of Galileo.

Castiglioni, Giovacchino O.P. (d. ca. 1472). Pupil of Guarino. Wrote many orations and letters that were contained in the Codice Cibrario, destroyed in 1943. Gargan, 76–83. T. Verani, "Notizie del P. M. Giovacchino Castiglioni Milanese dell'ordine de' PP. Predicatori tratte da due codici del secolo XV," *Nuovo Giornale de' Letterati d'Italia* 43 (1790), 74–176.

Cavalieri, Bonaventura Ord. Jesuatorum (d. 1647). Famous mathematician.

Celle, B. Giovanni dalle O. Vallombr. (c. 1310–c. 1396). Author of sermons and letters (ed. 1845). *Enciclopedia Cattolica*, III, 1266–67.

Centueriis, Guillelmus de, de Cremona O.F.M. (c. 1340–1402). *De iure monarchiae*, ed. C. Cenci (Verona, 1967).

Chelidonius (Schwalbe), Benedictus O.S.B. (d. 1521). His Latin poems include a play entitled *Voluptatis cum virtute disceptatio*, and the Latin texts accompanying the book editions of Dürer's *Kleine Passion*, *Grosse Passion* and *Marienleben* (1511). Willibald Pirckheimer, *Briefwechsel*, I, ed. E. Reicke (Munich, 1940), 146; E. Panofsky, *Albrecht Dürer* (Princeton, 1943), I, 59 and passim, II, 31–39; *Neue Deutsche Biographie* 3 (1957), 195–196. *Albrecht Dürer 1471–1971* (Munich, 1971), 194–197, nos. 374–376; *The Little Passion by Albrecht Dürer, With the Poems of the First Edition of 1511 by Benedictus Chelidonius Musophilus in Latin with English Version* (Verona, 1971; there is an English version by Robert Fitzgerald, and an article on Chelidonius by G. Mardersteig, 199–215).

Christophorus Fanensis Ord. Humiliatorum (s. XV). He wrote Latin poems, and a dialogue on the siege of Rimini in 1469 (Urb. lat. 1260). *Iter*, I–II, Index. G. Zannoni, "L'impresa di Rimini (1469) narrata da Piero Acciaiuoli," *Rendiconti della Reale Accademia dei Lincei, Classe di Scienze Morali, Storiche e Filologiche*, ser. 5, V (1896), 198–220, at 198–200, n. 1.

Clarius, Isidorus O.S.B. (1495–1555). Edited the Vulgate (1542). *Epistolae*, ed. Modena 1705. Ziegelbauer, III, 344–348.

Clavius, Christophorus S.J. (1538–1612). Famous mathematician. De Backer, I, 1291–96.

Colonna, Francesco O.P. (c. 1432–1527). He is usually considered as the author of the *Hypnerotomachia Poliphili*, ed. Aldus 1499; ed. G. Pozzi and Lucia A. Ciapponi, 2 vols. (Padua, 1964). This attribution has been questioned by Lamberto Donati ("Il mito di Francesco Colonna," *Bibliofilia* 64, 1962, 247–270) and by Emanuela Kretzulesco Quaranta ("L'Itinerario Spirituale di 'Polifilo.' " *Rendiconti dell'Accademia Nazionale dei Lincei, Classe di Scienze Morali*, ser. 8, vol. 22, 1967, 269–284).

Colonna, Giovanni O.P. (d. 1343). Friend of Petrarch and author of a work of literary history, *De viris illustribus*. W. Braxton Ross, "Giovanni Colonna, Historian of Avignon," *Speculum* 45 (1970), 533–563.

Cono, Joh. O.P. (1463–1513). He helped Erasmus on his editions of the New Testament and of St. Jerome, and translated many texts from the Greek Church Fathers and dramatists. Quétif, II, 27–28. H. Meyer, "Ein Kollegheft des Humanisten Cono," *Zentralblatt für Bibliothekswesen* 53 (1936), 281–289. A. Oloroff, "L'humaniste Dominicain Jean Canon et le Crétois Jean Grégoropoulos," *Scriptorium* 4 (1950), 104–107. M. Sicherl, "Los comienzos del humanismo griego en Alemania," *Estudios clasicos* 10 (1966), 273–299. Th. Gelzer, "Eine Aristophaneshandschrift und ihre Besitzer," in Κωμωδοτραγηματα *W. J. W. Koster* (Amsterdam, 1967), 29–46. E. Reicke, "Ein vergessener Nürnberger Gelehrter der Pirckheimerzeit," *Mitteilungen des Vereins für Geschichte der Stadt Nürnberg* 35 (1937), 106–122. Pirckheimer, *Briefwechsel*, I (1940), 284–288. P. Adam, *L'humanisme à Sélestat*, 2nd ed. (Selestat, 1967). H. D. Saffrey, "Un humaniste dominicain, Jean Cuno de Nuremberg, precurseur d'Erasme à Bâle," *Bibliothèque d'Humanisme et Renaissance* 33 (1971), 19–62. Sister Agnes Clare Way, "Gregorius Nazianzenus," in *Catalogus Translationum et Com-*

*mentariorum*, II, ed. P. O. Kristeller and F. E. Cranz (Washington, 1971), 43–192, at 113–114.

Coranus, Ambrosius. See Massarius.

Corbetta, Hilarion O.S.B. (s. XVI). *Epistolae* (Modena, Est. lat. 794). *Declamatio contra Thelimanum* (Padua, Universitaria, ms. 521).

Corella, see Dominicus Johannis.

Corradus, Eusebius Can. Reg. (s. XV). Wrote two treatises against the Augustinian Hermits, denying that St. Augustine had been a monk (GW 2864 and 2923). Cf. Kristeller, *Studies*, 359.

Cortesius, Gregorius O.S.B., cardinal (1482–1548). His collected works (Padua, 1774, 2 vols.) include letters and poems. Ziegelbauer III, 339–344. Kapsner, I, 136. Hurter, II, 1498–99. *Catalogus Translationum*, II, 144–146.

Cranebrooke, Henry O.S.B. (d. 1466). Manuscript letters and notes. Weiss, p. 130.

Crastonus (Crestonus), Johannes O. Carm. (c. 1500). *Lexicon graeco-latinum* (ed. 1480, GW 7812, and many later editions). *Lexicon latino-graecum* (ed. 1480, GW 7816, and many later editions). Edited a *Psalterium graeco-latinum* (ed. 1481, Hain 13454). De Villiers, I, 814–824; II, 77. Zimmerman, "Les Carmes humanistes," 24–28.

Delphinus, Petrus O. Camald. (1444–1525). Wrote some orations and poems, and above all, a large number of letters. A selection was published in 1524 (copy at Columbia University), others by E. Martène and U. Durand, *Veterum scriptorum . . . amplissima collectio*, III (1724), 914–1232. Many more are still unpublished (Berlin, cod. lat. fol. 668–671; Florence, Nazionale, Conventi Soppressi E 3, 405; Venice, Marc. lat. XI 92). Cf. Ziegelbauer, *Centifolium*, 60–63. Hurter, II, 1362–63. J. Schnitzer, *Peter Delfin* (Munich, 1926).

Dionysius (Ryckel) Cartusianus (1402–71). *Opera omnia*, 42 vols. in 44, Monstrolii, 1896–1913. Hurter, II, 909–917. Grabmann, *Geschichte*, 121–172.

Dionysius de Burgo S. Sepulchri O.E.S.A. (d. 1342). His commentary on Valerius Maximus survives in many mss. and was printed once (GW 8411). Ossinger, 167–168. Zumkeller (1961), 302–304. Arbesmann, 15–36.

Diophylax, Johannes O.Carm. (1504–27). Latin poet. Zimmerman, "Les Carmes humanistes," 88–91.

Dominici, Giovanni O.P. (c. 1356–1419), cardinal. Quétif, II, 777–779. Hurter, II, 777–779. Orlandi, II, 77–126. Johannis Dominici *Lucula Noctis*, ed. E. Hunt (Notre Dame, 1940). Augustine T. Riplinger, "Blessed John Dominici and the Renaissance," *Reality* 11 (1963), 60–75.

Dominicus Johannis de Corella O.P. (1403–83). He wrote a poem *De illustratione urbis florentinae* (Laur. 91 sup. 50), and another poem in four books entitled *Theotocon de laudibus Beatae Mariae Virginis*. The latter is found in numerous mss. and was published by J. B. Maria Contarenus, *Nuova Raccolta d'opuscoli scientifici e filologici*, ed. A. Calogerà, XVII (1768), no. 10; XIX (1770), 381–468; the last two books also in *Deliciae eruditorum*, ed. G. Lami, XII (1742), 1–48. Quétif, I, 864–965. Orlandi, II, 305–315. Kaeppeli, 326–327.

Dominicus de Flandria O.P. (ca. 1425–79). His commentaries on Aristotle and on Thomas were frequently printed. Orlandi, II, 300–301. U. Schikowski, "Dominikus de Flandria O.P.," *Archivum Fratrum Praedicatorum* 10 (1940), 169–221. L. Mahieu, *Dominique de Flandres* (Paris, 1942). Kaeppeli, 315–318.

Ellenbog, Nicolaus O.S.B. (1481–1543). He knew Greek and Hebrew and was interested in astronomy, astrology and philosophy. He wrote many treatises and letters and a few poems. His works include a commentary on Baptista Mantuanus' *Fasti*. His *Epitoma Platonicum* [sic], based on Ficino, is lost. His letters are preserved mainly in ms. Stuttgart hist. 4° 99 and in Paris. lat. 8643 and were recently calendared and partly published: *Briefwechsel*, ed. A. Bigelmair and F. Zoepfl, *Corpus Catholicorum*, XIX–XXI (Münster, 1968).

Fabri, Felix O.P. (1441/42–1502). Author of historical and topographical writings: *Evagatorium in Terrae Sanctae, Arabiae et Egypti peregrinationem; Descriptio Sueviae; De civitate Ulmensi*. *Allgemeine Deutsche Biographie* 6 (1877), 490 (by Wolff); Joachimsen, 45–50; M. Haeussler, *Felix Fabri aus Ulm und seine Stellung zum geistigen Leben seiner Zeit* (Leipzig-Berlin, 1914); *Neue Deutsche Biographie*, IV (1959), 726–727; Quétif-Echard, I, 871–872.

Fasitellus (Fascitellus), Honoratus O.S.B. (1502–64), bishop of Isola (1551). Tutor of a nephew of Julius III. Latin poet. Some of his poems were printed with those of Sannazaro (Bassano, 1782). Ziegelbauer, I, 342 .

Faucherius, Dionysius O.S.B. (d. 1562). He wrote letters and poems. Ziegelbauer, III, 351–353.

Fazellus, Thomas O.P. (d. 1576). *De rebus Siculis* (Palermo, 1558, several more editions). Quétif-Echard, II, 212–213.

Federico da Venezia, O.P. (d. after 1401). Wrote a widely diffused commentary on the Apocalypse in Venetian dialect. Kaeppeli, 407–409; Gargan, 47–48; A. Luttrell, "Federigo da Venezia's Commentary on the Apocalypse: 1393/94," *The Journal of the Walters Art Gallery* 27–28 (1964–65), 57–65.

Ferabos, Johannes Andreas O.Carm. (active 1466–95). He published an Italian version of the letters of Phalaris (undated, but c. 1474, Copinger 4736, BM) and wrote a few letters (Parma, ms. Parm. 283) and poems (Urb. lat. 1193, f. 113–115 and 219)—ed. A. Cinquini, *L'Arte* 9 (1906), 56–57, and *Classici e Neolatini* 3 (1907), 553–560. Rob. Gaguin, *Epistole et Orationes*, ed. L. Thuasne (Paris, 1903), II, 272–274. De Villiers, I, 728 refers to him under Secabos. Zimmerman, "Les Carmes Humanistes," *Etudes Carmélitaines* XX, 2 (1935), 22–24.

Fernandus, Carolus O.S.B. (d. 1496). He wrote treatises against Gaguin and Vinc. Bandello, letters and poems. Ziegelbauer, III, 203–204.

Ferrarius, Ambrosius O.S.B. (s. XVI). Cf. Ziegelbauer, III, 543. He translated Origen (Ambr. D 16 inf.), Cyril (Vat. 3528 and Ottob. 756) and Gregory of Nyssa (Ottob. 776).

Filosseno (Philoxenus), Marcello, O. Serv. (s. XV–XVI). Wrote Latin and vernacular poems. See *Iter Italicum*; Besutti 209–212.

Flandinus, Ambrosius O.E.S.A. (d. 1531). Perini, II, 72–73; IV, 75–76. Lauchert, 239–240. H. Jedin, *Girolamo Seripando* (Würzburg, 1937), I, 82. His writings include many sermons (*Conciones quadragesimales*, ed. Venice 1523; *Conciones per adventum*, Mantua F IV 19; *De mundi genitura*, Mantua F IV 20; *Sermones*, Pavia Aldini 535); writings against Pomponazzi (*De animarum immortalitate contra Petrum Pomponatium*, ed. Mantua 1519; *De fato contra Pomponatium pro Alexandro Aphrodisio*, Genoa A VII 5); writings against Luther (*Examen vanitatis duodecim articulorum Martini Lutheri*, Parma, ms. Parm. 974; *Contra Lutheranos de vera et Catholica fide conflictationes*, Genoa A VII 6; Lauchert cites from old sources an *Apologia adversus Lutherum* of 1520, but I have been unable to locate it); commentaries on *Liber de causis* (Mantua

G III 10), on Plato's *Alcibiades* I and II (Mantua G III 11), on Plato's *Parmenides* and on Timaeus Locrus (Turin, Accademia ms. 0285), and on Plato's *Timaeus* (Paris. lat. 12948); finally a defense of Plato against Georgius Trapezuntius (Paris. lat. 6284).

Folengo, Teofilo O.S.B. (1496–1544). Famous author of Italian and Maccheronic poems. *Enciclopedia italiana*, 15, 602–603. E. Menegazzo, "Contributo alla biografia di Teofilo Folengo (1512–20)," *Italia Medioevale e Umanistica* 2 (1959), 367–408.

Folengus, Johannes Baptista O.S.B. (s. XVI). Theological works. *Dialogi quos Pomiliones vocat* (ed. 1533). D. Marra, *Conversazioni con Benedetto Croce su alcuni libri della sua biblioteca* (Milan, 1952), 48–49.

Foresti, Jacopo Filippo (Jacobus Philippus Bergomas) O.E.S.A. (1434–1520). *Supplementum Chronicarum* (ed. 1483 etc., Hain 2805–10, and several later editions). *De claris selectisque mulieribus* (ed. 1497). Ossinger, 359–363. Perini, II, 77–79. Zumkeller (1962), 58–59. Hurter, II, 1147–48. Tiraboschi, VI, 884–888.

Fossa, Evangelista, O. Serv. (d. after 1497). Wrote an epic poem (*Innamoramento di Galvano*) and translated Vergil's *Bucolica* and Seneca's *Agamemnon* into Italian verse. Betussi, 129–139.

Francesco (Sicuro) di Nardò, O.P. (d. 1489). Taught metaphysics at Padua, 1465–89. Edited Antonius Andreae's questions on Aristotle's *Metaphysics*. Gargan, 114–115. Kaeppeli, 390–391. See above pp. 49, 53, 60, 90.

Franciscus Savonensis, see Sixtus IV.

Frezzi, Federico, O.P. (d. 1416). Wrote *Il Quadriregio*, a well-known poem, and a *Iudicium de liceitate tyrannicidii*. Kaeppeli, 403–405.

Gadolus, Bernardinus O. Camald. (c. 1455–91). His letters—S. Michele di Murano 734 and 735, cf. J. B. Mittarelli, *Bibliotheca codicum* (Venice, 1779), 418–423—are now in Camaldoli.

Gaguinus, Robertus Ord. Trin. (c. 1425–1501). Historical works and poems. *Epistolae et orationes*, ed. L. Thuasne, 2 vols. (Paris, 1903).

Galatinus, Petrus (Columna) O.F.M. (c. 1460–1540). *De arcanis catholicae veritatis*, ed. Ortona, 1518 (copy at Columbia), often reprinted. His other theological works are preserved in Vatican mss. *Libellus de morte consolatorius in obitu Laurentii Medicis ducis Urbini*, to Leo X (Vat. lat., 3190); *De anima intellectiva et eius immortalitate* and *De homine* (Vat. lat. 5577). He knew Hebrew and was interested in the Cabala. Secret, 102–104. A. Kleinhans, "De vita et operibus Petri Galatini, O.F.M.," *Antonianum* 1 (1926), 145–179, 327–356.

Gallineta, Lazzaro, O.P. (d. 1490). Wrote orations and made vernacular translations of Leonardo Bruni's *Laudatio urbis Florentinae* and of pseudo-Aristotle's *De virtute*. Gargan, 131–134.

Gattus, Johannes, O.P. (d. 1484). Bishop of Cefalù and Catania. Wrote several orations. Quétif-Echard, I, 867–868. *Iter Italicum*.

Genebrardus, Gilbertus O.S.B. (1537–97). Translated from Greek and Hebrew, wrote a funeral oration on Petrus Danesius, and a theological treatise against Jacob Schegk. Ziegelbauer, III, 361–366.

Georgius (Giorgio, Zorzi), Franciscus O.F.M. (1460–1540). *De harmonia mundi* (ed. Venice 1525, copy at Columbia University). *In scripturam sacram problemata* (ed. 1536). Interested in Platonism and in Cabalism. Sbaralea, I, 271. Tiraboschi, VII, 606–608. G. degli Agostini, *Notizie istorico-critiche intorno la vita e le opere degli scrittori viniziani* (Venice, 1754), II, 332–362. Secret, passim.

S. Giacomo della Marca O.F.M. (1391–1476). Famous preacher. His library is preserved in Monteprandone. The proceedings of a congress dedicated to him were published in *Picenum Seraphicum* 6 (1969), 7–160.

Giles of Viterbo, see Aegidius.

Giocondo, Fra Giovanni (Johannes Jucundus) O.F.M. (1435–1515). Famous architect. He dedicated a collection of ancient inscriptions to Lorenzo de' Medici, and edited Vitruvius and several other ancient Latin authors. The question whether he was a Franciscan or Dominican was long debated, but has now been settled in favor of the Franciscans. Lucia A. Ciapponi, "Appunti per una biografia di Giovanni Giocondo da Verona," *Italia Medioevale e Umanistica* 4 (1961), 131–158. M. A. Gukovskj, "Ritrovamento dei tre volumi di disegni attribuiti a Fra Giocondo," ibid. 6 (1963), 263–269.

Giovanni da S. Miniato O. Camald. (s. XIV–XV). Correspondent of Salutati who addressed to him a long defense of poetry. Coluccio Salutati, *Epistolario*, ed. F. Novati, VI, pt. 1 (1905), 170–205. He made an Italian translation of Petrarch's *De remediis utriusque fortunae* (Madrid, Biblioteca Nacional, ms. Reservado 212).

Giovannino, see Johanninus.

Giudici, see Baptista de Judicibus Finariensis.

Giunta da S. Gimignano O.E.S.A. (d. after 1318). Compiled an index of Valerius Maximus. Zumkeller (1961), 312.

Giustiniani, see Justinianus.

Godendach, see Bonadies.

Gratiadei, Antonius, Venetus, O.M. (s. XV). Composed grammatical treatises for Bernardus Masius of Florence, dated Bruges, 1477. British Museum, ms. Add. 14776.

Guido Pisanus, O.Carm. (s. XIV). Wrote a double commentary on Dante's *Inferno*, in Latin prose and in vernacular verse. British Museum, Ms. Add. 31918. Chantilly, ms. 597 (1424). E. Orvieto, "Guido da Pisa e il Commento inedito all'Inferno Dantesco," *Italica* 46 (1969), 17–32.

Gulielmus Cremonensis, see Centueriis.

Hieronymus (Amideus) Lucensis O.Serv. (d. 1543). Wrote against Pomponazzi on the immortality of the soul (1518) and against Luther and Ochino. F. Lauchert, 679–681; Piana, *Ricerche*, 248–249.

Hothby, Johannes O.Carm. (d. 1487). English musician and musical theorist active in Italy. His writings were partly published by E. de Coussemaker, *Histoire de l'harmonie au Moyen Age* (Paris, 1852), 295–349; *Scriptorum de Musica Medii Aevi*, N.S., III (repr. 1963), 328–334. See also Johannis Octobi *Tres tractatuli contra Bartholomaeum Ramum*, ed. A. Seay (Rome, 1964). Anton Wilhelm Schmidt, *Die Calliopea legale des Johannes Hothby* (Leipzig, 1897). Kristeller, *Studies*, 458–462. Reese, 178.

Jacobus de S. Cassiano Cremonensis, O.E.S.A. (s. XV). He was a pupil of Vittorino da Feltre, criticized Georgius Trapezuntius' translation of Ptolemy and translated Archimedes and also Diodorus Books XI–XIII (British Museum, ms. Harl. 4916). C. De Rosmini, *Idea dell'Ottimo Precettore nella vita e disciplina di Vittorino da Feltre e de' suoi discepoli* (Milan, 1845), 238–243; M. Clagett, *Archimedes in the Middle Ages*, I (Madison, 1964), 12; S. Prete, *Two Humanist Anthologies* (Vatican City, 1964), 51–52 and passim.

Jacobus Philippus Bergomas, see Foresti.

Javellus, Chrysostomus O.P. (d. after 1538). His many works cover theology and philosophy and include commentaries on Aristotle; *Solutiones rationum Pomponatii* (printed with the latter's *Tractatus*, 1525); *Moralis philosophiae Platonicae dispositio; Civilis philosophiae ad mentem Platonis dispositio; Philosophia civilis*

*Christiana; Totius rationalis, naturalis, divinae ac moralis philosophiae compendium.* Cf. Quétif, II, 104–105. Hurter, II, 1209–10.

Johannes Baptista Theatinus O.P. (s. XVI). *In opus Andronicum Contiocinia Hebraicis Chaldaicisque sententiis referta,* ed. Ancona 1520. Quétif, II, 43–44. Secret, *Les dominicains,* 326–327.

Johannes Caroli O.P. (1428–1503). His theological works are found in mss. in Florence and listed by Orlandi, I, 898–900; II, 353–380. He is the author of a section of the *Necrologio* of S. Maria Novella published by Orlandi. Five biographies of friars of S. Maria Novella are included in Leandro Alberti's *De viris illustribus ordinis Praedicatorum* (Bologna, 1517), f. 70–82, 86v–94, 116v–121, 121–123v, 198v–204v. The same biographies, some of them in a longer version and all with prefaces, two additional biographies, and a preface of the collection to Cristoforo Landino are found in cod. B 28 of S. Maria Novella. He also wrote *De temporibus suis,* in 3 books (Vat. lat. 5878).

Johannes de Casali O.F.M. (s. XIV). *De velocitate motus alterationis* (ed. Venice 1505 with Bassanus Politus, and Rice. 117, f. 135–144v, with the date 1346). Sbaralea, II, 52; M. Clagett, *The Science of Mechanics in the Middle Ages* (Madison, 1959), 332, 382–391, 644.

Johannes Ferrariensis O.M. (d. 1460). His family is given as de' Cocchi (de Curribus) or Canali. He wrote a chronicle of the Este family, and a philosophical treatise *De immortalitate animae,* later revised and published as *De celesti vita.* D. Fava, "Fra Giovanni Ferrarese e Sigismondo Pandolfo Malatesta," in *Scritti vari dedicati a Mario Armanni in occasione del suo sessantesimo* (Milan, 1938), 49–62; J. Kirshner, *Dizionario Biografico degli Italiani* (forthcoming).

Johannes Franciscus Brixianus O.S.B. (c. 1500). Translated Gregory Nazianzen. See Sister Agnes Clare Way in *Catalogus Translationum,* II, 65. Cf. Ziegelbauer, III, 590.

Johannes Gallicus O. Carth. (d. 1473). A Frenchman or Belgian who lived in Mantua, was a pupil of Vittorino da Feltre and a teacher of Nicolaus Burtius. His musical treatise, *Ritus canendi vetustissimus et novus,* was printed by E. de Coussemaker, *Scriptorum de Musica Medii Aevi,* N.S., IV, (repr. 1963), 298–421. Kristeller, *Studies,* 461–462.

Johannes Pratensis O.F.M. (d. after 1455). He preached against the pagan poets, was attacked in a letter by Guarino, and replied with a *Libellus contra Guarinum de non legendis impudicis auctoribus:*

Est. lat. 577 and 772, ed. F. A. Zaccaria, *Iter litterarium per Italiam* (Venice, 1762), 325–336. Cf. Guarino, *Epistolario*, ed. R. Sabbadini (Venice, 1916) II, 519–534; III (1919), 419.

Johannes (de Bertoldis) de Serravalle O.F.M. (d. 1445), bishop of Fermo and Fano. Wrote a Latin translation and explanation of Dante's *Divine Comedy: Translatio et Commentum totius libri Dantis Aldigherii . . .* ed. M. da Civezza and T. Domenichelli (Prato, 1891). Sbaralea, II, 41.

Johannes (Stojković) de Ragusa O.P. (d. 1443). Theological writer whose important library went to the Dominican convent in Basel. A. Vernet, "Les manuscrits grecs de Jean de Raguse (†1443)," *Basler Zeitschrift für Geschichte und Altertumskunde* 61 (1961), 75–108; R. W. Hunt, "Greek Manuscripts in the Bodleian Library from the Collection of John Stojković of Ragusa," *Studia Patristica*, VII (*Texte und Untersuchungen zur Geschichte der Altchristlichen Literatur*, XCII, Berlin, 1966), 75–82; Gargan, 58.

Johanninus de Mantua O.P. (s. XIV). He addressed to Albertino Mussato a prose letter against poetry: *Thesaurus Antiquitatum et Historiarum Italiae*, ed. Jo. Georg. Graevius (Leiden, 1722), IV, pt. 2, 54–57. Mussato replied with a poem in defense of poetry (59–62). Cf. M. Minoia, *Della vita e delle opere di Albertino Mussato* (Rome, 1884), 184–185. A. Zardo, *Albertino Mussato* (Padua, 1884), 302–310.

Jucundus, see Giocondo.

Judicibus, see Baptista de Judicibus.

Julianus de Istria O.F.M. (de Cirmisonibus of Muggia) (s. XV). Wrote an Italian poem in praise of Bologna (Vindob. 3121, f. 190–190v). Piana, *Ricerche*, 188–190.

Juncta, see Giunta.

Justinianus, Augustinus O.P. (1470–1536). Wrote annals of Genoa in Italian. Edited a *Psalterium Hebreum Graecum Arabicum et Chaldaicum*, with 3 Latin versions (ed. 1516). He also edited the Hebrew text of Job, and writings of Maimonides, Philo and Calcidius. Quétif, II, 96–100. Secret, passim. P. S. Allen, *Opus Epistolarum Desiderii Erasmi*, III (1913), 278.

Justinianus, B. Paulus (previously Thomas) O. Camald. (1476–1528). Author of letters and poems and of numerous religious writings. Mittarelli and Costadoni, *Annales Camaldulenses*, IX (1773), 37–38; 446–719. Ziegelbauer, *Centifolium*, 43–50. J. Leclercq, *Le*

*Bienheureux Paul Giustiniani* (Rome, 1951). Beato Paolo Giustiniani, *Trattati Lettere e Frammenti*, ed. E. Massa, I (Rome, 1967). H. Jedin, "Contarini and Camaldoli," *Archivio italiano per la storia della pietà* 2 (1959), 51–118. F. Gilbert, "Cristianesimo, umanesimo e la Bolla 'Apostolici Regiminis,' " *Rivista storica italiana* 79 (1967), 976–990.

Landuccius, Bernardinus O.Carm. (d. 1523). His early logical work, *De sensu composito et diviso*, was printed several times. Villiers, 268–269.

Lapius, Maurus O.Camald. (d. 1478). Letters, *Itinerarium Hierosolymitanum*, and lives of saints (Marc. lat. XIV 112 and 295). Cf. Ziegelbauer, *Centifolium*, 39.

Leonardus Chiensis O.P. (d. 1458). He wrote a letter to Nicolaus V on the fall of Constantinople, and a dialogue *De vera nobilitate* against Poggio, printed with Poggio's treatise in 1657 from a manuscript now lost. Quétif-Echard, I, 816–817.

Leonardus (Mainardus) Cremonensis O.F.M. (s. XV). Writings on geometry (Ambr. J 253 inf., Parma, Parm. 984). Sbaralea, II, 172. M. Clagett, *Archimedes in the Middle Ages* (Madison, 1964), I, 636.

Leoninus de Padua O.E.S.A. (d. after 1332). *Abbreviatio Aegidii de Roma de regimine principum*, cf. Zumkeller (1961), 59, and (1963), 436. A logical treatise is found in Edinburgh, University Library, ms. Laing, III, 150.

Liuti, see Thomas Ferrariensis.

Ludovicus S. Francisci O.F.M. (s. XVI). *Globus canonum et arcanorum linguae sanctae*, ed. 1586. A. Kleinhans, "De grammatica Hebraica P. Ludovici S. Francisci ... , " *Antonianum* 1 (1926), 102–108.

Maffei, Celso Can. Reg. (d. 1508). He wrote letters and treatises. *Defensorium canonicorum regularium contra monachos* (ed. 1487, etc., Hain 10441–42). *Dissuasoria ne christiani principes ecclesiasticos census usurpent* (ed. 1494, Hain 10413). *Pro facillima Turcorum expugnatione epistola* (ed. s.a., c. 1498, Reichling 239). Zeno, *Dissertazioni Vossiane*, II (1753), 345–348. S. Maffei, *Verona Illustrata*, III (Milan, 1825), 176–181.

Maffei, Paolo Can. Reg. (s. XV). Letters and religious treatises. S. Maffei, III, 167–171.

Maffei, Timoteo Can. Reg. (d. 1470). *In Cosmi Medicis detractores.*

*Epistola ad principes Italiae* (against the Turks). *In sanctam rusticitatem* (many mss.). Hurter, II, 1325. S. Maffei, *Verona illustrata*, III (1825), 164–171.

Mainardus, Leonardus, see Leonardus Cremonensis.

Mainardus, Vincentius de S. Geminiano O.P. (d. 1527). *Vita S. Antonini* (ed. 1525). Some letters and poems are found in mss. Quétif, II, 75.

Malerbi (Manerbius), Niccolò O. Camald. (s. XV). His Italian version of the Bible was repeatedly printed. Ziegelbauer, *Centifolium*, 42.

Malvetius, see Paracletus.

Mannellus, Lucas O.P. (d. 1362). Wrote a *Compendium moralis philosophiae*, and a commentary on Seneca's Epistles. Quétif, I, 652. T. Kaeppeli, "Luca Mannelli (†1362) e la sua Tabulatio et expositio Senecae," *Archivum Fratrum Praedicatorum* 18 (1948), 237–264.

Mansuetus, Leonardus Perusinus O.P. (d. 1480). General of the Order 1474. Kristeller, *Supplementum Ficinianum* (1937), I, 125. T. Kaeppeli, *Inventari di libri di San Domenico di Perugia* (Rome, 1965).

Marcatel, Raphael de O.S.B. (d. 1508), abbot of St. Bavo at Gent. Collected an important library. K. A. van Acker, *Nationaal Biographisch Woordenboek*, II (1966), 507–512.

Marcus de Benevento O.S.B. Congr. Coelest. (c. 1465–c. 1524). Edited Thomas Aquinas, Ockam, Paulus Venetus and Ptolemy's *Geography*, and wrote two treatises against the astrology of Albertus Pighius. A. Birkenmajer, "Marco da Benevento und die angebliche Nominalistenakademie zu Bologna," *Philosophisches Jahrbuch* 38 (1925), 336–344. L. Thorndike, *A History of Magic*, V (1941), 199–201. Several of his mathematical writings are found in London, Lincoln's Inn, ms. Hale 107; cf. N. R. Ker, *Medieval Manuscripts in British Libraries*, I (Oxford, 1969), 130–131. Piana, 210–213. Herbert S. Matsen, *Alessandro Achillini* (forthcoming).

Mariano da Firenze O.M. (d. after 1523). Wrote several theological and historical works, and an *Itinerarium Urbis Romae* (ed. E. Bulletti, Rome, 1931). Weiss, *The Renaissance Discovery of Classical Antiquity* (1969), 86.

Marianus de Genazzano O.E.S.A. (d. 1498). Wrote orations, sermons and letters. Ossinger, 393–394. Perini, II, 101–102. Zumkeller (1963), 442.

Marianus Vulterranus O. Carth. (s. XV). *Eptalogus Salvatoris in cruce,* in 7 books, and other poems. Kristeller, *Iter,* II (index).

Marinus de Castignano O.F.M. (s. XV). Several logical writings (Vat. lat. 3037; Jena, ms. GB d 1).

Marsili (Marsigli), Luigi O.E.S.A. (c. 1330–94). Wrote Italian letters and a commentary on two poems of Petrarch. Ossinger, 558–561. Perini, II, 182–185. Arbesmann, 73–119. Mariani, 66–96. Cesare Vasoli, "La 'Regola per ben confessarsi' di Luigi Marsili," *Rinascimento* 4 (1953), 39–44.

Massarius, Ambrosius (de Cora) O.E.S.A. (d. 1485). He published orations, a life of Augustine, a commentary on his rule, a chronicle of the order, a *Defensorium ordinis Heremitarum S. Augustini* (against the Augustinian Canons) (Hain 5683–88; Copinger 1767). He also wrote a *Vita B. Christinae Spoletanae* and several orations (Paris. lat. 5621), a commentary on Gilbertus Porretanus' *Liber sex principiorum* (ms. Angelica 12), and a treatise *De animae dignitatibus* (mss. Angelica 835, Perugia G 2, Vat. Chigi E V 153). Several other orations and treatises are found in cod. Est. lat. 894 (*Iter,* I, 383). Ossinger, 260–264. Perini, II, 194–197. Zumkeller (1961), 73–75. His *Sermo de pace coram Paulo II* is found in Bologna, Biblioteca Universitaria, ms. 1719 (lat. 884), f. 246. Piana, *Ricerche,* 287.

Matthias Monachus O.S.B. (early s. XVI). Translated Gregory Nazianzen (Venice, Museo Correr, ms. Cicogna 988). Kristeller, *Iter,* II, 284. Sister Agnes Clare Way in *Catalogus Translationum,* II, 140–142.

Meisterlin, Sigismund O.S.B. (d. after 1488). Wrote histories of Augsburg and of Nürnberg in Latin and German. *Allgemeine Deutsche Biographie* 21 (1885), 264–266 (by Wegele); Joachimsen, 42–45; P. Joachimsohn, *Die humanistische Geschichtsschreibung in Deutschland,* vol. 1 (the only one published, Bonn, 1895).

Mezzavacca, Leon. O.S.B. Congr. Olivet. (late s. XV). See Valerio M. Cattana, "Un trattato sugli studi dei monaci della seconda metà del secolo XV," *Benedictina* 14 (1967), 234–258.

Mirabilibus, Nicolaus de O.P. (s. XV). *Disputatio nuper facta in domo Magnifici Laurentii Medicis* (ed. Florence 1489, Hain 11221). *De praedestinatione iuxta doctrinam Thomae Aquinatis* (dated 1493, ms. Wien 1566). Quétif, I, 878–879.

Mondellus, Ludovicus O.F.M. (d. after 1510). He posthumously edited

Mario Filelfo's *Novum epistolarium sive Ars scribendi epistolas.* The first edition appeared around 1481, and there were altogether 18 editions (the last two in 1511 and 1662, BN).

Montaldus, Adam, Genuensis O.E.S.A. (d. c. 1493). He published a poem *Passio Christi* (Hain 11554) and *Carmina contra Turcos* (Hain 11555) and composed other poems and orations. A prose work on the fall of Constantinople is found in ms. Utrecht, 742, and was twice published from this source, the second time by C. Desimoni, *Atti della Società Ligure di Storia Patria*, 10 (1874), 287–354, who also lists his works (p. 312–316). Ms. HC 387/1677 of the Hispanic Society of America in New York contains a stylistic revision by Montaldo of the medieval Latin version of the *Secretum Secretorum* attributed to Aristotle, along with a collection of political prophecies and accompanying letters to Ludovico Sforza and to Innocentius VIII.

Mucagatta, Filippo O.Serv. (d. 1511). Wrote logical works, and an *Oratio coram pontifice in die epiphanie* (1488). Besutti, 145–155.

Nanni, see Annius.

Nicoletti, see Paulus Venetus.

Nigrono, Petrus de O.S.B., Abbas S. Gregorii de Urbe (late s. XV). He owned mss. Ottob. lat. 318 and Siena G VII 32. Kristeller, "Giovanni Pico della Mirandola and His Sources," in *L'opera e il pensiero di Giovanni Pico della Mirandola* (Florence, 1965), I, 118–119.

Oddus, Leonardus, Perusinus O.S.B. (s. XVI). Cf. Ziegelbauer, III, 600. Wrote Latin poems (Monte Cassino ms. 563; Padua, Universitaria, ms. 439).

Orlandinus, Paulus O. Camald. (d. 1519). Wrote letters and poems, philosophical and theological treatises. Ziegelbauer, *Centifolium*, 50–52. Kristeller, *Supplementum Ficinianum*, II (1937), 348. Thorndike, *History*, IV (1934), 540, 702–703. E. Garin, *La cultura filosofica del Rinascimento italiano* (Florence, 1961), 113–114, 213–224.

Ottobi, see Hothby.

Pacioli, Luca O.F.M. (c. 1445–1514). *Summa de arithmetica, geometria, proportioni et proportionalita* (ed. 1494). *La divina proportione* (ed. 1503). Sbaralea, II, 176–178. Cantor, II (1892), 280–315. Robert Emmet Taylor, *No Royal Road: Luca Pacioli and His Times* (Chapel Hill, 1942).

Paduanus, Franciscus, de Florentia O.F.M. (s. XV). Wrote letters, moral treatises, and a critique of astrology. Thorndike, *History*,

IV (1934), 313–330. Kristeller, *Iter Italicum,* I (1963), II (1967), see the indices.

Pagnini, Sante O.P. (1470–1541). *Institutiones Hebraicae,* ed. 1520. *Veteris et novi testamenti nova translatio,* ed. 1527. *Thesaurus linguae sanctae,* ed. 1529. *Isagoge ad S. Literas,* ed. 1528. *Catena argentea in Pentateuchum,* ed. 1536. *Isagoge ad linguam Graecam,* ed. 1525. Quétif, II, 114–117. Hurter, II, 1515–17.

Palmerius, Nicolaus, Siculus O.E.S.A. (d. 1467), bishop of Catanzaro and Orte. He wrote letters, orations, sermons, disputations and a few poems (Magl. VIII 1434; Perugia F 52; Vat. lat. 5815) as well as several treatises against the Fraticelli (Magl. XXXIV 11; Vat. 4158; Chigi A IV 113). Several of these manuscripts were copied by or for Andreas Guazalotus of Prato who also composed an epitaph for Palmieri and had a coin struck for him. Cf. L. Oliger, "Ein unbekannter Traktat gegen die Mendikanten von Nikolaus Palmerius O.S.A., Bischof von Orte," *Franziskanische Studien* 3 (1916), 77–92 (who edits a text from Vat. lat. 4158). Perini, III, 48. G. B. Vaccaro, "Nicolò Palmeri vescovo di Orte e Città Castellana," *Bollettino Storico Agostiniano* 12 (1935), 83–86. Kristeller, *Iter Italicum,* I and II (index). For Guazzalotti's medal, see *Renaissance Bronzes, Statuettes, Reliefs and Plaquettes, Medals and Coins from the Kress Collection* (Washington, 1951), 174. J. Friedlaender, *Andrea Guazzalotti scultore pratese* (Prato, 1862). A. Mundó, "Una Lletra d'Alfons de Palència a Vespasià da Bisticci," in *Studi di Bibliografia e di Storia in Onore di Tammaro De Marinis,* III (Verona, 1964), 271–281.

Panetius (Panetti), Baptista O.Carm. (d. 1497). He wrote letters, poems and sermons, a *Historia Matildis comitissae,* and an Italian version of Josephus. He also was active as a scribe and book collector. De Villiers, 216–217. G. Bertoni, *La Biblioteca Estense e la Coltura Ferrarese ai tempi del Duca Ercole I* (Turin, 1903), 128–129, 176. The same, "Notizie sugli amanuensi estensi nel Quattrocento," *Archivum Romanicum* 2 (1918), 29–57 at 55–57 (with facsimile). Kristeller, *Iter,* I (index). Piana, *Ricerche,* 65–66. For some poems in a ms. in Leningrad, see L. Katushkina, *Ot Dante do Tasso* (Leningrad, 1972), 69–70.

Paracletus (de Malvetiis) Cornetanus O.E.S.A. (d. 1487), bishop of Acerno. Wrote orations and poems, and a dialogue *De bono mortis.*

Zumkeller (1963), 459. Kristeller, *Iter*, I and II (index). Piana, 285.

Paulus (Attavanti) Florentinus O.Serv. (d. 1499). He wrote a history of Mantua, a history of Perugia, a dialogue *De origine ordinis Servorum*, and several works on theology and canon law. Kristeller, *Supplementum Ficinianum*, I (1937), 117. *Dizionario Biografico degli Italiani*, 3 (1962), 531–532. *Mostra dei Codici Gonzagheschi, Catalogo* (by U. Meroni, Mantua, 1966), 82. Besutti and Serra, 79–113, 213–254.

Paulus (Nicoletti) Venetus O.E.S.A. (d. 1429). His philosophical works (commentaries on Aristotle, *Logica, Summa totius philosophiae naturalis, De compositione mundi*) were frequently copied and printed. *Logica Magna (Tractatus de Suppositionibus)*, ed. and trans. Alan R. Perreiah, Franciscan Institute Publications, Text Series 15 (St. Bonaventure, 1971). Ossinger, 920–924. Perini, IV, 39–46. Zumkeller (1963), 459–462. Hurter, II, 807–808. F. Momigliano, *Paolo Veneto e le correnti del pensiero religioso e filosofico del suo tempo* (Turin, 1907). A. R. Perreiah, "A Biographical Introduction to Paul of Venice," *Augustiniana* 17 (1967), 450–461.

Paulus de Venetiis O.Serv. Wrote a Prognosticon for 1470. Piana, 290.

Perionius, Joachimus O.S.B. (d. 1559). He translated several Greek patristic authors including Origen and John Chrysostom. Ziegelbauer, III, 348–351.

Persona, Christophorus O.S. Guil. (1416–86). Translated Origen, Agathias, Procopius and other Greek authors. Hurter, II, 1029. Ermolao Barbaro, *Epistolae, Orationes et Carmina*, ed. V. Branca (Florence, 1943), II, 157–158. Tiraboschi, VI, 1097–98. Cf. Panzer, *Annales Typographici* (Nuremberg, 1793–1803), VIII, 257, 106; 247, 22.

Petrus O.P. (s. XIV). Commentary on Valerius Maximus. Maria De Marco, "Un nuovo codice del commento di 'Frater Petrus O.P.' a Valerio Massimo," *Aevum* 30 (1956), 554–558.

Petrus de Castelletto O.E.S.A. (d. after 1402). His funeral sermon on Gian Galeazzo Visconti was often copied. It appears with his *Genealogia Vicecomitum* in Paris. lat. 5888. Ossinger, 217. Perini, I, 211–212; IV, 73. Zumkeller (1963), 464–465.

Petrus (Gavasseti) de Nubilaria (da Novellara) O.Carm. (d. c. 1504). He was an associate of Baptista Mantuanus and composed in Italian a treatise on the blood of Christ. Cf. Kristeller, *Thomisme*, 84–86, 130–137. See above, pp. 68–69.

Philippus Bergomensis O.S.B. (d. c. 1380). His commentary on the *Disticha Catonis* was frequently copied and also printed a few times. Ziegelbauer, III, 615. Zumkeller (1962), 59.

Philoxenus. See Filosseno.

Pipinus, Franciscus O.P. (d. after 1328). Made a Latin translation of Marco Polo, probably from the French. Kaeppeli, 392–395.

Pornasio, Raphael de O.P. (d. 1467). Prolific writer on theological and philosophical subjects. Quétif, I, 831–834; II, 823. Hurter, II, 888. K. Michel, *Der liber de consonancia nature et gracie des Raphael von Pornaxio, Beiträge zur Geschichte der Philosophie des Mittelalters*, XIX, 1 (1915). An important manuscript containing many of his treatises and described by Quétif is now cod. D 156 (formerly Phillipps 11076) in the library of St. Hugh's Charterhouse, Parkminster, Partridge Green, Horsham, Sussex where it was kindly shown to me by the librarian, Dom Anselm Stoelen.

Priolus, Eusebius O.Camald. (s. XVI). Wrote a funeral oration on Petrus Delphinus. Ziegelbauer, *Centifolium*, 20.

Puteus, see Archangelus de Burgonovo.

Quirinus, Petrus (previously Vincentius) O.Camald. (c. 1479–1514). He wrote poems, letters and theological treatises. See the literature cited above under Paulus Justinianus, and also Ziegelbauer, *Centifolium*, 63–65; Kristeller, *Iter Italicum*, I, 237. H. Jedin, "Vincenzo Quirini und Pietro Bembo," in *Miscellanea Giovanni Mercati*, IV, *Studi e Testi*, CXXIV (Vatican City, 1946), 407–424.

Ransanus, Petrus O.P. (c. 1420–92). Wrote orations, poems and works on history and hagiography. Quétif, I, 876–878. F. A. Termini, *Pietro Ransano* (Palermo, 1915).

Raphael Placentinus O.S.B. (s. XVI). A collection of his Latin poems was published in Cremona, 1518. Maria Pia Billanovich, "Una miniera di epigrafi e di antichità, Il Chiostro Maggiore di S. Giustina a Padova," *Italia Medioevale e Umanistica* 12 (1969), 197–293, at 222–223.

Razzi, Serafino O.P. (1531–1613). Author of works on history and hagiography, and also on philosophy and theology. Quétif, II, 386–388.

Razzi, Silvano O.Camald. (1527–1611). Prolific author of historical and biographical works. Ziegelbauer, *Centifolium*, 74–76.

Reisch, Gregor O.Carth. (d. 1525). His encyclopedia, entitled *Margarita philosophica*, was printed many times from 1503 to 1583.

*Allgemeine Deutsche Biographie* 28 (1889), 117 (by Prantl). K. Hartfelder, "Der Karthaeuserprior Gregor Reisch, Verfasser der *Margarita philosophica*," *Zeitschrift für die Geschichte des Oberrheins*, N.F. 5 (44, 1890), 170–200.

Reutter, Konrad O.S.B. (s. XVI). Wrote Latin poems and letters. K. Steiff, *Der erste Buchdruck zu Tübingen* (Tübingen, 1889), 178–179; K. Hartfelder, "Adam Werner von Themar," *Zeitschrift für vergleichende Litteraturgeschichte und Renaissancelitteratur*, N.F. 5 (1892), 214–235, at 224–225.

Roberto da Lecce, see Caraccioli.

Rontus, Matthaeus O.S.B. Olivet. (d. 1443). Wrote a Latin verse translation of Dante's *Comedy*. Tiraboschi, VI, 1205–6.

Rosselius, Hannibal Calaber O.F.M. (c. 1524–c. 1600). Wrote a voluminous commentary on the *Pimander* and *Asclepius* attributed to Hermes Trismegistus that was printed in 6 parts 1584–90, etc. Volumes 7–10 were planned, and at least volume 9 appeared in 1589 (BN). Sbaralea, I, 352. K. H. Dannenfeld in *Catalogus Translationum et Commentariorum*, ed. P. O. Kristeller, I (Washington, 1960), 143–144, 148.

Rovere, Francesco della, see Sixtus IV.

Rutgerus (Venray) Sycamber Can. Reg. (c. 1500). *Dialogus . . . de quantitate syllabarum cum paucis carminibus adiunctis*, ed. Cologne, 1502 (BM). H. Huesschen, "Rutgerus Sycamber und sein Musiktraktat," *Festschrift für W. Schiedmair, Beiträge zur rheinischen Musikgeschichte*, XX (Cologne, 1956), 34–35. V. Scholderer, "Rutgerus Sicamber and his writings," *Gutenberg-Jahrbuch* (1957), 129–130. Kristeller, *Renaissance News* 14 (1961), 6–11. A part of his collected writings is preserved in Cologne, Historisches Archiv der Stadt, ms. W 340, which contains many poems, letters and treatises. Other poems are scattered.

Ryckel, see Dionysius Cartusianus.

Sangrinus, Angelus O.S.B. (s. XVI). For his poems, see Monte Cassino mss. 158 and 577, and Vat. lat. 3488.

Sardi, Tommaso O.P. (d. 1517). He wrote a long poem in terza rima entitled *Anima Peregrina*, which survives in several mss. Quétif, II, 38. V. Rossi, *Quattrocento*, 257 and 259. G. Romagnoli, "Frate Tommaso Sardi e il suo poema inedito dell'*Anima Peregrina*," *Propugnatore* XVIII, 2 (1885), 289–333. Parts of the poem were published by A. Bianconi, *Girolamo Savonarola giudicato da un suo contemporaneo* (Rome, 1910) and by Margaret Rooke, *De anima peregrina, Poema di Fra Tommaso Sardi* . . . , *Smith College Studies in Modern Languages*, X, 4 (1929).

Savonarola, Girolamo O.P. (1452–98). M. Ferrara, *Bibliografia Savonaroliana* (Florence, 1958).

Scheiner, Christophorus S.J. (1575–1650). Astronomer. De Backer, II, 601–604.

Schifaldus, Thomas O.P. (d. after 1495). Wrote *De viris illustribus (Siculis) Ordinis Praedicatorum*; commentaries on Persius, on Horace's *Ars poetica* and on Ovid's *Epistola Sapphos*; Latin poems. Quétif-Echard, I, 882; G. Cozzucli, *Tommaso Schifaldo umanista siciliano del sec. XV, Società Siciliana per la Storia Patria, Documenti*, ser. 4, VI (Palermo, 1897). Eva M. Sanford in *Catalogus Translationum*, I, ed. P. O. Kristeller (Washington, 1960), 238.

Schlitpacher, Johannes O.S.B. (s. XV). Vansteenberghe, *Autour de la docte ignorance* (Münster, 1915).

Scutellius, Nicolaus Tridentinus O.E.S.A. (d. 1542). He translated Jamblichus, *De mysteriis* and *De vita Pythagorae* (ed. 1556), a dialogue of Lucian and four hymns of Homer (Vindob. 10056), Pletho's treatise on the differences between Plato and Aristotle (ibid.), Orpheus' *De gemmis* (ibid.), Proclus (ibid., Ricc. 155, Naples I H 46 and VIII F 7), Porphyry (Barb. lat. 322), pseudo-Plato, *De iusto* (Naples V F 5) and other philosophical texts. Cf. Ossinger, 823–824. Perini, III, 175–176. Zumkeller (1963), 454–455. Jedin, *Seripando*, I, 82–84. A. Segarizzi, "Da libri e manoscritti," *Studi Trentini* 1 (1920), 279–280.

Sebastianus, Constantius O.S.B. Congr. Olivet. (s. XVI). Translated Gregory Nazianzen (Vat. lat. 3500). See Sister Agnes Clare Way in *Catalogus Translationum*, II, 157.

Sellyng, William O.S.B. (d. 1494). Wrote orations and translated a homily of John Chrysostom. R. Weiss, *Humanism in England during the Fifteenth Century* (second ed., Oxford, 1957), 153–159 and passim; George B. Parks, *The English Traveler to Italy*, I (all published, Rome, 1954), 302 and passim; Piana, *Ricerche*, 94–96.

Seripandus, Hieronymus O.E.S.A. (1493–1563). Wrote many letters and theological works. Ossinger, 836–846. Perini, III, 193–201. H. Jedin, *Girolamo Seripando* (Würzburg, 1937). Jedin shows that Seripando in his early period was a Platonist (I, 43–80), and publishes some of his early *Quaestiones* (II, 441–464). Cf. *Papal*

*Legate at the Council of Trent: Cardinal Seripando,* trans. Frederick C. Eckhoff (St. Louis, 1947).

Severus Monachus, see Varinus.

Siberti, Jacobus O.S.B. (s. XV–XVI). His poems, letters and prose treatises are preserved in Bonn, Universitätsbibliothek, ms. S 247 and 359. Cf. Ziegelbauer, III, 588.

Sibylla, Bartholomeus O.P. (d. 1493). Wrote several orations. Kaeppeli, 168–169.

Sigfridus de Castello O.E.S.A. (c. 1500). Corresponded with Wimpfeling on the question whether St. Augustine was a monk. Zumkeller (1963), 471–472.

Sixtus IV (Franc. della Rovere) O.F.M. (1414–84). *De sanguine Christi, De potentia Dei, De conceptione Beatae Mariae Virginis, De futuris contingentibus* (Hain 14796–800). Wadding, 211–212. Sbaralea, III, 104–106. Hurter, II, 1006–7. C. Sericoli, *Immaculata B. M. Virginis Conceptio iuxta Xysti IV Constitutiones, Bibliotheca Mariana Medii Aevi,* V (Sibenic and Rome, 1945).

Sixtus Senensis O.P. (1520–69). *Bibliotheca Sancta* (ed. 1566, etc.). Quétif, II, 206–208. Secret, *Les dominicains,* 328–330.

Soldus, Jacobus, Burgensis O.Serv. (s. XV). Wrote a treatise *De peste.* Besutti, 167–177.

Spagnoli, see Baptista Mantuanus.

Spina, Bartholomaeus O.P. (d. 1546). He published many theological and philosophical treatises and defended in 1519 the immortality of the soul against both Caietanus and Pomponazzi (*Propugnaculum Aristotelis de immortalitate animae contra Thomam Caietanum; Tutela veritatis de immortalitate animae contra Petrum Pomponatium; Flagellum in tres libros apologiae eiusdem Peretti,* BM). Quétif, II, 126. Hurter, II, 1385–87.

Stephanus de Flandria O.Serv. (d. after 1494). *Quaestio de subiecto et propria passione. Logica.* Piana, 292 and 449–451; Besutti, 187–193.

Steuchus, Augustinus Can. Reg. (1496–1549). He is known for his biblical studies, for his critique of Luther, and above all for his influential *De perenni philosophia* (ed. 1540 and repeatedly afterwards). Hurter, II, 1483–85. Charles B. Schmitt, "Perennial Philosophy from Agostino Steuco to Leibniz," *Journal of the History of Ideas* 27 (1966), 505–532. P. O. Kristeller, *Renaissance Philosophy and the Mediaeval Tradition* (Latrobe, Pa., 1966), 77–78 and 100–101;

Charles B. Schmitt, "Prisca Theologia e Philosophia Perennis: due temi del Rinascimento italiano e la loro fortuna," in *Il pensiero italiano del Rinascimento e il tempo nostro*, ed. G. Tarugi (Florence, 1970), 211–236; G. Di Napoli, "Il concetto di 'Philosophia perennis' di Agostino Steuco nel quadro della tematica rinascimentale," in *Atti del Quarto Convegno di Studi Umbri* (Gubbio, 1966), 459–489.

Strada, Philippus Mediolanensis O.P. (d. after 1503). He was active in Venice as a copyist and as an author of poems in Latin and Italian. He also translated several works of Cicero into Italian. A. Segarizzi, "Reliquie d'una biblioteca monastica veneziana," *Il Libro e la Stampa*, N.S. 3 (1909), 1–5. F. Novati, "Ancora di Fra Filippo della Strada . . . ," ibid., N.S. 5 (1911), 117–128. A. Segarizzi, "Un calligrafo milanese," *Ateneo Veneto* 32 (1909), I, 63–77. Another manuscript of Lactantius copied by Philippus and accompanied by his verses and prologues is cod. 1 of the Istituto Barbara Melzi in Legnano.

Strassoldo, Ludovicus de, Piranensis O.F.M. (d. 1446). Wrote *Regulae memoriae artificialis* (Marc. lat. VI 274, [2885]), *Dialogus de papali potestate* to Eugene VI (Vat. lat. 4143) and another dialogue *De regia ac papali potestate* to the emperor Sigismund (Chigi D VI 97, also in British Museum, ms. Add. 19063). Sbaralea, II, 192–193. B. Ziliotto, "Frate Lodovico da Cividale e il suo 'Dialogus de papali potestate,' " *Memorie storiche forogiuliesi* 33–34 (1937–38), 151–191. A. Campana, "Un nuovo dialogo di Lodovico di Strassoldo, O.F.M. (1434) e il 'Tractatus de potestate regia et papali' di Giovanni di Parigi," in *Miscellanea Pio Paschini* (Rome, 1949), II, 127–156.

Sybertus, Jacobus, see Siberti.

Tedescus, Nicolaus Abbas Panormitanus O.S.B. (d. 1445). Famous canonist. Ziegelbauer, III, 198–201. Schulte, II, 312–313.

Testadraconibus, Matthaeus de, Florentinus, O. Serv. (s. XV–XVI in.). Author of a musical treatise. See Coussemaker, III (Paris, 1869), p. XXXI ff. Kristeller, *Studies*, 459, n. 31.

Thomas de Vio, see Caietanus.

Thomas (Liuti) Ferrariensis O.P. (d. after 1481). Wrote a long theological work in Italian and in dialogue form entitled *Declaratorio*. T. Kaeppeli, "Tommaso dai Liuti di Ferrara e il suo 'Declaratorio'," *Archivum Fratrum Praedicatorum* 20 (1950), 194–212. Gargan, 91.

APPENDIX B: HUMANISTS AND SCHOLARS    155

Titelmannus, Franciscus O.F.M. (s. XVI). *De consideratione dialectica* (ed. Antwerp, 1533, etc.), *Compendium naturalis philosophiae* (ed. 1535, etc.). Sbaralea, I, 303–304. W. Risse, *Die Logik der Neuzeit,* I (Stuttgart, 1964), 413–414. The same, *Bibliographia Logica,* I (Hildesheim, 1965), 47.

Tolosanus, Johannes Maria O.P. (d. c. 1595). Several theological works survive in mss. in Florence. He also wrote a treatise *De correctione calendarii.* Quétif, II, 123–124. Kristeller, *Iter,* I, 153 and 164.

Torquemada, see Turrecremata.

Traversagnus, Laurentius Gulielmus, Savonensis O.F.M. (1425–1503). Active in England, France and Austria as well as in Italy. His *Nova rhetorica* and his *Ars epistolandi* were published repeatedly. He also wrote letters, poems and theological treatises. Sbaralea, II, 167. Weiss 162–163 and 175. B. Černik, "Die Anfaenge des Humanismus im Chorherrenstift Klosterneuburg," *Jahrbuch des Stiftes Klosterneuburg* 1 (1908), 57–94, at 65–66, 73–74, 87–94. J. Ruysschaert, "Lorenzo Guglielmo Traversagni de Savone . . . ," *Archivum Franciscanum Historicum* 46 (1953), 195–210. The same, "Les manuscrits autographes de deux oeuvres de Lorenzo Guglielmo Traversagni imprimées chez Caxton," *Bulletin of the John Rylands Library* 36 (1953–54), 191–197. His treatise *De arte metrica* is in ms. Poole 118 of the Indiana University Library in Bloomington: cf. W. H. Bond and C. U. Faye, *Supplement to the Census of Medieval and Renaissance Manuscripts in the United States and Canada* (New York, 1962), p. 178, no. 14, who attribute the text to Lorenzo Valla; yet the photostat which I have seen clearly shows *Laurentius Qugli. Ty.* and *Laur. Qua. Ty.* Ronald H. Martin, "The *Epitome Margaritae Eloquentiae* of Laurentius Gulielmus de Saona," *Proceedings of the Leeds Philosophical and Literary Society, Literary and Historical Section* 14, pt. 4 (1971), 99–187. (not seen).

Traversarius, Ambrosius O.Camald. (1386–1439). His correspondence, along with the *Vita* by Lor. Mehus, was published in 1759. Apart from his letters and a few orations, he is famous for his translations of Aeneas Gazaeus, Basil, Diogenes Laertius, Dionysius Areopagita, Ephrem, John Chrysostom, Manuel Calecas, Palladius, Johannes Climacus and other authors. Ziegelbauer, *Centifolium,* 1–7. Hurter, II, 822–823. Voigt, I, 314–322 and passim. F. P. Luiso, *Riordinamento dell'Epistolario di A. Traversari* (Florence, 1903).

L. Bertalot, "Zwölf Briefe des Ambrogio Traversari," *Römische Quartalschrift* 29 (1915), 91\*–106\*. Agnes Clare Way, "The Lost Translations made by Ambrosius Traversarius of the Orations of Gregory Nazianzene," *Renaissance News* 14 (1961), 91–96.

Trevet, Nicolaus O.P. (c. 1258–c. 1334). He wrote commentaries on Augustine (*De civitate Dei*), Boethius (*De consolatione philosophiae* and the apocryphal *De disciplina scholarium*), Livy, the elder and the younger Seneca (*Declamationes* and Tragedies). Smalley, 58–65. Ruth J. Dean, "Cultural Relations in the Middle Ages: Nicholas Trevet and Nicholas of Prato," *Studies in Philology* 45 (1948), 541–564. The same, "The Dedication of Nicholas Trevet's Commentary of Boethius," ibid., 63 (1966), 593–603.

Trithemius, Johannes O.S.B. (1462–1516). His numerous works cover theology, history and the occult sciences, and he also wrote many letters and some orations and poems. For his bibliography, see Ziegelbauer, III, 217–333. Kapsner, I, 590–591; II, 380. *De scriptoribus ecclesiasticis* (ed. 1494, etc.; Hain 15613–14). *Catalogus illustrium virorum Germaniam . . . exornantium* (ed. 1495), etc.; Hain 15615–16). The collection of his *Opera historica* (Frankfurt, 1601; repr. 1966) includes his *Epistolae familiares,* probably from cod. Vat. Pal. lat. 730. From the extensive literature I cite only a few titles: I. Silbernagl, *Johannes Trithemius* (Landshut, 1868; 2nd ed. Regensburg, 1885). B. Thommen, *Die Prunkreden des Abtes Johannes Trithemius,* 2 pts. (*Beilage zum Jahrsbericht der Kant. Lehranstalt Sarnen,* 1933–34 and 1934–35). R. N. Behrendt, "The Library of Abbot Trithemius," *American Benedictine Review* 10 (1959), 67–85. Paul Lehmann, "Merkwuerdigkeiten des Abtes Johannes Trithemius," *Bayerische Akademie der Wissenschaften, Philosophisch-Historische Klasse, Sitzungsberichte,* Jahrgang 1961, no. 2 (lists the mss. owned by Trithemius). P. Chacornac, *Grandeur et adversité de Jean Trithème* (Paris, 1963). Christel Steffen, "Untersuchungen zum 'Liber de scriptoribus ecclesiasticis' des Johannes Trithemius," *Archiv für Geschichte des Buchwesens* 10 (1969), 1247–1354. Klaus Arnold, *Johannes Trithemius (1462–1516)* (Würzburg, 1971). The same, "Johannes Trithemius und Bamberg," *107. Bericht des Historischen Vereins Bamberg* (1971), 161–189.

Trombetta, Antonius O.F.M. (1436–1517). Wrote several philosophical treatises including a *Questio de animarum humanarum plurifica-*

*tione* (ed. 1498; Hain 15646) and *Quaestiones metaphysicales* (ed. 1493; Hain 15647). Sbaralea, I, 98. Hurter, II, 1105–6. Brotto and Zonta, 203–207. A. Poppi, "Lo Scotista Patavino Antonio Trombetta," *Il Santo* 2 (1962), 349–367.

Turrecremata, Johannes de O.P. (1388–1468). Prolific writer on theology and canon law. Quétif, I, 837–841. Hurter, II, 880–884. J. M. Garrastachu, "Los manuscritos del Cardenal Torquemada en la Biblioteca Vaticana," *La Ciencia Tomista* 41 (1930), 188–217, 291–322.

Turrianus, Joachimus O.P. (d. 1500). Was the owner of important mss. Gargan, 104–107.

Urbanus Bononiensis "Averroista" O.Serv. (s. XIV). Pupil of Gentile da Cingoli. *Expositio commentarii Averrois super physiciam Aristotelis*, ed. Venice, 1492. Besutti, 195–208. Charles J. Ermatinger, "Urbanus Averroista and Some Early Fourteenth Century Philosophers," *Manuscripta* 11 (1967), 3–38. Juliana Hill Cotton, "Politian and Fra Urbano Averroista's Expositio," ibid., 12 (1968), 104–106.

Varinus, Severus O. Cist. (d. 1549). Wrote a few letters and poems, and translated Aristotle (*Nicomachean Ethics*, book I) and Lucian. Kristeller, *Studies*, 156–158. Livorno ms. CXII 3, 26 (*Iter*, I, 250). Tiraboschi, VII, 1497–1502.

Vegius, Mapheus O.E.S.A. (1407–58). Famous humanist. He wrote many religious and other poems, including a thirteenth book of Vergil's *Aeneid; De perseverantia religionis; De memorabilibus Basilicae S. Petri; De verborum iuris significatione; De educatione liberorum* (ed. Sister W. M. Fanning and Sister A. S. Sullivan, Washington, 1933–36). M. Minoia, *La vita di Maffeo Vegio* (Lodi, 1896). L. Raffaele, *Maffeo Vegio* (Bologna, 1909). Anna Cox Brinton, *Maphaeus Vegius and his thirteenth book of the Aeneid* (Stanford, 1930). *Studi su Maffeo Vegio*, ed. S. Corvi (Lodi, 1959). V. Rossi, *Il Quattrocento* (Milan, 1933), 283–284. *Enciclopedia Cattolica*, 12 (1954), 1162–64.

Venray, see Rutgerus Sycamber.

Vigerius, Marcus O.F.M. (d. 1516). Theological works. Sbaralea, II, 211–212.

Vincentius de Aggsbach O.Carth. (s. XV). See E. Vansteenberghe, *Autour de la docte ignorance* (Münster, 1915).

Vincentius de Castronovo, see Bandellus.

Vincentius de S. Geminiano, see Mainardus.

Vio, Thomas de, see Caietanus.

Wagner, Leonhard O.S.B. (1454–1522). Active as a copyist and teacher of calligraphy. His *Proba centum scripturarum*, dedicated to Maximilian I and preserved in manuscript, includes several samples of Gothic handwriting that may have served as models for the German Gothic print. A. Schroeder, "Leonhard Wagner's 'Proba centum scripturarum'," *Archiv für die Geschichte des Hochstifts Augsburg* 1 (1909–11), 372–385. Konrad F. Bauer, "Leonhard Wagner, der Schoepfer der Fraktur," *Zeitschrift für Bücherfreunde* 40 (1936), Beilage. The same, "Noch einmal: Leonhard Wagner," ibid., pp. 1–3. C. Wehmer, "Augsburger Schreiber aus der Frühzeit des Buchdrucks, I. Leonhard Wagner und seine *Proba centum scripturarum*," *Beiträge zur Inkunabelkunde*, N.F. 1 (1935), 78–111. The same, "Leonhard Wagner der Schoepfer der Fraktur?", ibid., N.F. 2 (1938), 153–167.

Walsingham, Thomas O.S.B. (d. ca. 1422). Apart from chronicles, he wrote *Prohemia poetarum* (BM Harl. 2693), a commentary on Ovid's *Metamorphoses* (*Archana poetarum*, ed. Robert A. van Kluyve, Durham, N.C., 1968) and a musical treatise (BM Lansdowne 763, f. 97v). Cf. *Dictionary of National Biography* 20 (1921), 699–701. R. Weiss, *Humanism in England* (2nd ed., Oxford, 1957), 10 and 31.

Whethamstede (Frumentarius), Johannes O.S.B. (d. 1465), abbot of St. Albans. His antiquarian work *Granarium* (*De viris illustribus*) partly survives in manuscript. Ziegelbauer, III, 195–198. Kapsner, I, 624; II, 386. *Dictionary of National Biography*, XX, 1358–60. Schirmer, 82–98 (2nd ed. 70–90). Weiss, 30–38 and passim.

Wiler (Willer), Franciscus O.F.M. (s. XV–XVI). Wadding, 95. Sbaralea, I, 308. Luxembourg, Bibliothèque, ms. 236 contains his *Lignum pomiferum Beatae Mariae Virginis* (dedicated 1494 to Trithemius), several religious poems, a treatise on the Immaculate Conception (1490), a *Cosmographia* (1500) and a *Directorium confessorum* (1490).

# ADDENDA AND CORRIGENDA

# ADDENDA AND CORRIGENDA

*Paul O. Kristeller and Edward P. Mahoney*

ADDENDUM: "THE SCHOLAR AND HIS PUBLIC IN THE LATE
MIDDLE AGES AND THE RENAISSANCE"

See now Paul O. Kristeller, "Latein und Vulgärspraches im Italien
des 14. und 15. Jahrhunderts," *Deutsches Dante-Jahrbuch* 59 (1984), 7–
35. This article appeared in a revised form as "Latin and Vernacular
in Fourteenth- and Fifteenth-Century Italy," *Journal of the Rocky
Mountain Medieval and Renaissance Association* 6 (1985), 105–126.

ADDENDA AND CORRIGENDA: "THE CONTRIBUTION OF
RELIGIOUS ORDERS TO RENAISSANCE THOUGHT
AND LEARNING"

The following members of Religious Orders may be mentioned for
their contributions to philosophy and science: Antonius Andreas
O.F.M.; Domingo Bañez O.P.; Cristophorus Clavius S.J.; Ioannes
Canonicus O.F.M.; Filippo Fantoni O. Camald.; Joannes Gratiadei
O.P.; Isidorus de Isolanis O.P.; Benito Pereira S.J.; Antonio Rubio
S.J.; Domingo de Soto O.P.; Franciscus Toletus S.J.; Paulus Valla S.J.;
Joannes Versor O.P.; Mutius Vitelleschi S.J. On the contribution of
Andreas, Canonicus and Toletus to scientific discussions, see Pierre
Duhem, *Le système du monde*, 6 (Paris, 1954), pp. 386–390 and 423–
438; Anneliese Maier, *Zwei Grundprobleme der scholastischen Naturphil-
ophie*, 2nd ed. (Rome, 1951), pp. 197–200; Edward Grant, *Much Ado
about Nothing: Theories of Space and Vacuum from the Middle Ages to the
Scientific Revolution* (Cambridge, 1981); and E. P. Mahoney, "Aristotle
as 'The Worst Natural Philosopher' (*pessimus naturalis*) and 'The Worst
Metaphysician' (*pessimus metaphysicus*): His Reputation among Some
Franciscan Philosophers (Bonaventure, Francis of Meyronnes, Antonius Andreas, and Joannes Canonicus) and Later Reactions," in
*Die Philosophie im 14. und 15. Jahrhundert. In memoriam Konstanty Mich-
alski (1879–1947)*, Bochumer Studien zur Philosophie, 10 (Amsterdam, 1988), pp. 261–273. The scientific contribution of Pereira, Rubio, de Soto and Toletus is presented by William A. Wallace in his
"Traditional Natural Philosophy," in *The Cambridge History of Renaissance Philosophy*, eds. Charles B. Schmitt, Quentin Skinner and Eck-

hard Kessler (Cambridge, 1988), pp. 201–235. For further data on science and the Jesuits, see Wallace's *Galileo and His Sources: The Heritage of the Collegio Romano in Galileo's Science* (Princeton, 1984). Among those studied are Clavius, Pereira, Toletus, Paulus Valla and Vitelleschi.

## ADDENDA TO GENERAL BIBLIOGRAPHY:

Bérubé, Camille (ed). *Regnum Hominis et Regnum Dei: Acta Quarti Congressus Scotistici Internationalis, Patavii, 24–29 septembris 1976,* vol. II: *Sectio specialis: La tradizione scotista veneto-padovana.* Studia Scholastico-Scotista, 7. Rome, 1978.

Bevilacqua, Mario. "Tipografi ecclesiastici nel Quattrocento," *La Bibliofilia* 45 (1943), 1–29.

Elm, Kasper. "Mendikanten und Humanisten im Florenz des Tre- und Quattrocento," in *Die Humanisten in ihrer politischen und sozialen Umwelt, Zum Problem der Legitimierung humanistischer Studien in den Bettelorden, Kommission für Humanismusforschung, Mitteilung,* 3. Boppard, 1976, 51–85.

Poppi, Antonio (ed.). *Storia e cultura al Santo.* Vicenza, 1976.

## ADDENDUM TO APPENDIX A: LIBRARIES OF RELIGIOUS ORDERS:

Padova, Italy. Biblioteca Antoniana. Giuseppe Abate and Giovanni Luisetto, *Codici e manoscritti della Biblioteca Antoniana.* Vicenza, 1975.

## ADDENDA TO APPENDIX B: HUMANISTS AND SCHOLARS OF THE RELIGIOUS ORDERS:

Adrianus Carthusiensis (d. 1411). Revised Petrarch's *De remediis utriusque fortunae.* See Nicholas Mann, "New Light on a Recently Discovered Manuscript of the 'De remediis'," *Italia Medioevale e Umanistica* 12 (1969), 317–322.

B. Albertus de Sarteano O.F.M. (1385–1450). See F. Biccalturi, "Un Francescano umanista, il B. Alberto de Sarteano (1385–1450)," *Studi Francescani* 35 (1938), 22–48; Floro Biccellari, "Il Beato Alberto da Sarteano: Apostolo ed apologista," *Studi Francescani* 35 (1938), 97–127; idem, "Il B. Alberto Sarteano: letterato e Santo," *ibid.* 36 (1939), 265–287.

Antonius de Bitonto O.F.M. (d. 1459) Sbaralea, I, 71–72. Attanasio

Gaeta, *Antonio da Bitonto O.F.M., oratore e telogo del secolo XV* (Baronissi, 1952). C. Piana, "Antonius de Bitonto O.F.M., praedicator et orator saec. XV," *Franciscan Studies* 13 (1953), 178–197.

Augustinus Cremenis O.E.S.A. *Liber Ephimerorum,* s. XV. Bergamo Delta V 44, now MA 316. *Iter,* V, 481.

Bartholomaeus Sulmonensis O.P. Wrote a grammar and Latin poem. W. Keith Percival, "The *Artis Grammaticae Opusculum* of Bartolomeo Sulmonese: A Newly Discovered Latin Grammar of the Quattrocento," *Renaissance Quarterly* 31 (1978), 39–47.

Borghini, Vincenzo Maria O.S.B. (1515–1580). See Gianfranco Folena in *Dizionario biografico degli italiani* 12 (1970), 680–689.

Gisalbertus de Pergamo O.F.M. *Commentary on 'Disticha Catonis'.* Bergamo ms. Alpha I 37, now MAB 29. *Iter,* V, 477.

Ludovicus de Ferraria O.P. *Compendium Ethicorum Aristotelis.* Newberry Library, ms. 99.1, dedicated to Card. Oliverius Carafa. *Iter,* V, 246. Quétif-Echard, I, 882–883.

Nicolaus or Nicolutius de Esculo, O.P. *Declamationes Senece in claro stilo reducte,* in ten books. Copied in Venice, 1392. Columbia University Library, Plimpton ms. 114. *Iter,* V, 304–305. Quétif-Echard, I, 566–567.

Frater Nicolaus Montanus. Composed a vocabulary, Columbia University Library, Plimpton ms. 152. *Iter,* V, 306.

Ransanus, Petrus O.P. (c. 1420–1492). *Epithoma rerum Hungaricarum,* ed. P. Kulesar, Budapest, 1977. mss. Palermo, Biblioteca Comunale 3 Qq C 60, f. 224v–331 and Budapest, Szechenyi Library Clmae 249. *Iter,* II, 26 and IV, 291. Quétif-Echard, I, 876–878.

Pornasio, Raphael de O.P. (d. 1467). *De arte magica, De angelica virtute.* Owned by Jac. Parleo. Vienna ms. lat. 3155. Quétif-Echard, I, 831–834 and II, 823.

Sixtus IV (Franc. della Rovere) O.F.M. (1414–1484). Lucio Pusci, "Profilo di Francesco della Rovere poi Sisto IV," in *Storia e cultura al Santo,* ed. A. Poppi (Vicenza, 1976), pp. 279–287. Egmont Lee, *Sixtus IV and Men of Letters* (Rome, 1978).

Tolosanus, Johannes Maria O.P. (mentioned on p. 155) died in 1545.

Trombetta, Antonius O.F.M. (1436–1517). Antonino Poppi, *La filosofia nello studio francescano del Santo al Padova* (Padua, 1989), pp. 63–85; E. P. Mahoney, "Antonio Trombetta and Agostino Nifo on Averroes and Intelligible Species: A Philosophical Dispute at the University of Padua," in *Storia e cultura al Santo,* pp. 289–301.

# STUDIES ON ST. THOMAS AND THE ITALIAN RENAISSANCE (1974–1991): AN OVERVIEW

# STUDIES ON SAINT THOMAS AND THE ITALIAN RENAISSANCE (1974–1991): AN OVERVIEW

*Edward P. Mahoney and James B. South*

During the years since the publication of the English version of Paul O. Kristeller's "Thomism and the Italian Thought of the Renaissance," a remarkable number of studies touching on Saint Thomas and the Renaissance have been published. We shall cite a large proportion of those articles and books listed in the *Répertoire bibliographique de la philosophie*, which has now the title *International Philosophical Bibliography*, the *Rassegna di letteratura tomistica*, the *Bulletin de théologie ancienne et médiévale*, and the *Bibliographie internationale de l'Humanisme et de la Renaissance* for the years 1974–1991 that relate to the topic. Since no general history of Thomism in the Italian Renaissance has yet been published, Kristeller's study remains the basic reference tool. Unfortunately some scholars seem not to know the 1974 English translation which contains some bibliographical references not found in the original 1967 French version. It is to be hoped that those offering courses in Renaissance Intellectual History or the History of Late Medieval and Renaissance Philosophy will draw their students' attention to the English translation and the supplementary remarks in this "overview" that are intended to bring Kristeller's valuable study up-to-date.

Two studies merit particular attention, since their titles suggest comprehensive surveys of Thomas's impact on the late medieval and Renaissance periods. The first is the more helpful. Stefan Swiezawski, "Le thomisme à la fin du moyen âge," in *San Tommaso, Fonti e riflessi del suo pensiero. Saggi*, Studi Tomistici, 1 (Rome, 1974), 225–48 chronicles a wide range of late medieval and Renaissance authors and the interest shown in Thomas at Paris, Toulouse, Louvain, Cologne, Padua, Pavia, and Cracow among other places. The Renaissance figures whom he discusses include academic Aristotelians such as Nicoletto Vernia, Pietro Pomponazzi, and Agostino Nifo; Dominicans such as Dominic of Flanders, Francesco (Securo) di Nardò and Thomas de Vio (Cajetan); Florentine figures such as Saint Antoninus and Savonarola (both of whom were Dominicans) and also Marsilio Ficino; and other noteworthy Renaissance figures such as Pletho, Cardinal Bessarion, George of Trebizond and Giovanni Pico della Mirandola. The second study, Giovanni di Napoli's "Tommaso d'Aquino nel Rinascimento," in his *Studi sul Rinascimento* (Naples, 1973), pp. 279–309, is informative but limited to Valla, Ficino, Pico, Pomponazzi, Cajetan and Campanella. Unfortunately his essay could not be cited in the original printing of the English version of Kristeller's study.

Among the most straight-forward contributions to the history of Thomism in the Renaissance are those that concern Italian Dominican Thomists. The most famous of them is surely Thomas de Vio, better known as Cajetan. Jared Wicks, *Cajetan und die Anfänge der Reformation*, Katholisches Leben und Kirchenreform im Zeitalter der Glaubensspaltung, 43 (Münster, 1983), pp. 10–19 situates the young de Vio in the intellectual milieu of the University of Padua toward the end of the fifteenth century. In his earlier article, "Thomism between Renaissance and Reformation: the Case of Cajetan," *Archiv für Reformationsgeschichte* 68 (1977), 9–31, Wicks carefully brought out Cajetan's key role in Catholic theology of the period, the Thomistic aspect of his writings, but also his disagreement with Thomas on the question whether the immortality of the human soul was demonstrable by human reason. Antonino Poppi, in his "Scienza e filosofia nelle scuole tomista e scotista all'Università di Padova nel. sec. XV," in *Scienza e filosofia all'Università di Padova nel quattrocento*, Contributi alla storia dell'Università di Padova, 15, ed. A. Poppi (Trieste, 1983), pp. 329–343 takes particular care to contrast Cajetan's views to those of the Franciscan theologian, Antonio Trombetta. That study has been reprinted in Poppi's valuable collection, *La filosofia nello Studio francescano del Santo a Padova* (Padua, 1989), pp. 115–126. Also of note is Denis R. Janz, "Cajetan: a Thomist Reformer?," *Renaissance and Reformation* 6 (1982), 94–121.

Several Dominican scholars have made valuable contributions to our knowledge of other members of the Thomist school in Renaissance Italy. See Armando F. Verde, "Domenico di Fiandra: intransigente tomista non gradito nello Studio Fiorentio," *Memorie Domenicane* 7 (1976), 304–21; Giacinto Arturo Scaltriti, "S. Tommaso d'Aquino in Savonarola," in *Tommaso d'Aquino nel suo settimo centenario: Atti del Congresso Internazionale* [1974], II (Naples, 1976), 152–158; and Michael Tavuzzi, "Chrysostomus Javelli O.P. (ca. 1470–1538)—A Biobibliographical Essay: Part I, Biography," *Angelicum* 67 (1990), 457–482; "Part II, Bibliography," *Angelicum* 68 (1991), 109–121.

The role that Thomas played in the teaching of the Jesuits at the

Roman College has been clarified by Charles Lohr in his "Jesuit Aristotelianism and Sixteenth-Century Metaphysics," in *PARA-DOSIS: Studies in Memory of Edwin A. Quain* (New York, 1976), pp. 203–220. In like fashion, Leonard Kennedy indicates in his "Early Jesuits and Immortality of the Soul," *Gregorianum* 69 (1988), 117–131 how closely Francisco de Toledo, Francisco Suarez, and Gregory of Valencia, all of whom taught at the Roman College, followed Thomas on this key topic. F. Edward Cranz, in his study, "The Publishing History of the Aristotle Commentaries of Thomas Aquinas," *Traditio* 34 (1978), 157–192, at 179–180 examines the teaching aims and methods of the Jesuits in relation to the decline both in printings of Aquinas and also in his influence at the end of the sixteenth century. Cranz lists the editions of Thomas's commentaries, which were mainly printed in Italy, and analyzes the different translations of Aristotle used in these editions. This phenomenon of printing Thomas's commentaries on Aristotle with Renaissance humanistic translations was noted by Charles B. Schmitt in his basic book *Aristotle and the Renaissance* (Cambridge, Mass., 1983), pp. 19–20. Unfortunately he does not stress the role of Thomism in the development of Renaissance Aristotelianism. On a late-sixteenth century Roman edition of Thomas's works, see Gian Ludovico Masetti Zannini, "Intorno all'edizione romana delle opere di S. Tommaso (1569–1571)," in *San Tommaso, Fonti e riflessi del suo pensiero* pp. 285–290. Zannini shows that the edition was undertaken and subsidized by the Dominican Order with some help from Pope Pius V.

Some attention has been paid to Thomas's influence on the theological thought of both Jesuits and Dominicans during the Renaissance by Johannes Stöhr, "Die Theozentrik der theologischen Wissenschaften des Hl. Thomas von Aquin und ihre Diskussion bei neuzeitlichen Kommentatoren," in *Thomas von Aquin: Werk und Wirkung im Licht neuerer Forschungen*, ed. Albert Zimmermann with Clemens Kopp, Miscellanea Mediaevalia, 19 (Berlin and New York, 1988), pp. 494–498. Among the Dominicans mentioned are Thomas de Vio (Cajetan), Sylvester Mazzolini Prierias, and Crisostomo Javelli, while among the Jesuits mentioned are Gregory of Valencia, Francisco Suarez, Robert Bellarmine and Francisco de Toledo. The relation of Suarez's philosophical ideas to those of Thomas has interested recent historians. See for example Jorge J. E. Gracia, "Suarez's Criticism of the Thomistic Principle of Individuation," in *Tommaso d'Aquino nel suo settimo centenario: Atti del Congresso Internazionale* [1974], IX (Naples, 1978), 563–568; Francisco Peccorini, "Knowledge of the Singular: Aquinas, Suarez and Recent Interpreters," *The Thomist* 38 (1974), 606–655; and Jean-François Courtine, *Suarez et le système de la métaphysique* (Paris, 1990).

Many of the Aristotelians who dominated university teaching often showed a respectful and keen interest in Thomas's ideas. This has been brought out in regard to Pomponazzi by Martin Pine in his "Pietro Pomponazzi and the Medieval Tradition of God's Foreknowledge," in *Philosophy and Humanism: Renaissance Essays in Honor of Paul Oskar Kristeller*, ed. E. P. Mahoney (New York and Leiden, 1976), pp. 100–115 and in his book, *Pietro Pomponazzi: Radical Philosopher of the Italian Renaissance* (Padua, 1986). For the impact of Thomas on Agostino Nifo, Pomponazzi's life-long rival, see Edward P. Mahoney, "Agostino Nifo and Saint Thomas Aquinas," *Memorie Domenicane* 7 (1976), 195–226. For a sketch of traces of Thomas's ideas in Nicoletto Vernia, Antonio Trombetta and the early Pomponazzi and Nifo, see the same author's "Saint Thomas and the School of Padua at the End of the Fifteenth Century," *Proceedings of the American Catholic Philosophical Association* 48 (1974), 277–85. Also relevant to the question of Thomas's influence at Padua are comments to be found in Antonino Poppi's helpful *Introduzione all'aristotelismo padovano*, 2nd revised ed. (Padua, 1991). For a critical evaluation of Pomponazzi's critique of Thomas in his celebrated *De immortalitate animae*, published in 1516, see John L. Treloar, "Pomponazzi's Critique of Aquinas's Arguments for the Immortality of the Soul," *The Thomist* 54 (1990), 453–470.

Thomas's metaphysics and its role in Renaissance discussions are given passing notice in Charles Lohr's lengthy essay, "Metaphysics," in *The Cambridge History of Renaissance Philosophy*, ed. Charles B. Schmitt, Quentin Skinner and Eckhard Kessler (Cambridge, 1988), pp. 537–638. On Thomas's conception of metaphysical hierarchy and its role in discussions by Renaissance philosophers such as Bessarion, Ficino and Nifo, see Edward P. Mahoney, "Metaphysical Foundations of the Hierarchy of Being according to Some Late Medieval and Renaissance Philosophers," in *Philosophies of Existence: Ancient and Medieval*. ed. Parviz Morewedge (New York, 1982), pp. 165–257, and "Il concetto di gerarchia nella tradizione padovana e nel primo pensiero moderno," in *Aristotelismo veneto e scienza moderna*, ed. Luigi Olivieri (Padua, 1983), pp. 729–741.

The relevance of Thomas to the study of late medieval and Renaissance history of science is now generally accepted. Of particular interest here is William A. Wallace's "Galileo and the Thomists," in *St. Thomas Aquinas (1274–1974): Commemorative Studies*, eds. Armand Maurer et al. (Toronto, 1974), 293–330, which appeared in a "heavily revised" version in his *Prelude to Galileo*, Boston Studies in the Philosophy of Science, 62 (Dordrecht, Boston, London, 1981), pp. 160–191. Wallace also gives attention to Thomas's influence on early Jesuits in his *Galileo and His Sources: The Heritage of the Collegio Romano in Galileo's Science* (Princeton, 1984). Other contributions to be noted are Giuseppe Mario Galli, "San Tommaso d'Aquino e la scienza. S. Tommaso precursore di Copernico?," *Memorie Domenicane* 7 (1976), 322–38 and Edward Grant, "Celestial Matter: a Medieval and Galilean Cosmological Problem," *Journal of Medieval and Renaissance Studies* 13 (1983), 157–86, at 172–175.

Although no general work examining the impact of Thomas's ethical thought on the Renaissance has yet appeared, scholars have noted that influence. Jill Kraye, in her study, "Moral Philosophy," which appeared in *The Cambridge History of Renaissance Philosophy*, points out the influence of Thomas's division of moral philosophy (p. 304). She also observes that Thomas was the most influential commentator on Aristotle's *Nicomachean Ethics* (pp. 326–328). And in another study in the same volume, "Fate, Fortune, Providence and Human Freedom," Antonino Poppi carefully shows how important an authority Thomas was for Pomponazzi, even if he did reject Thomas's positions (pp. 653–660). Martin Pine, in his article and book cited above, also indicates how seriously Pomponazzi treated Thomas in his own discussions regarding providence and freedom. It should be noted that Louis Verecke has studied Cajetan among others in his "Les commentaires thomistes du traité de la 'lex nova' de saint Thomas d'Aquin au début de XVIe siècle," *Studia Moralia* 23 (1985), 163–86. In like fashion, Leonard Kennedy situates the Thomist tradition in relation to Scotus, Ockham and fourteenth-century developments in his "Thomistic Ethics and Divine Absolute Power," in *Atti del IX Congresso Tomistico Internazionale*, IV, Studi tomistici, 43 (Vatican City, 1991), pp. 194–199 and makes brief reference to Cajetan and Capreolus.

In his study on "Political Philosophy" in *The Cambridge History of Renaissance Philosophy*, Quentin Skinner points out Thomas's impact on the political thought of Remigio de'Girolami, Ptolemy of Lucca and Henry of Rimini, especially regarding the question of what is the best form of government (pp. 395–399). But he contrasts the humanists' stress on the Roman ideals of honor, glory and fame as motives for rulers with rejection of such motivation by Thomas and his followers (p. 413). Skinner also treats of Thomas and his influence in his magisterial *The Foundations of Modern Political Thought*, 2 vols. (Cambridge, 1978). The Thomistic element in Dante's background is delineated by Joan M. Ferrante in her important work, *The Political Vision of the 'Divine Comedy'* (Princeton, 1984). There is a significant attempt to connect the political thought of Thomas and other medieval Aristotelians both with later Italian discussions regarding "mixed constitution" and also with the development of republicanism in James M. Blythe's recent book *Ideal Government and the Mixed Constitution in the Middle Ages* (Princeton, 1992). Odd Langholm studies Thomas's economic views and their influence on such fourteenth-century Italian Thomists as Ptolemy of Lucca, Remigio de'Girolami and John of Naples in his *Economics in the Medieval Schools, Wealth, Exchange, Value, Money and Usury according to the Paris Theological Tradition 1200–1350*, Studien und Texte zur Geistesgeschichte des Mittelalters, 29 (Leiden, 1992), pp. 198–248 and 454–478.

Given Marsilio Ficino's important place in the history of Renaissance philosophy, it is no surprise that several scholars have studied the relationship of his thought to that of Thomas. Perhaps the most ambitious is Ardis B. Collins, *The Secular is Sacred. Platonism and Thomism in Marsilio Ficino's "Platonic Theology"*, International Archives of the History of Ideas, 69 (The Hague, 1974). There are also relevant discussions in Alessandra Tarabochia Canavero, "Agostino e Tommaso nel Commento di Marsilio Ficino all' *Epistola ai Romani*," *Rivista di filosofia neo-scolastica* 65 (1973), 815–24; eadem, "L'amicizia nell'epistolario di Marsilio Ficino," *ibid.*, 67 (1975), 422–429; Jerry Griswold, "Aquinas, Dante, and Ficino on Love: an Explication of the *Paradiso*, XXVI, 25–39," *Studies in Medieval Culture* (Kalamazoo), 8–9 (1976), 151–161; and Cesare Vasoli, "Ficino e il 'De christiana religione'," in *Die Philosophie im 14. und 15. Jahrhundert: In memoriam Konstanty Michalski (1879–1947)*, ed. Olaf Pluta, Bochumer Studien zur Philosophie, 10 (Amsterdam, 1988), pp. 151–190. Kristeller established the debt of Ficino, Landino and others to Thomas in his "The Active and Contemplative Life in Renaissance Humanism," in *Arbeit*,

*Musse, Meditation: Betrachtungen zur "Vita activa" und "Vita contempla-tiva,* ed. Brian Vickers (Zurich, 1985), pp. 133–152. And in his "Vita attiva e vita contemplativa in un brano inedito di Bornio da Sala e in S. Tommaso d'Aquino," in *Essere e libertà: Studi in onore di Cornelio Fabro* (Perugia, 1984), pp. 211–224, Kristeller shows that Ficino's concept of the transformation of the lover into the object of his love is derived not from Dante or the Dolce stil nuovo poets but from Thomas (*In III Sent.*, dist. 27, q. 1, a. 1, solutio). Ficino's views on magic and his use of Thomas in his *De vita* have received the attention both of Brian P. Copenhaver in his studies, "Scholastic Philosophy and Renaissance Magic in the *De vita* of Marsilio Ficino," *Renaissance Quarterly* 37 (1984), 523–554 and "Renaissance Magic and Neoplatonic Philosophy: 'Ennead' 4.3–5 in Ficino's 'De vita coelitus comparanda'," in *Marsilio Ficino e il ritorno di Platone: Studi e documenti*, II, ed. Gian Carlo Garfagnini (Florence, 1986), pp. 351–369, and also of Carol V. Kaske in the Introduction to *Marsilio Ficino: Three Books on Life. A Critical Edition and Translation with Introduction and Notes by Carol V. Kaske and John R. Clark* (Binghamton, N.Y., 1989), pp. 52, 55 and 61–66.

Thomas's influence on another celebrated Renaissance philosopher, Giovanni Pico della Mirandola, was studied by Giovanni Di Napoli in his "Giovanni Pico della Mirandola e la teoresi tomistica dell' *Ipsum esse*," in *San Tommaso. Fonti e reflessi del suo pensiero*, pp. 249–281. There are various references to Thomas in Henri de Lubac's *Pic de la Mirandole. Études et discussions* (Paris, 1974) that enable the reader to appreciate the role he played as an authority for Pico. The metaphysics of Thomas and Giordano Bruno are compared by Michelangelo Ghio, "Causa emanativa e causa immanente: S. Tommaso e G. Bruno," *Filosofia* 30 (1979), 529–54. Finally, two studies on Tommaso Campanella merit attention here since they delineate his attitude toward Thomas. They are Michel-Pierre Lerner, "Campanella, juge d'Aristote," in *Platon et Aristote à la Renaissance: XVI^e Colloque International de Tours*, De Pétraque à Descartes, 32 (Paris, 1976), pp. 335–57 and John M. Headley, "Tommaso Campanella and Jean de Launoy: The Controversy over Aristotle and His Reception in the West," *Renaissance Quarterly* 43 (1990), pp. 529–550. Both indicate that Campanella held that Thomas was not an Aristotelian but a Christian who did not believe Aristotle to be infallible.

The reaction of different humanists to Thomas has been examined by various scholars. John W. O'Malley, in his valuable study, "Some Renaissance Panegyrics of Aquinas," *Renaissance Quarterly* 27 (1974), 174–92, examines some fourteen panegyrics to Thomas delivered at Rome and elsewhere by such authors as Lorenzo Valla (who actually presents a critique of Thomas), Aurelio Lippo Brandolini, Tommaso Inghirami and Josse Clichtove. He provides a helpful discussion regarding the judgments on Thomas's relation to philosophy and to Aristotle that are found in these panegyrics. Salvatore I. Camporeale, an authority on Valla, has written two informative articles relating him to Thomas: "Lorenzo Valla tra Medioevo e Rinascimento. Encomion S. Thomae (1457)," in *Centenario di s. Tommaso d'Aquino 2: Tomismo e antitomismo. Memorie Domenicane*, 7 (1976), 11–194, which was also published separately as a monograph (Pistoia, 1977), and "Umanesimo e teologia tra '400 e '500," in *Temi medievali umanistici: Cultura e teologia. Memorie Domenicane* 8–9 (1977–78), 411–436. The topic of Valla and Thomas has also been treated by Glori Cappello, "Umanesimo e scolastica: il Valla, gli umanisti e Tommaso d'Aquino," *Rivista di filosofia neo-scolastica* 69 (1977), 423–42. Passing attention is paid to Valla's attitude toward Thomas by Charles Trinkaus, "Italian Humanism and Scholastic Theology," in *Renaissance Humanism: Foundations, Forms, and Legacy*, Vol. III: *Humanism and the Disciplines*, ed. Albert Rabil, Jr. (Philadelphia, 1988), p. 339. Two articles relating Thomas to other humanists are Romano Rosa, 'Tomismo e antitomismo in Battista Spagnoli Mantovano (1447–1516)," *Memorie Domenicane* 7 (1976), 227–64 and Eugene E. Ryan, "Bartolomeo Cavalcanti as a Critic of Thomas Aquinas," *Vivarium* 20 (1982), 84–95. The influence of Thomas on Coluccio Salutati has been underscored by Ronald Witt in his *Hercules at the Crossroad: The Life, Works, and Thought of Coluccio Salutati*, Duke Monographs in Medieval and Renaissance Studies, 6 (Durham, N.C., 1983), pp. 296–298 and 343–346.

Our knowledge of the reputation and influence of Thomas in Renaissance Rome was dramatically advanced by a further and more important contribution that John W. O'Malley made in his later article, "The Feast of Thomas Aquinas in Renaissance Rome: A Neglected Document and its Import," *Rivista di storia della chiesa in Italia* 35 (1981), 1–27.[1] The evidence that he presents leaves no doubt that Thomas was the dominant medieval theologian for late fifteenth- and early sixteenth-century Rome, that is, from 1447–1521. This was in great part the result of a definite policy of Oliviero Carafa, Cardinal protector of the Dominican Order, who had a personal devotion to Saint Thomas. Pope Nicholas V (1447–1555), "the first Renaissance pope," began the innovation of requiring that Thomas's feast day— March 7—be celebrated at the Dominican church Santa Maria sopra Minerva with a liturgy that included singing the Creed, thus putting Thomas on the same doctrinal basis as that of Augustine, Ambrose, Jerome and Gregory the Great. He also demanded that the entire college of Cardinals be present for the liturgy. Valla's "counter-panegyric," which was understandably not well received by those present, thus reflected his disapproval of the extraordinary honors being accorded Thomas. O'Malley suggests that the Renaissance popes may have favored Thomas since they found his views on poverty and the role of the papacy in the Church to their liking. It should be added that in his book, *Praise and Blame in Renaissance Rome: Rhetoric, Doctrine, and Reform in the Sacred Orators of the Papal court, c. 1450–1521*, Duke Monographs in Medieval and Renaissance Studies, 3 (Durham, N.C., 1979), O'Malley had already underscored Thomas's reputation at Rome and pointed out that he was the medieval theologian on whom preachers at the Papal court seemed most dependent. The significance of the fresco in honor of Saint Thomas that Cardinal Carafa commissioned for the Minerva, namely, Filippino Lippi's *Triumph of Saint Thomas Aquinas* has been examined by Gail L. Geiger in her *Filippino Lippi's Carafa Chapel: Renaissance Art in Rome*, Sixteenth Century Essays and Studies, 5 (Kirksville, Missouri, 1986).

The results of O'Malley's research are incorporated by Charles L. Stinger, *The Renaissance in Rome* (Bloomington, 1985), in his helpful analysis of theological developments under the Renaissance papacy and the role that Thomas and contemporary Dominican Thomists, such as Thomas de Vio (Cajetan) and Sylvester Prierias, played in those developments. Thomas's reputation and influence at Renaissance Rome are also chronicled by John F. d'Amico in his *Renaissance Humanism in Papal Rome: Humanists and Churchmen on the Eve of the Reformation* (Baltimore, 1983). Besides alluding to the panegyrics of Valla and Brandolini, he discusses at some length the theological ideas of Paolo Cortesi and Raffaele Maffei and their attitudes toward Thomas. He takes Thomas to be Cortesi's "favorite scholastic" and relates that while Maffei also presents the position of Duns Scotus his general preference is for Thomas. In an earlier article, "A Humanist Response to Martin Luther: Raffaele Maffei's *Apologeticus*," Six-

*teenth Century Journal* 6 (1975), 37–56, d'Amico had already stated that Maffei "found Thomism the most acceptable form of scholasticism" and had underscored that Prierias's heavy dependence on Thomas in his *Dialogus* against Luther evoked from the latter an attack on Thomism in his reply. With the founding and early development of the Society of Jesus in the sixteenth century, Thomas and his thought would come to gain another institutional base outside the Dominican Order, one that would have an impact both at Rome and elsewhere. In his forthcoming book, *The First Jesuits: Their Ministries, Their Culture, Their "Way of Proceeding," 1540–1565* (Cambridge, Mass.: Harvard University Press), O'Malley delineates the role that Thomas played in the foundational years of the Society of Jesus and how the early Jesuits gradually came to the conclusion that Thomas was their theologian.

Thomas also had a noteworthy influence on Jewish philosophers in Italy during the middle ages and the Renaissance.[2] Colette Sirat, *A History of Jewish Philosophy in the Middle Ages* (Cambridge and Paris, 1985), pp. 268–269 notes that already in the late thirteenth century Hillel of Verona drew upon Thomas's *De unitate intellectus contra Averroistas* in arguing against Averroes's doctrine of the unity of the intellect and followed Thomas in maintaining personal immortality. But see also Giuseppe Sermonetta, "Per una storia del tomismo ebraico," in *Tommaso d'Aquino nel suo settimo centenario*, II, pp. 354–359, which also appeared in a French version in *Aquinas and Problems of His Time*, eds. G. Verbeke and D. Verhelst (Louvain and The Hague, 1976), pp. 130–135, and "Jehudah ben Moseh ben Dani'el Romano, traducteur de saint Thomas," in *Hommage à Georges Vajda: Études d'histoire et de pensée juives*, eds. Gérard Nahon and Charles Touati (Louvain, 1980), pp. 235–262. Sermonetta discusses the late thirteenth- and early fourteenth-century philosopher, Judah ben Daniel Romano, who made translations from Thomas. David ben Judah Messer Leon, who flourished in Italy in the late fifteenth century and drew upon Thomas and Maimonides in formulating his own position on faith, is discussed briefly by David B. Ruderman, "The Italian Renaissance and Jewish Thought," in *Renaissance Humanism: Foundations, Forms, and Legacy. Vol. I: Humanism in Italy*, ed. Albert Rabil, Jr. (Philadelphia, 1988), pp. 388–390. His strong dependence on Thomas is established in a definitive manner by Hava Tirosh-Rothschild, *Between Worlds: The Life and Thought of Rabbi ben Judah Messer Leon* (Albany, 1991).

Finally, it will complete the picture to note that Thomas's influence on major figures of the Reformation has also been noted and studied. For his impact on Luther, see Harry J. McSorley, "Thomas Aquinas, John Pupper von Goch, and Martin Luther: An Essay in Ecumenical Theology," in *Our Common History as Christians: Essays in Honor of Albert C. Outler*, eds. John Deschener et al. (New York, 1975), pp. 97–130; Michael G. Baylor, *Action and Person. Conscience in Late Scholasticism and the Young Luther*, Studies in Medieval and Reformation Thought, 20 (Leiden, 1977), especially pp. 20–69; Lawrence F. Murphy, "Gabriel Biel as Transmitter of Aquinas to Luther," *Renaissance and Reformation*, 7 (1983), 26–41; Denis R. Janz, *Luther and Late Medieval Thomism* (Waterloo, 1983); idem, *Luther on Thomas Aquinas: the Angelic Doctor in the Thought of the Reformer* (Stuttgart, 1989); David C. Steinmetz, "Luther among the Anti-Thomists," in his *Luther in Context* (Bloomington, 1986), pp. 47–58; John L. Farthing, *Thomas Aquinas and Gabriel Biel. Interpretations of St. Thomas Aquinas in German Nominalism on the Eve of the Reformation*, Duke Monographs in Medieval and Renaissance Studies, 9 (Durham, 1988). Thomas's impact on Calvin and his followers—such as Peter Martyr Vermigli and Jerome Zanchi—has been studied by John P. Donnelley, "Calvinist Thomism," *Viator*, 7 (1976), 441–55; idem, *Calvinism and Scholasticism in Vermigli's Doctrine of Man and Grace*, Studies in Medieval and Reformation Thought, 18 (Leiden, 1976); idem, "Italian Influences on the Development of Calvinist Scholasticism," *Sixteenth Century Journal* 7 (1976), 81–101; Charles Partee, "Predestination in Aquinas and Calvin," *Reformed Review* 32 (1978), 14–22; Joseph C. McLelland, "Calvinism Perfecting Thomism? Peter Martyr Vermigli's Question," *Scottish Journal of Theology* 31 (1978), 571–578; and David C. Steinmetz, "Calvin among the Thomists," in *Biblical Hermeneutics in Historical Perspective*, ed. Mark S. Burrows and Paul Rorem (Grand Rapids, 1991), pp. 198–214. Zanchi's dependence on Thomas is brought out by Richard A. Muller, *Christ and the Decree: Christology and Predestination in Reformed Theology from Calvin to Perkins*, Studies in Historical Theology, 2 (Durham, N.C., 1986), pp. 110–121, who also notes a Scotist tendency.

Recent scholarship has also traced the impact of other medieval philosophers on the Italian Renaissance. For that of Albert the Great, see Graziella Federici Vescovini, "Su alcune testimonianze dell'influenza di Alberto Magno come 'metafisico', scienziato e 'astrologo' nella filosofia padovana del cadere del secolo XIV: Angelo di Fossombrone e Biagio Pelacani da Parma," in *Albert der Grosse. Seine Zeit, sein Werk, seine Wrikung,* ed. Albert Zimmermann, Miscellanea Mediaevalia, 14 (Berlin and New York, 1981), 155–176; William A. Wallace, "Galileo's Citations of Albert the Great," *Southwestern Journal of Philosophy,* 10 (1979), 261–83, which reappeared in his *Prelude to Galileo,* pp. 264–285; and also Edward P. Mahoney, "Albert the Great and the *Studio Patavino* in the Late Fifteenth and Early Sixteenth Centuries," in *Albertus Magnus and the Sciences: Commemorative Essays 1980,* ed. James A. Weisheipl, Studies and Texts, 49 (Toronto, 1980), 537–563. Mahoney has also written a study on "Pico, Plato and Albert the Great," *Medieval Philosophy and Theology* 2 (1992), 166–93.

The influence of the thought of John Duns Scotus during the Renaissance received special attention at the Fourth International Scotist Congress held at Padua in 1976. See *Regnum Hominis et Regnum Dei,* Vol. 2: *Sectio specialis—La tradizione scotista veneto-padovana,* Studia Scholastico-Scotistica, 7, ed. Camille Bérubé (Rome, 1978), for articles by Antonio Antonaci, Francesco Bottin, William F. Edwards, Christopher J. T. Lewis, Edward P. Mahoney, Herbert Matsen, Giovanni di Napoli, Charles B. Schmitt, Cesare Vasoli, Graziella Federici Vescovini, and William A. Wallace. Leo Elder's study, "La théorie scotiste de l'acte indifférent et sa critique par Cajetan," pp. 207–214, touches directly on Thomas and the history of Thomism. There are also relevant articles on Scotism at Padua during the Renaissance by Carlo Balic, Edward P. Mahoney, Antonino Poppi, Lucia Rossetti, Pietro Scapin, and Charles B. Schmitt in *Storia e cultura al Santo,* ed. Antonino Poppi (Vicenza, 1976).

To ignore the influence of Albert the Great or Thomas Aquinas or John Dun Scotus during the Renaissance is to ignore a major aspect of Renaissance philosophical thought, namely, the continuity of the medieval philosophical tradition, including its diversity. It is also to refuse to consider in a serious and comprehensive fashion one of the sources of the intellectual vitality of the Renaissance itself, that is, to draw upon a wide range of philosophical and theological traditions, challenging those traditions and engaging in dialogue with them.

1. Professor John O'Malley, Weston School of Theology, Cambridge, Mass., was kind enough to discuss with us his two articles on panegyrics in honor of Saint Thomas and his recent research on the beginnings of the Society of Jesus.

2. Professor Kalman Bland, Duke University, graciously supplied us with some of our bibliographical references on Jewish philosophy during the late Middle Ages and the Renaissance.

# INDEX*

*This index is that of the 1974 edition. References to Roman numbered pages are therefore unreliable. Moreover, the index does not contain any entries for the new material found on pp. 167–178.